The Last Flight of Bomber 31

Also by Ralph Wetterhahn

The Last Battle: The Mayaguez Incident and the End of the Vietnam War
Winner of the 2002 Colby Award

Shadowmakers

The Last Flight of Bomber 31

Harrowing Tales of American and Japanese Pilots in World War II's Arctic Air Campaign

RALPH WETTERHAHN

CARROLL & GRAF PUBLISHERS
NEW YORK

THE LAST FLIGHT OF BOMBER 31
Harrowing Tales of American and Japanese Pilots in World War II's Arctic Air Campaign

Carroll & Graf Publishers
An Imprint of Avalon Publishing Group Inc.
245 West 17th Street
11th Floor
New York, NY 10011

AVALON
publishing group incorporated

First Carroll & Graf edition 2004

Appendix 4: Interned Crews, by Release Group and photograph of Nona Solodovinova on page 193 reprinted from *Home from Siberia* by Otis Hays by permission of the Texas A&M University Press.

Library of Congress Cataloging-in-Publication Data is available.

ISBN: 0-7867-1360-7

Designed by Paul Paddock
Maps by Mike Morgenfeld
Printed in the United States of America
Distributed by Publishers Group West

For Carol
Tireless, supportive, my inspiration throughout

CONTENTS

LIST OF ILLUSTRATIONS

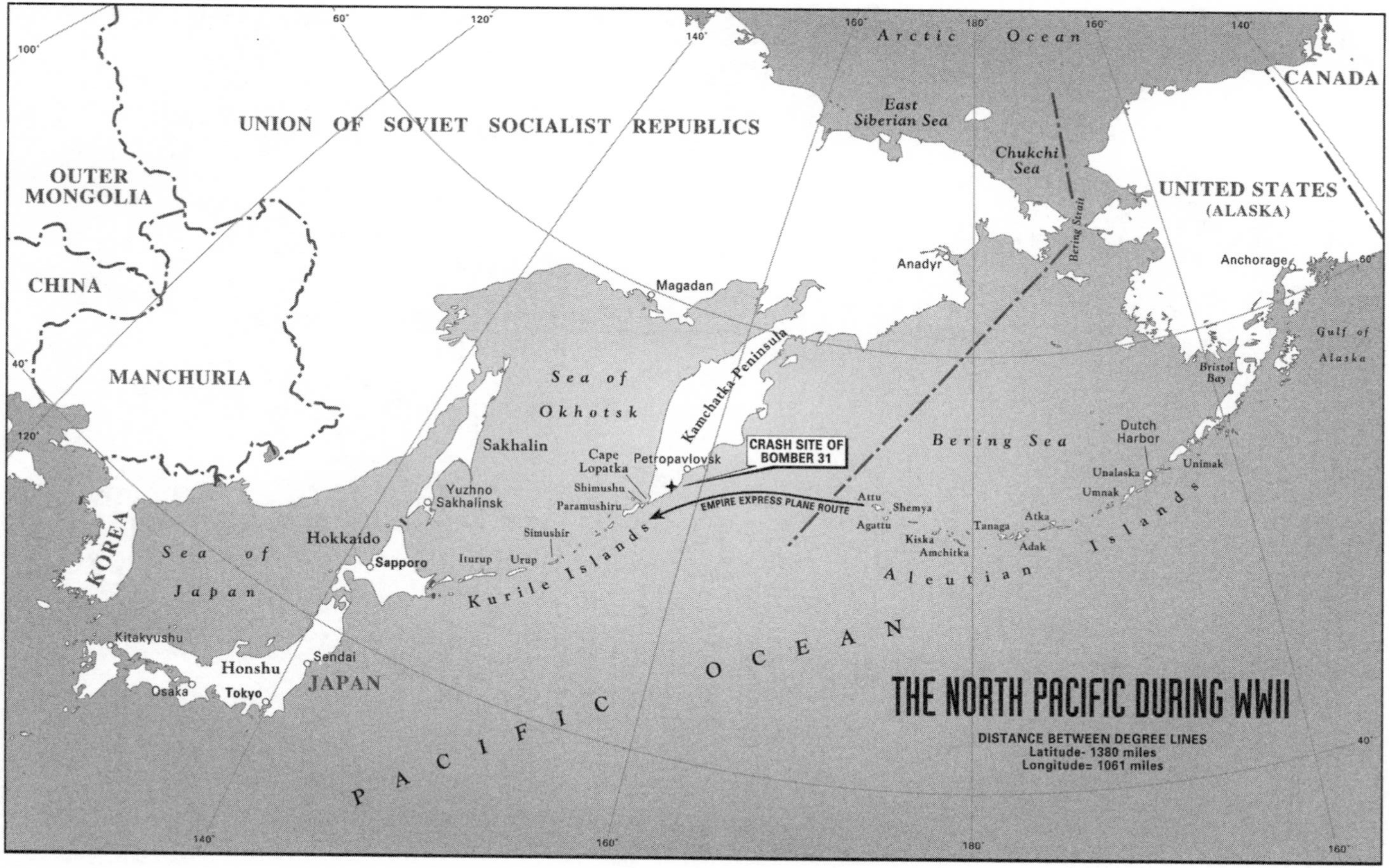
THE NORTH PACIFIC DURING WWII
DISTANCE BETWEEN DEGREE LINES
Latitude- 1380 miles
Longitude= 1061 miles
UNION OF SOVIET SOCIALIST REPUBLICS
OUTER MONGOLIA
CHINA
MANCHURIA
KOREA
JAPAN
UNITED STATES (ALASKA)
CANADA
Arctic Ocean
East Siberian Sea
Chukchi Sea
Bering Strait
Bering Sea
Sea of Okhotsk
Sea of Japan
Gulf of Alaska
PACIFIC OCEAN
Anadyr
Magadan
Anchorage
Bristol Bay
Dutch Harbor
Unalaska
Unimak
Umnak
Atka
Adak
Tanaga
Amchitka
Kiska
Shemya
Attu
Agattu
Aleutian Islands
Kamchatka Peninsula
Petropavlovsk
Cape Lopatka
Shimushu
Paramushiru
Simushir
Urup
Iturup
Kurile Islands
Sakhalin
Yuzhno Sakhalinsk
Hokkaido
Sapporo
Honshu
Sendai
Tokyo
Osaka
Kitakyushu
CRASH SITE OF BOMBER 31
EMPIRE EXPRESS PLANE ROUTE
100°
60°
120°
140°
160°
180°
40°

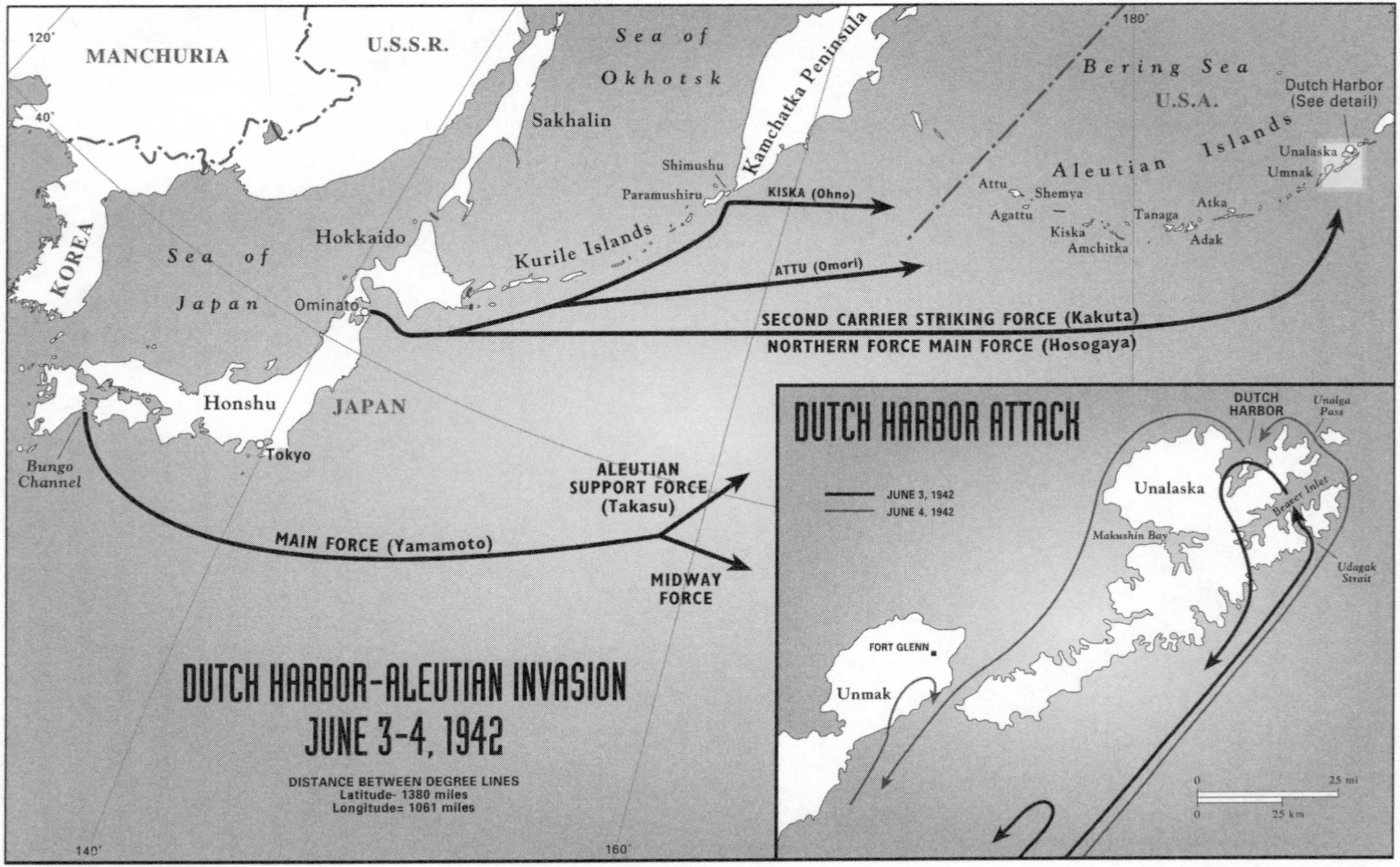

DUTCH HARBOR-ALEUTIAN INVASION
JUNE 3-4, 1942
DISTANCE BETWEEN DEGREE LINES
Latitude- 1380 miles
Longitude= 1061 miles
MANCHURIA
U.S.S.R.
KOREA
Sea of Japan
Sea of Okhotsk
Sakhalin
Hokkaido
Honshu
JAPAN
Tokyo
Ominato
Bungo Channel
Kurile Islands
Shimushu
Paramushiru
Kamchatka Peninsula
Bering Sea
U.S.A.
Aleutian Islands
Dutch Harbor
(See detail)
Attu
Shemya
Agattu
Kiska
Amchitka
Tanaga
Atka
Adak
Unalaska
Umnak
KISKA (Ohno)
ATTU (Omori)
SECOND CARRIER STRIKING FORCE (Kakuta)
NORTHERN FORCE MAIN FORCE (Hosogaya)
MAIN FORCE (Yamamoto)
ALEUTIAN SUPPORT FORCE (Takasu)
MIDWAY FORCE
120°
40°
140°
160°
180°
DUTCH HARBOR ATTACK
JUNE 3, 1942
JUNE 4, 1942
DUTCH HARBOR
Unalga Pass
Unalaska
Makushin Bay
Beaver Inlet
Udagak Strait
FORT GLENN
Unmak
0
25 mi
25 km

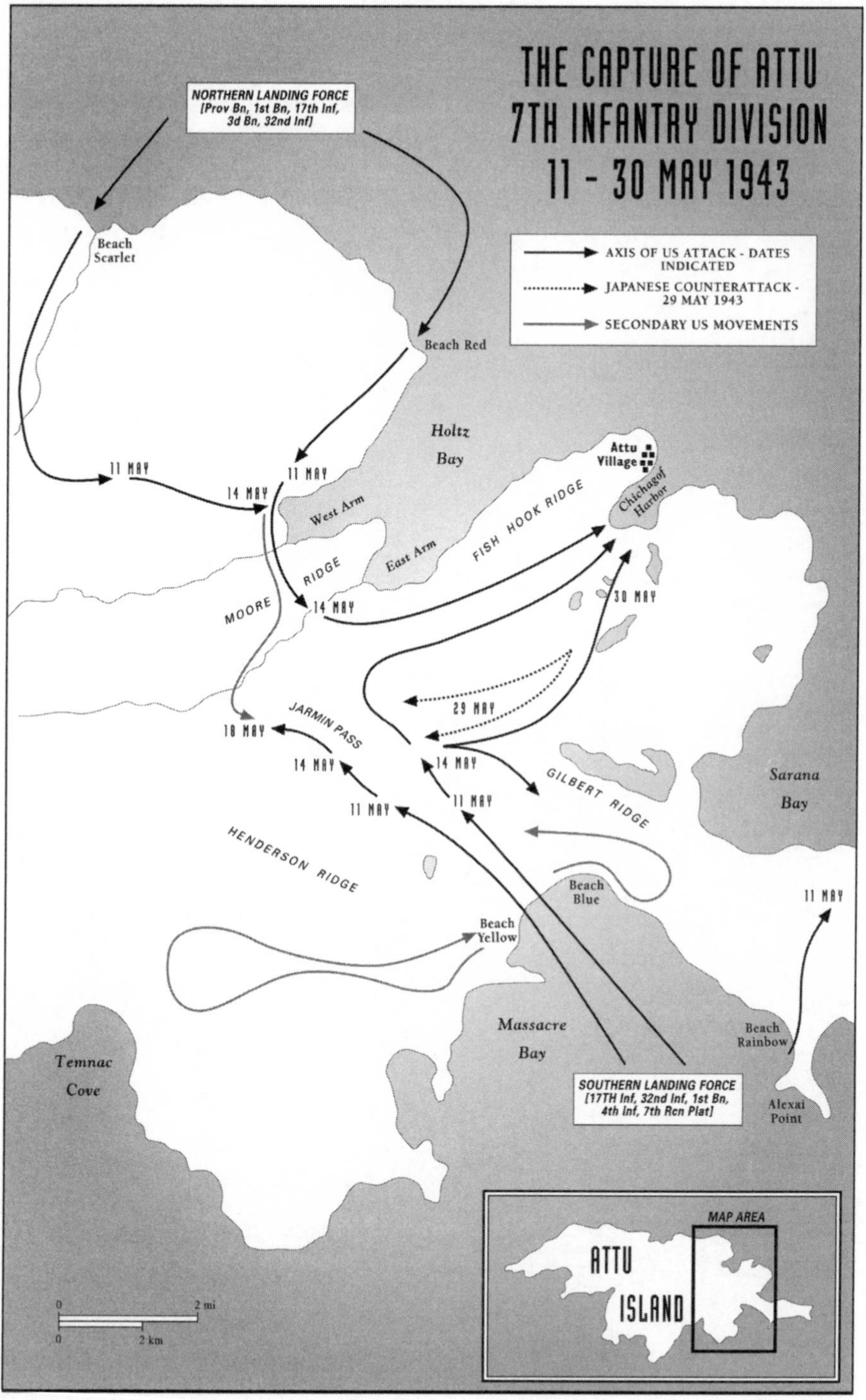

THE CAPTURE OF ATTU
7TH INFANTRY DIVISION
11 - 30 MAY 1943
NORTHERN LANDING FORCE
[Prov Bn, 1st Bn, 17th Inf, 3d Bn, 32nd Inf]
AXIS OF US ATTACK - DATES INDICATED
JAPANESE COUNTERATTACK - 29 MAY 1943
SECONDARY US MOVEMENTS
Beach Scarlet
Beach Red
Holtz Bay
Attu Village
Chichagof Harbor
West Arm
East Arm
FISH HOOK RIDGE
MOORE RIDGE
11 MAY
14 MAY
11 MAY
14 MAY
30 MAY
29 MAY
JARMIN PASS
18 MAY
14 MAY
14 MAY
11 MAY
11 MAY
GILBERT RIDGE
Sarana Bay
HENDERSON RIDGE
Beach Blue
Beach Yellow
11 MAY
Massacre Bay
Beach Rainbow
Alexai Point
Temnac Cove
SOUTHERN LANDING FORCE
[17TH Inf, 32nd Inf, 1st Bn, 4th Inf, 7th Rcn Plat]
MAP AREA
ATTU ISLAND
0
2 mi
0
2 km

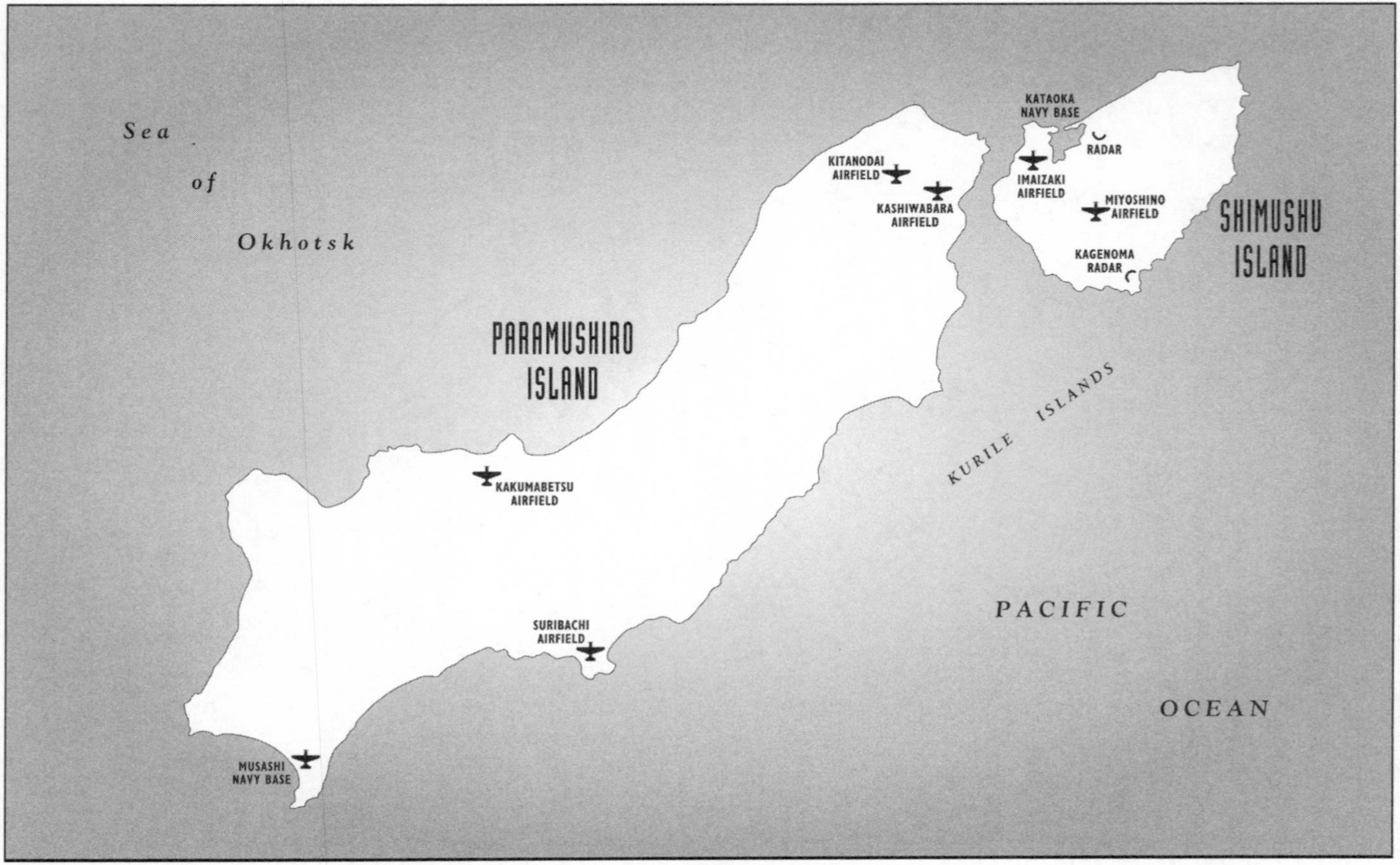
Sea of Okhotsk
PARAMUSHIRO ISLAND
KITANODAI AIRFIELD
KASHIWABARA AIRFIELD
KAKUMABETSU AIRFIELD
SURIBACHI AIRFIELD
MUSASHI NAVY BASE
KATAOKA NAVY BASE
RADAR
IMAIZAKI AIRFIELD
MIYOSHINO AIRFIELD
KAGENOMA RADAR
SHIMUSHU ISLAND
KURILE ISLANDS
PACIFIC OCEAN

The Last Flight of Bomber 31

Prologue

Summer 1962, five miles southeast of the Mutnovskiiy Volcano, Kamchatka Peninsula, Soviet Far East

The Russians had flown by helicopter from Petropavlovsk, the capital of Kamchatka, and came to a hover just above the tundra on a windswept clearing. An extinct volcano loomed above. An active one smoldered some five miles to the north. Expedition leader Yuri Slepov hefted his equipment and hopped clear of the aircraft. He was followed by team members Mikhail Khotin, Valerie Sheymovich, and German Nevseev. Though armed, their job was only to conduct a geological survey in this highly restricted area of the Soviet Union. Little happened in this cold and desolate region without the express approval of the Soviet KGB, which had given them permission to be there. Thirty miles to the north was the new Soviet nuclear submarine base at Avacha Bay. At Petropavlovsk Airfield near the sub pens, MiG interceptors sat alert in revetments, armed with missiles to shoot down American B-47 and B-52 bombers should they attack the motherland.

The terrain where the expedition landed was difficult to explore. Thick brush blanketed the hillsides, and progress was impaired by swift-running streams that spilled off the heights, still topped with snow. The four men kept wary eyes out for bears. The brown or Kodiak bear, a species larger and more fierce than the grizzly, is common throughout the region. The abundance of blueberries in the high muskeg draws them.

After the men crossed the Akhomen Stream, they continued hauling their gear uphill. A rock-strewn cleft rose steeply toward the peak that hovered above them. Suddenly one of them spotted something in the distance. In an open field, the objects appeared much like the gray boulders and detritus that lined the nearby gully. As they neared the clearing, however, they were startled by what they saw.

The closest two features were not boulders but propeller engines, sitting side by side some fifty meters below a shape that was by now clearly recognizable as an aircraft.

The team members put down their equipment, then huffed and puffed their way toward the rest of the aircraft, which was pointed uphill, wings intact. They could see the barrels of two machine guns poking from a Plexiglas blister on top of the fuselage. Thirty meters below the wreckage they came upon the first bodies.

Chapter 1

One Down on Kamchatka

During the first week in August 2000, I spent two days at the Elmendorf Air Force Base History Office in Anchorage, Alaska. With eminent Air Force historian John Cloe, we dug out and copied the World War II aircraft loss records compiled during the Aleutian campaigns. Then, on August 6, I caught a long-sold-out Reeve Aleutian Airlines jet bound for Kamchatka. In the weeks before, my wife thought from my slick-tongued lack of eloquence that the airline was called "Revolution." The plane, a Boeing 727 "combi" (half cargo space, half passenger seating), was crammed with well-heeled hunters out for Kodiak bear and bighorn sheep, a group of trout fishermen, a film crew, and a smattering of students and tourists. Up front in the cargo hold were enough high-powered rifles, bullets, and shotgun shells to start a real "revolution."

The fully loaded plane lifted into the air that morning after a surprisingly long takeoff roll. Once airborne, I glanced out the window as the rugged terrain of Alaska slid beneath our wings, then watched as we left the relative safety of terra firma and continued out over the Bering Sea. I had seen an initial report from Moscow about the discovery of a missing American aircraft found on the Kamchatka Peninsula and wondered if we were tracing the flight route of one of the aircraft on my list nearly six decades after the fact. One thing I knew from my hours spent in the history office in Anchorage: a lot of aircraft and crews had disappeared over these cold and turbulent waters (see first map).

As in many of the forensic investigations I have been part of in my postmilitary life, this odyssey started with a phone call. Heather Lyons, my magazine editor at *Retired Officer Magazine* (now *Military Officer* magazine), called to inquire about my interest in providing another article on U.S. efforts to recover remains of America's missing in action. I had previously written for several national magazines about MIA search expeditions I had accompanied in Asia, and was in the process of writing a book about the *Mayaguez* incident, a combat engagement that took place off the coast of Cambodia in 1975 and closed out the Vietnam War. Three marines involved in that military operation had been inadvertently left behind during a night helicopter extraction. Over the course of five years, I was able to determine the marines' sad fate via interviews with their Khmer Rouge captors, American veterans, and after a detailed examination of the battle site.

Being unfamiliar with the government's current MIA activity, I called the Public Affairs office at the Central Identification Laboratory (CILHI) at Hickam Air Force Base in Hawaii. Known by its acronym (pronounced *sil hi*), it is the unit responsible for forensic work on all of the recovery operations.

A Public Affairs specialist, Staff Sergeant Earl Bushong, revealed that they were planning missions to Southeast Asia, North Korea, and Russia. Southeast Asia (Vietnam, Laos, and Cambodia) had all received wide coverage in the media, so I thought expeditions to a new area might attract more interest from Editor Lyons's readers. A letter and call to the North Korean representative at the United Nations resulted in a runaround. Foreign journalists visiting "the North" were definitely something they did not seek. I then began looking into the Russian effort. Author and researcher Alla Paperno, a Russian who lives in Petropavlovsk on the Kamchatka Peninsula in the Russian Far East, had sent a letter to the U.S. embassy reporting on a document that described the location of a plane crash. The wreck might possibly be American. She later entrusted slides taken at the site to a Russian friend who was traveling to Moscow. At Sheremetvedo, U.S. embassy officer Dr. James Connell met Alla's friend and took possession of the slides. Soon thereafter an IE (initial evaluation) mission was set up by CILHI to look into the issue.

I got back to Heather Lyons with my Kamchatka assignment proposal. "There was a wreck that 'might' be American," I told her. "Because of limited airline flights into and out of the peninsula, I have to make a decision now regarding joining the IE team." I added, "sometimes mission failure can be as important as success. It might show the extent to which the government's efforts go in bringing our long-deceased servicemen home." With that, my confident editor gave me the go-ahead.

The date of my combi flight was barely a week after the July 29, 2000, fatal crash of the French supersonic transport (SST) near Paris. Initiated by a blown tire on takeoff, that tragedy would soon occupy our thoughts. Two hours out from Alaska, the flight attendant announced that due to adverse winds there was not enough fuel to reach Petropavlovsk. We diverted to Anadir, a bleak Russian settlement above the Arctic Circle. After landing, the plane rolled out over a washboard of a runway, clanking to a stop straight ahead where we waited for a fuel truck. Ten minutes later, an olive-drab fuel tanker appeared. A hefty woman manhandled a huge steering wheel on the vintage tanker as she pulled alongside the aircraft. Inside the cab was a three- or four-year-old youngster who seemed not the least fazed by all of the activity. Once refueled, the plane spun around and the pilot ran the power up full until the aircraft shook. The brakes released with a rush, and the tires of the now fully loaded plane began slamming into each succeeding crack in the concrete slabs with ever more violence, the sound increasing in intensity and frequency as we built up speed. It sounded like those shotgun shells up front were exploding, and I had no doubt that I was not the only one aboard who was imagining a repeat of the Paris nightmare at that moment. For me, a veteran of many, many heart-thumping catapults and hard landings on aircraft carriers, this was one of the most nerve-racking takeoffs I had ever experienced. After what seemed like an eternity, the plane finally lifted safely into the air. Even the flight attendants had their breaths taken away. They now plied us liberally with free liquor, and I noticed one of them knocking back the hard stuff in the galley.

Two hours and a day later (we had crossed the international date line), the plane landed at the airport at Petropavlovsk and taxied past a SU-15 Russian interceptor nestled in a revetment. "Photos not permitted," we were advised. I wondered for a moment if I was eyeing the one that had risen from that same runway to shoot down Korean Airlines flight 007 back in 1983.

Our delay put the hunters way behind schedule. They were given preference through customs so their chartered helicopters might yet get them to their mountain campsites before dark. I was in no hurry, since the team from Hawaii was not due to arrive for a week.

The second part of the odyssey began in the capital of Kamchatka, Petropavlovsk-Kamchatsky, commonly referred to as P-K. Since the airline out of Anchorage flies to Kamchatka only once every two weeks and is always sold out, I had bracketed the planned arrival date of the CILHI team. I spent the first week touring the local sites and observing the rapidly changing weather on the peninsula. Each morning, a peek out the hotel window gave only an inkling of what to expect with the weather. Some mornings the visibility was unlimited and snow-capped volcanoes stood out

Avacha Volcano in August. This was a landmark used by the U.S. crews intent on finding Petropovlovsk and its airfield.

clearly from as far away as forty miles. On other mornings the fog would be so thick you could barely see the roadway beneath the hotel. An hour later, all of that could be reversed. On a clear morning in midweek, I hired a guide and had time to climb two-thirds up Mount Avacha, an 8,500-foot active volcano that smolders to the north, above the bay. The summit resembles a giant Chianti bottle whose candles had dripped a profusion of red and yellow wax down the sides. Steam and shimmering heat plumes rose into pristine air above the sulfur- and lava-stained rim. Without a doubt, any aircraft that chose to overfly that cinder cone would have a very "uplifting" experience, indeed.

On Monday, August 14, I went to the airport to greet the U.S. and Russian groups that arrived on an Aeroflot airliner from Moscow at 9:30 A.M. The IE team from Hawaii included the CILHI forensic's expert and two military personnel from the Joint Task Force–Full Accounting (JTF-FA).

Accompanying the IE threesome was retired major general

Roland LaJoie, who serves as chairman of the U.S.–Russia Joint Commission on POW-MIAs. LaJoie was hired as a consultant by the Defense POW/Missing Personnel Office (DPMO) in Washington, the department responsible for these undertakings. LaJoie is a take-charge type who speaks Russian fluently and oozes authority. Along from Washington for an orientation was archivist R. Michael McReynolds, commissioner and cochair of the World War II Working Group. Major James D. MacDougall, chief of Commission Affairs at DPMO, came as well. MacDougall was clearly the underdog rankwise in all this, yet he was the senior active duty officer from the head office.

Representing the Russian government was Colonel Konstantin Golumbovsky and a member of his staff from the Department of POWs, Internees, and MIAs, Presidential Administration, Moscow. Golumbovsky's American counterpart, Dr. James Connell, director of the Joint Commission Support Directorate (JCSD) at the U.S. embassy, also was among the group. He had joined the team as it transited through Moscow. Connell, a graduate of the Naval Academy, is a retired navy captain who has worked as a civil service employee in Moscow since the early 1990s. Fluent in Russian, he got along well with Colonel Golumbovsky and other local officials.

The IE team had crossed twenty-two time zones in thirty-six hours getting to P-K. They were a weary threesome. The team included anthropologist Dr. Ann Bunch from CILHI, whose role was to ensure that strict scientific archeological methods were used at the excavation site. JTF-FA's explosive ordnance disposal technician, Army sergeant first class Michael Swam, was assigned the unnerving job of locating and neutralizing unexploded bombs, fuses, and ammunition. A mortuary affairs specialist, Army staff sergeant Carlos Roman, was to photograph and record data while collecting personal items for return to next of kin.

It is never easy to figure out who is really in charge at any given point in these recovery operations, since the structure of the POW/MIA recovery business is fragmented among all the services.

Everyone involved seems to have a different headquarters to report to; hence, different bosses. Timing and location also are factors. JTF-FA provides the commander who is in overall charge of the mission. CILHI's forensics expert is in charge of the recovery activities at the crash site. Often these responsibilities overlap, and friction can result and has arisen between or among the relevant parties. I had observed this difficulty on previous expeditions, but must add that they are always worked out to the service's credit, though often in trying circumstances.

After introductions, General LaJoie commented on the sunny day. I agreed with his observation, then added, "And if you don't like the weather in Kamchatka, wait five minutes. Dense fog, I've already learned, can descend in a flash and last for days." Since the sky was cloud-free at the moment, LaJoie suggested the group go immediately to the crash site. I sensed an urgency beyond purely wanting to get on with the task. Though the team members from Hawaii clearly would have preferred to go to a hotel and get some sleep, no one seemed inclined to overrule the general.

The group boarded a bus and rode forty-five minutes to a grass airfield southwest of the city. There, a motley green Russian Mi-2 helicopter waited. After a quick preflight inspection of the machine by the Russian air force pilot, half the group—four plus myself—were loaded aboard. With no seat belts in the cabin area, we simply found a place to sit while the pilot started the engine, then added power and took off, heading south.

Kamchatka is one of nature's contradictions. Fire and ice live side by side on a peninsula that begins at the same latitude as Anchorage, Alaska, then extends 920 miles south. It is 390 miles across at its wide midpoint. More than three hundred volcanoes dot the landscape, twenty-nine of them active, and most of them are snow-covered nearly year-round. With hundreds of hot springs, the Kamchatkans claim their local swans do not migrate since ample food thrives in the warm waters that flow down the mountains.

Bomber 31 lies in the open area in the center between two rock slides. Its color matches the surrounding boulders. Mi-2 helicopter is at lower left.

As we climbed away from P-K, fishermen could be seen angling in the Avacha River. There are no dams on the peninsula to impede the spawning of seven species of salmon that muscle their way up pristine rivers. It being summer, one of the eye-catching contrasts was how lush green vegetation grows in profusion right beside deep pockets of snow and roaring streams. Brown bears proliferate in great numbers, and a female with two cubs interrupted her foraging to look up at our helicopter as we continued south. This one stood her ground as the two cubs scampered to her side.

The Mi-2 swung past Mutnovsky Volcano to an area where the pilot pointed toward a twenty-degree slope. From the air, it was nearly impossible to spot the remnants of the wreckage amid a backdrop of rocky slag that had rolled down the mountainside. The pilot circled while we got our bearings, then landed beside a snowfield. We found ourselves at 2,050 feet altitude on the western side of the mountain, about five miles from the eastern coast at coordinates N 52°22' and E 158°17'.

My initial thought upon hearing about the crash while still Stateside was that it might be an American Lend-Lease aircraft that had gotten lost and hit the mountain in bad weather. During World War II, the United States was supplying the Soviets with all manner of equipment, including C-47 cargo planes, A-39, P-40, and P-63 fighters, plus B-25 bombers. Lend-Lease aircraft amounted to 18 percent of all aircraft in the Soviet air force, 20 percent of all bombers, and 16 to 23 percent of all fighters (depending on calculation methods), and 29 percent of all naval aircraft. Many of the planes were flown by American crews to Fairbanks, Alaska. There they were handed over to a Soviet commission and ferried to Krasnoyarsk in Siberia by specially selected Soviet pilots. That we might be recovering the remains of Soviet crew members was not lost on me.

We began a visual examination of the wreckage. The paint scheme and shape of the twin tails readily identified it as belonging to a PV-1 Ventura, a U.S. Navy plane of which none was delivered to the Soviets, at least not intentionally. That meant that any remains found of the airmen did not belong to Soviet crewmen.

Once the CILHI team was on site, Sergeant Roman began setting

A 500-pound bomb with fuse still installed lay among the wreckage of Bomber 31.

Sergeant First Class Michael Swam places a yellow warning flag to mark the location of a fused but unexploded 500-pound bomb.

up a satellite phone. "We always have comm [communication], our lifeline out here," Roman said. "CILHI back in Hawaii knows what time we left and where we are at all times." Try as he might, though, he was unable to make contact with Hawaii.

Sergeant First Class Swam unloaded his equipment and began his dangerous work. His first order of business was to search for unexploded ordnance. He donned a headset and began sweeping the terrain with a metal detector. Swam hardly needed it. Live 50-millimeter cannon rounds tipped either red, black, or blue were strewn about the main site. Small fragmentation and incendiary bombs littered the landscape. This further confirmed that the plane was not a Lend-Lease aircraft, since they were never delivered with munitions aboard.

Swam placed a yellow warning flag beside each explosive he saw, or above buried metal contacts he discovered with the detector. When asked about the risks of bouncing around in Mi-2 helicopters over desolate countryside, then tracking down explosives in bear country beneath volcanoes, Swam shrugged. "It's all part of the job," he said, a wily grin creasing his lips as he took out a tape measure to determine the size of the site. Near the western or lower edge of the area he came upon an unexploded five-hundred-pound general-purpose bomb, its nose fuse still installed. A few yards away, both aircraft engines lay side by side.

Jim Connell, Captain, USN (Ret.), beside the tail of Bomber 31.

A look at the engines revealed that the propeller hub or spinner on one showed evidence of an explosion that had torn open the spinner housing. Jagged metal lay exposed. Inside the opening, I felt around with my fingers and a small metal fragment—like a piece of shrapnel—came loose. There was an oily residue on the metal artifact. At points on both engines, large-caliber holes were punched through the cylinder exhaust stacks. No careless hunter had used the engines for target practice. The damage had been done by heavy weapons. But how could a round hit the spinner? How could hits impact on the top portions of the engines? If not here, where had the damage taken place? By whom and by what means was it inflicted?

Once Swam had marked the hazardous areas, Sergeant Roman began a search for personal belongings of the victims. He found an oxygen mask, a parachute harness, and a life preserver.

Dr. James Connell from the U.S. embassy in Moscow moved beside the flattened double tail, a type found on several American medium bombers of the era. Connell lifted the left vertical

The wreckage of Bomber 31 being examined by the initial evaluation team from the U. S.

Dr. Ann Bunch at the moment of discovery. "We definitely have human remains here."

stabilizer. The number 34641 was clearly visible. Another, larger number 31, was stenciled on the other tailpiece. Connell checked both numbers against his list of missing aircraft. They matched a Navy PV-1 Ventura bomber flown by Lieutenant Walt S. Whitman and his six-man crew that went missing on a World War II combat mission on March 25, 1944. Bomber 31 had been found, but what was it doing here in Kamchatka?

Later that day, Roman finally established communications with Hawaii and relayed the information to CILHI headquarters, whose personnel contacted the navy casualty office to begin the process of locating next of kin.

By this time the helicopter had completed its round trip and Dr. Bunch, the anthropologist, arrived with the rest of the team, including General LaJoie.

"Big site," she said after a look, "a lot bigger than I thought."

According to Colonel Golumbovsky, the KGB had sent a team to investigate the wreck after it was discovered by a geologic survey team back in 1962. They removed the machine guns, cut open the fuselage, and hoisted out live bombs before trying to blow them up. The area had remained relatively undisturbed ever since. It is suspected that the plane was sectioned into pieces so that U.S. satellite photography would not reveal the identity of the aircraft and hence the Americans would not ask about it. During the Cold War, Kamchatka was a highly restricted area. Russian nuclear submarines have operated for decades out of Avacha Bay, and as mentioned, it was from the airport at Petropavlovsk that the Soviet fighter was launched before firing two missiles to down KAL 007.

The team from Hawaii continued its work in spite of the fact that once General LaJoie was on site, he began his own personal inspection, moving about at will and disturbing things around the main debris area. At one point he picked up an object that looked similar to the incendiary bomblets littering the ground nearby. Sergeant Swam observed this and politely asked the general to avoid handling anything. LaJoie would have none of that, turning the object over and reading the inscription on it, indicating it was a wooden float for use with the survival raft. He announced his observation, then placed the float back on the ground. Once again, no one was going to challenge the general.

Dr. Bunch made her way to the main debris field. The fuselage had been shifting on ice and snow for fifty-six years and had swung around so that the wings now faced downhill. Above and below the main wreckage, three craters gave evidence of the KGB effort to destroy the bombload. Dr. Bunch eased around yellow flags until she was astride the forward wing section. She bent low, deep in concentration, peering inside mangled rubble for a long minute.

"We definitely have human remains here," Dr. Bunch said. When I asked if she was sure, she remarked, "There's fabric around a bone fragment." Dr. Bunch glanced at me with the no-nonsense look of someone who has seen a lot of this sort of thing. "I know of only one species that wears clothes," she said, then pointed, "That's a human scapular [collarbone] over there." Looking in from above, she discovered more remains—"Right there's a section of vertebrae [backbone]."

Meanwhile, General LaJoie made no secret about how he thought the initial inspection should be completed as quickly as possible. As a result, the team spent only two days visiting the site and a third day going from place to place in Petropavlovsk. In P-K they gathered additional information about the logistics and manpower needed for the full recovery operation to be recommended upon their return to Hawaii. The brusque nature of this most important portion of the effort was to have a profound effect the following year, when the team returned.

I left feeling somewhat unfulfilled, my head bursting with questions. The obvious one: what was a bomb-laden U.S. Navy plane doing over Soviet territory? For that, there was no ready answer. It is not CILHI's job to determine either the circumstances or the cause of the crash, but curiosity based on prior experience as chief of safety, Pacific Air Force, and training at the Norton Air Force Base school for accident investigators led me to begin to try to unravel the story of the last flight of Bomber 31. Determining the final days and hours of a plane and seven men who vanished almost sixty years ago presented some obvious problems. None of the crew survived the war. There were no cockpit instruments among the remaining wreckage to use in obtaining readouts of heading, airspeed, or aircraft attitude, and no laboratory equipment was available in Kamchatka to use in analyzing the engines or structural parts of the wreckage. Why had the plane come to rest there, and how was one to reasonably confirm any possible theory about the crash landing with no test equipment or living crew members to verify details? That was the dilemma. I reasoned that there could have been other planes in the air at the same time. Might I be able to reconstruct Whitman and crew's intended mission if any witnesses were still alive who knew the crew and were in the air at the same time? As it turned out, even though the obstacles often seemed insurmountable, a mosaic of what transpired emerged slowly during my years of investigation. I began with interviews of World War II servicemen who had been involved in similar missions. If I encountered circumstances, the results of which mirrored documented facts and/or my personal observations of several wrecked Venturas, I included those to represent plausible descriptions of what Bomber 31 and its crew experienced. The search for answers took me throughout the Pacific "rim of fire," from Attu to Kamchatka to heartland America and mainland Japan. I was even fortunate enough to be one of the first Americans in nearly a century authorized to visit the disputed northern Kurile islands of Shimushu and Paramushiro, now controlled by Russia. What evolved is the story of an unheralded air war where young men on opposing sides battled not only each other, but also ice and fog in wind-lashed, primeval places.

Chapter 2
Yamamoto's Grand Scheme

The affairs of war, like the destiny of battles, as well as empires, hang upon a spider's thread.

—Napoleon Bonaparte

On the eve of the Pearl Harbor, General Hajime Sugiyama told Emperor Hirohito that the Pacific war would last "three months." The emperor replied that "when the war against China broke out, you told me that it would be over in a month. . . . But it has taken four years, and is still going on." Sugiyama said, "It didn't go as we expected, because China is so large a country." In anger, the emperor countered, "The Pacific is even larger. On what grounds do you assure me that it will only take three months?" The general lowered his head, unable to respond. In spite of Hirohito's reservations, the Pacific war plan went ahead, since Hirohito's military role was merely to provide his stamp of approval, which he eventually did.

In Hirohito's Japan, the military ran the show, dominating the cabinet and the office of the prime minister, who was always drawn from active army or navy ranks. Unlike those in the navy, most senior army officers came from the middle and lower classes of

Japanese society and had risen through the ranks during the depression. They had watched as their parents were weighed down by the economic chaos that descended on Japan after the American stock market crash. Now the Japanese army officer corps, under the aegis of the new prime minister, General Hideki Tojo, was determined to secure for Japan her dominant role in the "Greater East Asia Co-Prosperity Sphere." Expanding the war into the Pacific was considered unavoidable. Though the level of the emperor's complicity will be argued by historians for many years to come, Hirohito's naval aide recorded in his diary that throughout the day on which Pearl Harbor was attacked "the emperor wore his naval uniform and seemed to be in a splendid mood."

After the successful attack on Oahu, the Japanese quickly rolled over Hong Kong (December 1941), Wake Island (December 1941), Singapore (February 1942), the Philippines (April 1942), and Tulagi and Rabaul (May 1942). Then came a two-pronged plan to invade Midway (2,200 miles east of Tokyo) and Alaska's Aleutian Island's chain (1,440 miles north of Midway) in June 1942. The Aleutian part of the campaign would launch from northern Honshu's Ominato Naval Base, with one fleet segment refueling at Paramushiro Island in the Kuriles. The giving and taking of islands in these waters was nothing new to Japan.

For centuries prior to World War II, the status of the Kurile Island's archipelago was contested by Russia and Japan. Their squabbles included interference from French, British, and American naval forces, the latter under Admiral Matthew Perry in 1853. After Russia's defeat in the 1856 Crimean War bankrupted Czar Alexander II, he needed to consolidate territory and obtain hard currency. The czar put Alaska and the Aleutians on the block. The United States purchased both in 1867 for $7.2 million. The acquisition extended American territory to within 675 miles of Shimushu, the northernmost of the Kurile Islands.

Following the Treaty of St. Petersburg, signed in 1875 by Japan's Admiral Enomoto Buyo and Russia's Prince Aleksandr Gorchakov,

Russia abandoned claims to the Kurile Archipelago in return for control of Sakhalin Island. Japan's acquisition of the northern Kuriles ensured her dominance of the Sea of Okhotsk and disrupted Russia's naval operations. Ships from Vladivostok had to negotiate Japanese-controlled straits to reach the Pacific, and the route around southern Kamchatka's Cape Lopatka, often fogged in and stormy, was narrow and treacherous.

When the Japanese took over the northern Kuriles in 1875, they found an Asian people living there who had existed under Russian rule for a century. Though they looked Oriental, they spoke and dressed like Russians and hung portraits of the czar, Christ, and the Virgin Mary in their homes, much like Russia's Orthodox faithful. To the Japanese, they even drank and swore like Russians.

By the start of World War II, the Japanese had settled the islands in large numbers, making the entire arc an integral part of the Japanese homeland. The status of Sakhalin had changed, too. After Japan took the upper hand in the 1904 Russo-Japanese War over the control of Manchuria, President Theodore Roosevelt served as mediator at the subsequent peace conference held at Portsmouth, New Hampshire, from August 9 to September 5, 1905. The resulting Treaty of Portsmouth gave Japan control of Manchuria's Liaotung Peninsula (northwest of Korea), as well as the half of Sakhalin Island below the fiftieth parallel.

The Kuriles, being in close proximity to Siberia, experience harsh winters, even more severe than those in the Aleutians. The American archipelago, which is actually farther north than the Kuriles, benefits from the warm Japanese current that flows northeast from Japan toward North America.

Japanese military construction in the Kuriles accelerated in the 1930s all along the island chain. With the exception of aircraft hangars, triangular buildings were erected, the roofs of most reaching the ground. The earth beneath was dug out, making the structures semisubmerged. The low silhouette and pitch of the roofs withstood high winds and heavy snow. Inside, men slept on bunks above dirt floors and used potbellied stoves for heat and cooking. The location of these facilities was carefully chosen to preclude water from filling them during the wet spring and summer.

The Japanese used these island bases as jumping-off points for the Pearl Harbor attack. But when America sent Colonel Doolittle and his B-25 bombers to strike Tokyo on April 18, 1942, the raid redirected the focus of the Japanese High Command. Thinking that the mission had originated in the Aleutians, the admirals and generals crystalized their intent to occupy Midway and the Aleutians. On May 5, 1942, imperial headquarters issued Navy Directive 94, for the invasion of the Aleutians. They planned to "capture and demolish any points of strategic value on the western Aleutian Islands in order to check the enemy's air and ship maneuvers in this area."

By now, the Japanese had built up forces on Paramushiro and Shimushu, the closest points to America and Soviet territory. Thousands of troops were stationed there to defend the two islands. Airfield and fleet installations at Kataoka Navy Base were beefed up, as was Miyoshino Army Airfield on Shimushu, where reconnaissance and medium bombers were stationed. On Paramushiro, the Kashiwabara staging area and army airfields at Kakumabetsu and Suribachi were operational or under construction, along with Musashi Navy Base and its airfield in the south.

Kitanodai Airfield near Kashiwabara was being laid out with a wooden runway of thick interlocking planks designed to remain in service during the winter (see fourth map).

While the buildup was being completed, Japanese naval forces, under the overall command of Admiral Yamamoto, embarked on a grand scheme to attack and occupy Midway Island in the north-central Pacific, and Kiska, Attu, and Adak Islands in the Aleutians. From Ominato Navy Base on May 25, 1942, the Aleutian contingent departed on their mission to establish a foothold on Alaskan territory. Three task forces were committed, and part of

Yamamoto's Midway invasion force would supply supporting ships to back up the Aleutian operation. The element under Captain Takeji Ohno, involved in the Kiska part of the invasion, made a stop at Paramushiro to load additional troops before moving into the North Pacific. The second force, under Rear Admiral Sentaro Omori, proceeded up the Kuriles chain, then swung eastward toward the Aleutians. The third echelon, under Vice Admiral Moshiro Hosogaya and Rear Admiral Kakuji Kakuta, headed due east, then planned to angle north, toward Dutch Harbor, where an attack was planned to knock out the U.S. Navy installation there. The aircraft carriers *Junjo* and *Ryujo* were part of the latter group, along with the seaplane tender *Kimikawa Maru*, with its eight H6K4 Mavis seaplanes (see second map).

The command arrangement in Alaska was a merger of U.S. Army, Navy, and Canadian forces, with the U.S. Navy as the senior service.

In Hawaii, Admiral Nimitz met with and assigned Rear Admiral Robert A. Theobald overall command of the Northern Theater. Theobald's naval force was to be comprised of two heavy cruisers, three light cruisers, fourteen destroyers, and six World War I–vintage submarines.

Admiral Theobald departed from Pearl Harbor on his flagship, the cruiser USS *Nashville*, and with a small task force set course for Kodiak on May 21, 1942. Theobald's fleet plowed through heavy seas for four days as he pondered just how he was to defend Alaska and a fifteen-hundred-mile-long island chain with nineteen surface ships, none of which was an aircraft carrier, and half a dozen obsolescent submarines.

Admiral Theobald was not kept fumbling in the dark over these matters for long. The plan for Japan's two-pronged thrust into U.S. Pacific waters was complex, requiring the transmission by radio of an abnormally high number of top-secret orders. American cryptographers had already broken the Japanese code, and hence word of the planned operation was unraveling. Theobald was ordered to "oppose the Japanese advance into the Aleutians-Alaska area, taking advantage of every favorable opportunity to inflict strong attrition," and "be governed by the principle of calculated risk."

A day and a half from Kodiak, Theobald received the following coded message from Admiral Nimitz:

> 25 May 1942
> FROM: CINCPAC
> TO: COMNORPACFOR
>
> THE JAPANESE HAVE COMPLETED PLANS FOR AN AMPHIBIOUS OPERATION TO SECURE AN ADVANCED BASE IN THE ALEUTIAN ISLANDS. . . . FOLLOWING ESTIMATED JAPANESE TASK FORCE HAS LEFT JAPAN WITH PROBABLE OBJECTIVE ALEUTIAN ISLANDS AND/OR ALASKA.
>
> 2 AIRCRAFT CARRIERS, 2-3 SEAPLANE TENDERS, 3 HEAVY CRUISERS, 2 LIGHT CRUISERS, 12 DESTROYERS, 8 SUBMARINES, HEAVY BOMBERS (PROBABLY FLYING BOAT TYPE), AND TRANSPORTS AND CARGO VESSELS. . . . ON MAY 25 THE ABOVE FORCES WILL ARRIVE IN NORTHERN JAPAN, FUEL, AND PROCEED TO THE ALEUTIANS.

Army major general Simon Bolivar Buckner, Jr. was at Kodiak to greet Theobald when he arrived a day later, on the twenty-seventh, but Buckner had been building his Alaska defense force for more than two years, and resentment immediately blossomed. Gray-haired Buckner, the "Silver Stallion of Alaska," was the risk-taking, flamboyant son of the Confederate general who surrendered Fort Donelson to Ulysses S. Grant during the Civil War. Buckner had already begun expanding his air umbrella west, having built a secret airfield on Umnak, a harbor-less island some two-hundred miles out on the chain. He had installed a squadron of P-40 pursuit planes there in March 1942. Theobald was the more cerebral of the two, cautious and conservative; he was less inclined to overextend his scant forces.

When he conferred with Buckner, Theobald was openly skeptical of Nimitz's latest assessment that Dutch Harbor and the western Aleutians were prime targets. Theobald placed his faith in U.S. Naval War College doctrine that stated, "It is wrong to act solely on information provided by intelligence that was often incorrect, incomplete, or worse still, false if planted by the enemy." To be fair to Theobald, until the Battle of Midway proved otherwise a week later, the accuracy of these intelligence reports was not yet fully appreciated by field commanders. Based on Japanese capability, Theobald was adamant that an attack on Kodiak or even Anchorage was more likely. Securing those bases would put the Japanese within easy bombing range of the navy shipyard at Bremerton, Washington, and the Boeing bomber plant in Seattle. Buckner disagreed but was overruled.

Theobald's assessment caused him to concentrate his surface fleet close to Kodiak, allowing the Japanese unimpeded movement in their thrust toward more western portions of the Aleutians. Compounding Theobald's failure to appreciate the intelligence estimate was the fact that he chose to ignore it without advising Nimitz or his staff.

The Japanese plan unfolded exactly as Nimitz's messages had predicted. On the night of June 2, 1942, Rear Admiral Kakuta, a stern, fireplug of a naval commander, turned his task force north to get clear of the weather front he was using for cover. He increased speed to twenty-two knots, but at the planned launch point two hours later, the fleet was still in heavy weather. Kakuta was worried that his pilots might not be able to find Dutch Harbor, the intended target, or their own carriers after the attack. Flight crews were given copies of a thirty-year-old map that outlined merely the shores of Unalaska and Umnak Islands. Interior sections were blank and were marked as "unknown areas."

Forty-five minutes later, the ceiling rose to four hundred feet and visibility increased to a thousand yards, enough to get planes airborne but below the weather needed to recover aircraft. Admiral Kakuta gave the order to launch. The still air came alive with the roar of aircraft engines. At 3:25 A.M., Lieutenant Yoshio Shiga thundered down the deck of the *Junyo* in his A6M Zero. He then circled below the weather and waited for a dozen more fighter escorts, which were joined by thirteen D3A1 Val dive bombers. The bombers, led by Lieutenant Zenji Abe, each carried a single 500-pound bomb. At three hundred feet above the sea, the loose formation headed north.

From the carrier *Ryujo*, seven Nakajima B5N Kate torpedo bombers, led by Lieutenant Hiroichi Samejima, rumbled down the deck at 3:40 A.M. Each plane was armed with one 550-pound bomb and four 150-pounders. One of the first Kates lost power and crashed into the icy, heaving sea. A destroyer maneuvered to rescue the three-man crew while six escort Zeros took to the air. Samejima gathered his remaining bombers, joined with the Zeros into a loose formation, and headed north. Seven more Kates, led by Lieutenant Masataki Yamagami, were launched without mishap thirty minutes later.

Spread out in deteriorating weather were thirty-nine aircraft. After groping in and out of the fog for more than twenty minutes, strike leader Lieutenant Abe had seen enough. A veteran of the Pearl Harbor attack, he guessed they would never have the six-thousand-foot ceiling he needed in the target area for dive bombing. He ordered his thirteen Val bombers and Zero escorts to turn back. Two of the Zeros had gotten separated but still had the *Ryujo* formation in sight, so they continued with the Kates.

At 4:00 A.M. on June 3, the banshee wail of an air raid siren woke the men at Dutch Harbor. It was already daylight at that latitude

A Japanese bomb strikes the USS *Northwestern* at Dutch Harbor, June 4, 1942. Bombs also impact shore facilities located there.

and time of year as navy aerographer Paul E. Carrigan shook himself awake and hurriedly put on boots, foul-weather jacket, and steel helmet. He grabbed his rifle and headed for the Quonset hut door just as it flew open. In stormed a breathless radioman.

"What's up?" someone asked.

"This is it," the radioman replied. "Seventeen unidentified planes off Eider Point."

Bodies flew through the door as men headed for their battle stations.

All thirteen Kate bombers and six escorts from the *Ryujo,* plus two Zeros from the *Junyo,* arrived overhead shortly after another storm front had passed Dutch Harbor.

Carrigan witnessed the attack from his trench as the sound of antiaircraft fire filled the air and red tracers arced across the morning sky.

"The high-flying Kates, locked into their bombing runs, unswervingly kept coming, unhurried, somehow quietly detached from the noise around us, strangely remote, inevitable. With my neck craned way back, mouth open, and my eyes riveted on the bombers, the unseen Zeros appeared as if by magic. They had come flashing in low and were snarling and swarming among us."

Bombs began raining down on the ships in the harbor, the dock, warehouse, and barracks area. A PBY flying boat that tried to get airborne was shot to pieces before it could reach flying speed. Smoke billowed from the station ship USS *Northwestern*, which had taken a direct hit. Two fuel storage tanks were burning fiercely.

Thirty-five American lives were lost and considerable damage was done to facilities at Dutch Harbor while Admiral Theobald's forces were mispositioned to counter Kakuta's fleet.

The Japanese photographs taken during the raid were put to full advantage the next day when an even more effective raid was carried out. This time Lieutenant Abe and his force of Val dive bombers had no trouble finding Dutch Harbor. Along with the Kates under the command of Lieutenant Samejima, Abe led the bombers through a hole in the clouds and began the attack. Four new fuel storage tanks freshly filled with twenty-two thousand barrels of aviation gasoline were hit and destroyed. A diesel tank also was consumed in flames. But, whereas no planes were lost to combat on the previous day, two of Lieutenant Abe's Vals and one of the Lieutenant Shiga's Zeros were shot out of the sky by 11th Fighter Squadron P-40s launched from General Buckner's secret base at Fort Glenn, on nearby Umnak Island. Two other Vals were badly crippled and went down on the way back to the carrier. Two P-40s were shot down by Zeros and in one, Lieutenant John J. Cape was killed.

A second wave that day got lost in the clouds and turned for home. Four Pete F1M2-type 97 floatplanes from the cruisers *Takao* and *Maya* also became lost, but finally found a stretch of land, which they assumed to be Umnak Island. It was, but the planes orbited to get their bearings and neared the base at Fort Glenn.

Observed circling, the float planes were quickly engaged by P-40s that rose from the Umnak Island runway. One Pete was immediately shot down by Lieutenant John B. Murphy and his wingman, Lieutenant Jacob Dixon. The three others were shot full of holes, but managed to return to their cruisers, where one crash-landed in the water and sank. Pilot and gunner were rescued.

The U.S. Navy search had been underway for Admiral Kakuta's task force ever since receipt of the first intelligence warning. Eventually located at 11:00 A.M. on June 4 by a PBY, several attacks on the fleet were made by American planes, including one successful torpedo mission by B-25 bombers from the 77th Bombardment Squadron. One of the Japanese cruisers was hit and another ship was damaged. Kakuta reversed course and sped southwest, into the weather.

Meanwhile, Admiral Nimitz was not lured by the northern feint at Dutch Harbor, since the intelligence estimate had predicted that event. He kept two naval task forces near Midway: TF-16 under Rear Admiral Raymond A. Spruance, and TF-17 under Rear Admiral Frank J. Fletcher. The task force carriers USS *Enterprise, Hornet,* and *Yorktown* added 233 planes to the 119 aircraft based on Midway, bringing a total of 352 into the battle equation against 261 aboard the Japanese carriers *Hiryu, Kaga, Soryu,* and *Akagi,* all veterans of the Pearl Harbor attack.

Though operating separately, the American task forces were positioned north of Midway to block Yamamoto's southerly thrust, led by Vice Admiral Chuichi Nagumo's 1st Carrier Striking Force, which bore down on the island.

On June 3, a Catalina flying boat sighted the main Japanese striking force seven hundred miles west of Midway. When Admiral Nimitz in Hawaii was informed of the reported sighting, it confirmed his faith in the accuracy of the decoded Japanese message traffic. It also reaffirmed his belief that Yamamoto's plan was to initiate an attack on Midway the following morning from about two hundred miles northwest of the island.

Nine B-17s were launched from Midway on the third, soon after the sighting report was received, but attacks by these bombers and subsequent efforts later that day inflicted no damage on the invading force.

At dawn on the morning of the fourth, Nagumo's fleet was sighted by both an army air force B-17 (at 5:07 A.M.) and a navy PBY patrol bomber (at 5:34 A.M.). Yamamoto's carriers were in the process of launching 108 aircraft, including Val dive bombers, Kate torpedo bombers, and Zero fighters, toward Midway. They passed unseen abreast a force of 15 American B-17s, 4 Marine Marauder bombers, and 6 TBF Avenger torpedo planes dispatched from the island to engage Nagumo's fleet.

The Japanese struck first. Midway came under attack at 6:30 A.M. The island defenses were nearly destroyed during furious combat that resulted in some 75 American aircraft being shot down. While this attack was under way, the American bomber force arrived over the Japanese fleet but was crushed by defending Zeros without damaging the ships. Nagumo recovered his planes and ordered another strike against the island. To do so, he would have to download antiship armor-piercing bombs and torpedoes from his reserve aircraft and replace them with ground-attack ordnance. At that moment, he received word of the approaching American task forces but delayed for fifteen minutes before reversing his decision. The antiship weapons were to be put back on the planes. Meanwhile, the aircraft from Fletcher and Spruance's task forces came upon Nagumo's vulnerable fleet. Rarely in the history of warfare has the course of conflict changed in so short a time span as during the five minutes between 10:25 and 10:30 A.M. on June 4, 1942. During what would forever be known as the Battle of Midway, three Japanese carriers—*Akagi, Kaga*, and *Soryu*—were set aflame and began sinking after attacks by Dauntless dive bombers from the carriers USS *Enterprise* and *Yorktown*. One of the [Japanese] carriers "was burning with bright pink flames, sometimes blue flames," Lieutenant Commander John Thach recalled. He glanced down from overhead in his F4F Wildcat fighter. "I remember gauging the height of those flames by the length of the ship. The distance was about the same." The *Akagi* had been hit twice, and the resulting fires ignited ordnance and fuel lines on the flight deck, creating a fatal inferno. Later in the afternoon, the Japanese carrier *Hiryu* was located just after she had launched planes to bomb and torpedo the USS *Yorktown*. Dive bombers from the *Enterprise* made *Hiryu* a flaming wreck. She sank the following morning, while the *Yorktown* went to the bottom on June 6.

When the smoke cleared, Japan had lost four carriers, the battleship *Haruna*, the cruiser *Mikuma*, and 261 aircraft. American losses amounted to one carrier, the destroyer *Hammann* and 147 aircraft. For Japan, it was the beginning of the end as a naval power in the Pacific.

Stunned and embarrassed by these staggering losses, Admiral Yamamoto now took a second look at the Aleutians operation. Though reticent lest he lose again, he elected to press ahead with the occupation plan. Yamamoto needed a victory.

Chapter 3
The Kiska and Attu Invasions

They were seven young men from far away, the crew of Bomber 31, and they had shivered on that speck of muskeg and ice the entire winter of 1943–44. Who had lived there before the war came to what many described as "the lonesomest place on earth," and what bitter secrets lie scattered beneath the driven snow?

—Kamchatka crash site

The Northern Area Fleet commander, Vice Admiral Moshiro Hosogaya, received his orders to proceed with the Aleutian part of the operation from Admiral Yamamoto on June 5. His force included five naval groups: the Northern Force main body, the 2nd Carrier Striking Force, the Attu Landing Force, the Kiska Landing Force, and a submarine detachment. At 9:20 that same morning, Hosogaya ordered Rear Admiral Omori's Attu and Captain Ohno's Kiska invasion elements from their holding positions 225 miles south of the Aleutians. On the night of June 6, 1942, Ohno's fleet steamed into position off Kiska, fewer than 200 miles from the western end of America's 1,500-mile Aleutians chain.

The Kiska invasion force included the elite Maizuru 3rd Special Landing Force, led by Lieutenant Commander Hikumi Mukai.

Once this 550-man unit was loaded aboard landing craft, the Japanese made for the beach at Kiska's Reynard Cove. The assault party waded ashore at 10:27 P.M. and, meeting no resistance, spread out in three groups toward Kiska Harbor and the U. S. Navy weather station there. The weather detachment was comprised of ten enlisted men and their pet dog, Explosion. The dog, a small mongrel, had come by her name when she was born at Dutch Harbor, Unalaska, the night that a dynamite storage shack had exploded. She had been brought to Kiska and left with the detachment by Ensign William C. Jones when he visited the island months earlier on temporary duty to help set up the radio.

By noon on the second day of the invasion, the weather station was overrun and all but five of the weather detachment had been captured. Four surrendered ten days later and one, Aerographer's Mate First Class William C. House, eluded capture for forty-nine days before walking into the Japanese camp, his weight eighty pounds, his thighs the size of a child's arms. Meanwhile, the dog Explosion had been adopted by a Japanese soldier.

One hundred eighty miles to the west was Attu Island. Thirty-six miles long and twenty-five miles at its widest span, Attu was the westernmost American possession in the chain. Mountainous and covered with tundra, Attu had a few shallow bays and harbors but no airfields. The second element of Vice Admiral Hosogaya's invasion force steamed into position off Holtz Bay on the northern side of Attu in the early morning hours of June 7, 1942. The assault began at 3:00 A.M. using the Army North Sea Detachment, led by Major Matsutoshi Hotzumi. His unit was composed of the 301st Independent Infantry Battalion, the 301st Independent Engineer Company, and a service unit. The 1,143 men of the detachment split into two groups. The first, a scouting party, went ahead but got lost and ended up in uninhabited Massacre Valley, to the south. The main group climbed the snow-covered pass to the east and descended toward Chichagof Harbor.

At that time, the island population resided in Attu Village at Chichagof Harbor and consisted of forty-two native Aleuts and two American employees of the Bureau of Indian Affairs (BIA): Charles

Attu Village as it looked prior to the Japanese occupation.

Foster Jones, a sixty-year-old teaching assistant/weather reporter and his nurse/schoolteacher wife, Etta Jones. The tiny village was made up of a dozen frame houses, a church, and a weather station with its 120-foot radio tower, all clustered around the harbor. The Aleuts maintained a spartan existence by fishing, trapping fox, and weaving baskets. Missionaries, government patrol boats, small fishing craft, and the shortwave radio operated by Charles Jones from the weather station provided the inhabitants with their infrequent contacts with the outside world.

As the villagers prepared for Sunday morning church services, several of them spotted ships outside the harbor. An Aleut, Innokenti Golodoff, took a pair of field glasses and joined a group on their way to observe the vessels from the harbor point. The natives had already declined evacuation two weeks earlier when the seaplane tender USS *Casco* sailed into Chichagof Harbor and offered to take them aboard. Now the observers thought this fleet might be

American, coming back in force to coax them off the island. Not until a float plane from the light cruiser *Abukuma* swung overhead sporting a rising sun insignia did the villagers become alarmed. Golodoff reported what he had seen to Charles Jones, who ran to his radio and began sending out a message for help to the Indian Affairs outpost on Atka Island and to the weather station at Dutch Harbor, nine hundred miles to the east.

Major Hotzumi's main force entered the village from the west and began rounding up the inhabitants. They placed a Japanese flag on the schoolhouse. Minutes later, the valley behind the village echoed with reports of gunfire. The "lost" scouting party had found its way and was pouring over the hill, the troops shouting wildly and firing their rifles in the direction of the village.

An Aleut women was wounded in the foot. Bullets tore through the homes. One struck a Japanese soldier. Finally, the rising sun flag was spotted by the leader of the scouting party, and a cease-fire was ordered.

The Japanese continued gathering the inhabitants, some of whom had been seen fleeing to the hills. Etta and Charles Jones were captured in the village, then separated from the natives, who were herded into the church. The Joneses were interrogated in the schoolhouse by a Japanese officer, who seemed convinced that they were American spies and had them beaten. Given the presence of two Caucasians, one of whom operated the shortwave radio in this remote territory nearest Japan and the Soviet Union, it is no surprise the Japanese would suspect espionage.

Accounts vary, but according to Etta Jones, the Japanese took Charles away the next morning. He was never seen alive again. Charles Jones either committed suicide, was executed, or was shot while trying to flee. Jones was the only fatality during the island invasions, and his demise has been a point of controversy ever since.

Toranosuke Ozaki commanded the 3rd Platoon, 4th Company, and survived the war. Ozaki did not speak English but referred to

Charles Jones as the "spy priest," a term he picked up from the Japanese interrogator. He had been told that Jones held services in the church and ran the radio station. Ozaki readily admitted that Charles Jones "was killed," but claims he was not an eyewitness. Innokenti Golodoff stated after the war that several Aleuts were allowed to view part of the body and were told by the Japanese that Jones had committed suicide. The viewers saw cuts on his wrists, but the rest of the body was covered with a blanket. Aleut native Frank Latinoff was forced to dig Jones's grave.

Because Jones was a civil servant employee of the government, his body was disinterred after the war when Latinoff pointed out the burial site. Jones was reburied in Plot A, Grave 2, at the Fort Richardson National Cemetery near Anchorage, Alaska. No death certificate is available, but the remains were examined by Colonel T. C. Franks, an officer from the U.S. Graves Registration Service. His report stated that there was a hole, probably caused by a bullet, in his skull. The bullet hole was behind the ear. There is no comment in the report about the skull being shattered from an exit wound. Either Jones was killed by a rifle shot from very long range such that the bullet had spent most of its energy en route, or the wound was from a small-caliber handgun. The angle at which the bullet entered the skull indicated that the wound would not have been self-inflicted.

Upon learning of Charles's death, Etta Jones slit *her* wrists in a suicide attempt but was saved by a Japanese doctor. Once the island was considered secure, Etta and the Aleuts were allowed to roam about the village, but were restricted in their movements while the Japanese improved fortifications to defend against the American reaction to the invasion.

With the Midway area under control, Admiral Nimitz initially sent two carriers, the *Enterprise* and the *Hornet,* north to engage the Japanese fleet, but on June 10 he withdrew them to focus on operations in the South Pacific, at Guadalcanal. The strategy for the

Aleutians became one of containment, using forces already in place in Alaska, yet the idea that American territory was under foreign occupation gnawed upon public opinion. Something more, no matter how limited, had to be done.

Major General William O. Butler began receiving added fighter and bomber aircraft into his Eleventh Air Force bases on mainland Alaska. The navy moved Patrol Wing 4, commanded by Captain Leslie M. Gehres, to Kodiak Island, at the base of the Alaska Peninsula. The navy force included twenty PBY-5A Catalina flying boats. Long-range bombing and reconnaissance missions were tasked to keep the Japanese from securing a firm foothold. Strike missions against Kiska and Attu were assigned to 11th Air Force bombers using mainland bases, from Cape Field on Umnak Island, and by navy Patrol Wing 4 aircraft operating from Dutch Harbor, and from Kodiak and Atka Islands.

On June 10, the seaplane tender *Gillis* arrived at Atka. Her mission was to provide maintenance, fuel, parts, bombs, and bullets for navy seaplanes. Early the following morning, PBYs flew in from Dutch Harbor, taxied to the side of the ship, and began refueling and loading bombs.

A steady stream of Patrol Wing 4 seaplanes then began shuttle missions between Atka and Kiska. Though some PBYs had the Norden bombsight, it often proved impractical for the dive-bombing tactic preferred over Kiska. The PBYs dove on enemy ships and beach parties, "dropping bombs by the seaman's eye method," according to the Patrol Wing 4 war diary. After returning to Atka, the aircraft refueled, rearmed, and took off again. The strain on pilots and crews was intense, one pilot flying 19 1/2 hours in a single 24-hour period. One battle-damaged PBY sank after returning to Atka with two dead and one critically wounded crewmen aboard. By the second night, the flight crews were exhausted, so the tender's seamen gave up their bunks to allow the aviation personnel to get some rest. Some crews were put up by Ralph and Ruby Magee, the Indian Affairs employees at Atka

Village. The operation continued for 48 hours until the *Gillis* ran out of bombs and fuel.

The missions served more to harass than to inflict substantive Japanese losses. Postwar records show that the destroyer *Hibiki* was the only ship damaged. Near misses heavily damaged her bow, but she managed to return to Ominato, in Japan, for repairs.

When the *Gillis* withdrew from Atka, the villagers were evacuated, and their houses were set on fire to prevent their use by the Japanese, who were expected to occupy the island. The Russian Orthodox Church and its priceless records burned in the inferno.

On June 19, B-24 bombers launched from Cape Field and found clear weather over Kiska. Sitting in the harbor was the *Nissan Maru*, a sixty-eight-hundred-ton merchant vessel. Bombardier Master Sergeant Alpha G. Story centered his sight on the ship and released his bombs from fourteen thousand feet. The chances of hitting the target from that height were minimal, yet one of Story's thousand-pounders slammed into the vessel, midway between bow and stern. The *Nissan Maru* exploded and sank.

Intelligence photos revealed sixty-nine antiaircraft emplacements grouped in a five-square-mile area surrounding the main Japanese encampment and the submarine base. The Japanese revetted the gun pits and ran telephone communication wires from a command bunker to each of them. Moving things around was not a simple chore, given the weather and constant air attacks. The 11th Air Force intelligence staff soon determined the limitations of the particular guns and noted that the weapons were rarely repositioned. The American bomber crews then planned their run-ins to avoid the gun emplacements. When weather permitted, daily bombing missions became the routine over Kiska.

On August 4, a B-17 piloted by Major H. McWilliams flew as navigation lead for a pair of P-38 fighters flown by Lieutenants Kenneth Ambrose and Stanley Long. Upon arrival near Atka, McWilliams spotted three H6K4 Mavis flying boats headed for the island. Ambrose and Long rolled toward the Japanese formation from twenty-two thousand feet. The P-38s were spotted by the Mavis crews, and the seaplanes scattered. Long made a head-on attack on one, shattering its canopy. Ambrose set another on fire, which was last seen headed out of control into an overcast. The two American pilots headed west toward Kiska, hoping to catch the third Mavis running for home. After flying 150 miles, they spotted it. Both pilots made passes on the lumbering plane. The flying boat disappeared into the clouds. Upon landing at Umnak, each was credited with shooting down a Mavis. These were the first victories for the P-38 in any theater.

Due to unpredictably bad weather and the long distances required to attack Kiska and Attu, the bombers could carry only half their normal loads, making the need for a forward operating base apparent. Admiral Theobald had to balance his options since the Aleutian theater had low priority for resources compared to Europe and the South Pacific. Over vocal objections from General Buckner, Theobald chose to establish a forward base at Adak Island because of its natural harbor, 220 miles east of Kiska. Buckner wanted to use nearby but harborless Tanaga Island, since it was flatter and, in his view, more suitable for airfields.

Theobald held sway with navy headquarters in Washington, D.C. On August 30, Adak was occupied. Within two days, the 807 Engineer Aviation Battalion had diverted a creek that fed a tidal lagoon, filled in the lagoon, and began work constructing an airfield. Nine days later, the first aircraft, a B-18, landed on packed sand. Marston matting (pierced steel planking or PSP that interlocked to form a runway surface) was then laid above the sand. Eleventh Air Force fighter and bomber units flew in on September 12 and 13, throwing up huge plumes of spray as they touched down on the water-covered matting. Incredibly, combat operations off the new five-thousand-foot runway began on the fifteenth.

On Attu, the Japanese had made their headquarters at Attu Village and continued digging fortified positions around the harbor. Many of the troops were fishermen from southern Hokkaido. They used their skills catching salmon, trout, and octopus. With little interference from enemy aircraft, life was relatively good for these troops. Then, after learning of the nearby American buildup at Adak, the Imperial Command ordered a consolidation of forces on Kiska. On September 17, 1942, the Japanese pulled out of Attu, leaving only a communications detachment behind. The Attuans, along with Etta Jones, were loaded onto the *Yoko Maru* and taken to Kiska, where they were transferred aboard the *Osada Maru* to begin an arduous journey to Japan and confinement for the duration of the war.

On September 23, Major Donald Dunlap flew over Attu on a reconnaissance mission in a B-17 bomber. He circled Chichagof Harbor but saw no sign of Japanese presence. On the twenty-eighth, the village was bombed, destroying all but the church and one other building. On October 15, a B-24, with bombardier lieutenant Sam Newman aboard, arrived overhead. Newman watched as the remnants of Attu village drifted under his crosshairs. He released his weapons. Then, still bent over his bombsight, he saw the incendiary bombs burst and the last of the buildings disappear from sight beneath a spreading curtain of smoke. Though he reported the church destroyed, it had once again managed to survive.

Two weeks later, the Japanese High Command reversed its decision and sent forces back to Attu. With the village in shambles except for the church, they set up this time at Holtz Bay, three miles west of Chichagof Harbor. Construction of a tent city and two airfields became the major undertaking. With limited mechanized equipment, the task became onerous. Using manual labor, hand-pulled carts, picks, shovels, and a small bulldozer, the Japanese contingent made slow progress fashioning a runway in the valley south of the bay and starting work on another along the coast at the eastern arm of the bay. Wet conditions, loose soil, and deep ruts from runoff caused constant delays in construction. One Japanese survivor recalled after the war, "It was like sweeping the sea with a broom."

On November 9, a Boeing B-17 bomber led four Lockheed P-38 Lightning fighters 440 miles from Adak to Attu to attack eight Japanese A6M2-N Rufe float fighters that had been spotted by reconnaissance in the bay and onshore a few days earlier. The Rufe was a redesigned A6M2 Zero, and though its top speed was reduced to 271 miles per hour due to the central float and two smaller midwing floats, it still was a formidable adversary. The Japanese had begun using Attu as a safe haven for their supply ships to drop off planes destined east. The planes would then fly the remaining distance to Kiska Harbor.

The four P-38s swept in low over the eastern arm of Holtz Bay, strafed the Japanese tent city, then focused on the Rufes. All eight planes were destroyed according to the mission report.

Concurrently in November, the Japanese attempted to establish a base thirty miles east of Attu, on Shemya Island, hoping to take advantage of the island's flatter surface to more quickly build an airfield. Shemya has no natural harbor and after two failed attempts to offload supplies and personnel in rough sea conditions, the Japanese abandoned the idea. The Japanese experience was noted by reconnaissance and relayed to Admiral Theobald. It buttressed his choice to use Adak, with its natural harbor, over General Buckner's favored but harbor-less Tanaga Island for the U. S. effort.

A month later, on December 25, another U.S. reconnaissance plane reported eight more Rufes at Holtz Bay, apparently brought in by the *Kimikawa Maru* that day.

Twelve B-24 Liberator bombers and nine P-38 Lightning escorts were sent over Attu the day after Christmas. The bombers circled above clouds for an hour, then turned back. The P-38s, led by Captain Ralph D. Matthews, penetrated the cloud layer. Once underneath, the fighters bore in at high speed and low level along the western arm of the bay to strafe the Japanese planes and facilities. As the Japanese defenses opened up, the Lightnings crossed to the eastern arm and continued the attack. After clearing the area,

Japanese naval airmen pose for the camera on Attu in the Aleutians during the Japanese occupation from 1942 to 1943. The photo was captured when the U.S. 7th Infantry Division assaulted the island in May of 1943.

Captain Matthews and Lieutenant Artie L. Kayser decided to return for another run.

As the two fighters rolled back in, the Japanese antiaircraft batteries were ready. Matthews's P-38 took immediate hits. It burst into flames and slammed into the bay, killing Matthews. The Japanese gunners then homed in on Kayser's plane. Both engines took hits. The right one failed, and the left engine ran rough before finally quitting fifty miles from Adak, abeam Tanaga Island. Kayser ditched the plane near the beach and swam fifty yards in freezing water to shore. He was picked up by a navy PBY seaplane more than two hours later.

Though Lieutenant Oliver Wayman had been seriously wounded and Lieutenant Earl C. Nedlund's plane had one engine out, the seven remaining planes made it back to Adak.

Meanwhile, attacks were being conducted against the heavily entrenched Japanese forces on Kiska. More than six thousand troops were on the island, many of them manning antiaircraft batteries surrounding Kiska Harbor. American bombers fought their way through the flak to strike the submarine base, runway (under construction), military barracks area, supply ships, and float planes in the harbor. With the amount of flak in the air, U. S. losses were bound to occur.

On the morning of December 30, a B-25 flown by Lieutenant Julius Constantine was forced to ditch ten miles from Kiska after taking hits from antiaircraft fire. The OA-10 rescue plane sent to recover the crew crashed into the side of Kiska Volcano during bad weather, killing the crew and leaving the men of the B-25 to succumb to the frigid waters offshore. That same afternoon, P-38s from Adak arrived on the scene, but the Rufes that had been delivered from Attu were in the air. Two P-38s were lost, one of them flown by Lieutenant Kayser, the same pilot who had been shot down four days earlier. This time, his luck ran out.

Vice Admiral Thomas C. Kinkaid replaced Admiral Theobald on January 4, 1943. A more aggressive commander who had experience in the South Pacific, Kinkaid had an attitude similar to that of army general Buckner. Command relations improved immediately, and both men began preparations for occupying Amchitka Island, 178 miles farther west of Adak. With airpower available only 60 miles from Kiska and 240 miles from Attu, continual pressure could be applied to the Japanese garrisons while preventing resupply by surface ships. The stage was being set for the retaking of the Japanese-held islands.

The U.S. military occupation of Amchitka began on January 11, 1943, when thirty-five Alaska Scouts, an army unit made up of bush pilots, trappers, Sioux Indians, and native Alaskans, went ashore. They were followed by the rest of a 2,100-man landing force the next morning. Time was crucial, since the Japanese were sure to react once they discovered U.S. forces so near. High seas and gale-force winds played havoc with the landing force, swamping small boats, and sinking larger vessels, including the destroyer USS *Worden*, which was swept onto a rocky outcropping.

Fourteen men drowned trying to swim ashore after the order was given to abandon ship. The army transport *Middleton* ran aground while rescuing 175 sailors from the *Worden*. Fuel leaked out of the *Worden* and washed up onto the beach, drenching the men who were trying to unload barges in pounding surf. The transport USS *Reardon* also was driven onto rocks. She later sank with no reported casualties.

In spite of the hardships caused by wind-lashed surf, fog, snow, and bitter cold, the 813th Engineer Aviation Battalion undertook to accomplish the impossible on Amchitka. The engineers erected a dam, then drained a shallow marsh inland from the head of Constantine Harbor. Soldiers digging foxholes happened upon a gravel deposit that the engineers used to fill the marsh. First, they completed a four-thousand-foot-long fighter strip. Then, farther inland, they began a ten-thousand-foot bomber runway. Another storm swept in from the North Pacific, a blessing really, since it kept the Japanese on the ground.

As construction progressed, bombers from Adak continued to keep the pressure on the Japanese, but at heavy cost. On January 18, four B-24s and two P-38s along with eighteen men were lost due to bad weather.

On the twenty-first, a midair collision during an instrument approach to Adak caused the loss of another B-24 and its fifteen occupants. Eleventh Air Force units also lost two B-25D medium bombers, two A-26s, and a P-40 to accidents, bringing the month's total aircraft losses to eleven, none to combat.

Fighter cover was provided sporadically over Amchitka during the brief periods of decent weather. On January 24, the men working on the new runways looked up to see a lone Japanese plane circling. It departed before the arrival of American P-38 fighters. Two more Japanese planes came back the next day while the base was unprotected. The Japanese dropped small bombs that landed harmlessly in the harbor. On the twenty-seventh, six Rufe float planes appeared over Constantine Harbor. They commenced bombing and strafing attacks. One American was killed, another wounded, and the runway was cratered. As repairs progressed, nine floatplanes showed up on February 1 to strafe and bomb, but there were no casualties. The Japanese, it seemed, had determined the time periods when the P-38s would be providing top cover and suspended attacks during those hours. Then, on the thirteenth, Captain Morgan A. Griffin responded to a report from a navy PBY crew. He found a single Japanese Jake floatplane off the northwestern end of Amchitka and shot it down. On the fifteenth, a lone Rufe floatplane dropped a bomb in the camp area, killing the occupants of a nearby foxhole. In spite of these incursions, time had run out for the Japanese in their attempt to disrupt operations on the island.

The first American fighter, a P-40K flown by Lieutenant Kenneth Saxhaug, landed on the fighter strip at Amchitka on the February 16. He was followed by seven more P-40s and four P-38s. Japanese incursions over the island stopped on the eighteenth when Major Clayton J. Larson and Lieutenant Elmer J. Stone were on patrol and spotted two floatplanes near the island. They shot both down.

During the winter months, the Japanese continued efforts to secure a permanent foothold in the Aleutians. Admiral Kinkaid countered by setting up an air and sea blockade, deploying his meager forces south, west, and north of the fifteen-hundred-mile island chain. Between November 1, 1942, and February 20, 1943, thirty-three Japanese shiploads of men and supplies meant for Kiska and Attu tried to run the blockade. Fourteen vessels never made it to either island. A U.S. Navy PBY attacked and sank the *Montreal Maru*, while Eleventh Air Force B-24s sank the *Kotohira Maru* outside Attu's Holtz Bay. The *Urajio Maru* was so badly crippled by B-24 bombing attacks that it was abandoned near Kiska. On the night of February 18, Task Group 8.6's heavy cruiser USS *Indianapolis* heavily damaged the transport *Akagane Maru* southwest of Attu. The cargo ship went to the bottom a few hours later the next morning.

The Japanese responded by escorting their transports using cruisers and destroyers. One convoy reached the islands on March 9th. On the twenty-sixth, Vice Admiral Moshiro Hosogaya, aboard the heavy cruiser *Nachi*, led a force of escorts and three more transports in an effort to run the blockade. Aboard one of the transports was Attu's newly assigned commander, Colonel Yasuyo Yamasaki, and his staff. The other vessels carried troops, equipment, ammo, and supplies intended for Attu.

Despite being outnumbered, Rear Admiral Charles Horatio McMorris' Task Group 16, including one heavy and one light cruiser, blocked the path of the convoy. In a running gun battle lasting 3 1/2 hours, the two sides slugged it out. The heavy cruiser USS *Salt Lake City* was hit four times and lost power. While her escort destroyers laid a smoke screen, the *Salt Lake City*'s commander, Captain Bertram Rodgers, used his last few knots of speed to turn the vessel so that all the cruiser's guns could bear on the approaching Japanese task force. The crew hurriedly swung their heavy gun turrets and waited for the Japanese ships to emerge from the smoke screen. Meanwhile, the destroyer USS *Bailey* led two other escorts into the teeth of the Japanese fleet. The *Bailey* was hit twice, but the Japanese ran low on ammunition and disengaged while the *Salt Lake City* got under way again. Though air support had been requested via radio by Admiral McMorris, maintenance and weather delays kept American bombers from reaching the scene. The Japanese, however, intercepted the transmission and Hosogaya's convoy turned back for Japan, the *Nachi* damaged.

General Hap Arnold, the army air force chief in Washington, D. C., heard of the missed opportunity by his airmen that might have sent Hosogaya's fleet to the bottom. He sent an angry query to General Butler, the 11th Air Force commander under army general Buckner, demanding answers to why his planes never reached the scene. Butler explained that the delay was caused by armament problems encountered while a storm raged. His bombers had been loaded with general-purpose bombs for use against Kiska, but needed armor-piercing weapons for attacking ships. General Arnold was satisfied with the response, but Butler ordered six B-25s to begin a round-the-clock antishipping alert.

Admiral Hosogaya, who had failed to prevail with his superior force, was relieved of command and retired. The Japanese switched to using submarines to resupply the Aleutians, but with only about half its needed complement of troops and supplies getting through, the beleaguered garrisons on Attu and Kiska dug in and waited for the expected invasion.

By now the American buildup was beginning to make its presence known. Kodiak was a permanent base, with substantial facilities and comfortable quarters. Dutch Harbor on Unalaska Island, though more primitive, was crowded with troops and sailors. It was from here that supplies funneled west into the island chain. The war had moved beyond the once front-line air base at Umnak, and supplies bypassed the island. Men there sat around eating Spam three times a day, sometimes for weeks on end. At Atka Island, called "Atkatraz" by the troops, the army guarded the navy PBY base. Not much of any importance beyond that went on since the seaplanes had deployed west. Months could go by without any mail. At Adak, the harbor was crowded with Liberty ships, and bearded merchant mariners strolled the beaches where engineers were busy with all manner of construction projects. The island was slowly replacing Dutch Harbor as the funnel for supplies. Amchitka Island was the current end of the American line, only sixty miles from Kiska. Amchitka was crowded with men who slept in sleeping bags on mud tent floors and lived off C-rations. In less than a year the Aleutian population jumped from five thousand to forty thousand. All this movement and influx had but one purpose: the retaking of two Japanese-held islands to the west.

In considering a plan for invading Kiska and Attu, Admiral Kinkaid's staff analyzed reconnaissance photos. It was estimated that on Attu the Japanese had no more than five hundred troops ashore, no coastal batteries, and only a scattering of antiaircraft guns at Holtz Bay and Chichagof Harbor. Compared to the six-thousand-man garrison on Kiska, Attu was deemed the easier challenge. If Attu could be retaken, Kiska would be isolated. Kinkaid presented his concept to Admiral Nimitz, and on March 11, word was relayed to Kinkaid to proceed with the invasion plan.

Kinkaid moved his headquarters to Adak during March 1943. General Buckner moved his staff in from Fort Richardson, and Captain Gehres relocated from Kodiak. Promotions came through for all of them. Kinkaid and Buckner pinned on third stars as vice admiral and lieutenant general, respectively, and Gehres was elevated to one-star commodore.

During April 1943, air strikes by medium bombers and fighter aircraft continued unabated against Kiska and Attu. Due to the proximity of Amchitka to Kiska, Eleventh Air Force maintenance crews launched up to fourteen missions per day.

The Japanese had begun construction of an airfield on Kiska near Salmon Lagoon, and a concerted American effort was made to prevent the airfield's completion. U.S. records were established for missions flown and tonnage dropped that would not be broken during the remainder of the war in the North Pacific. In April 149 missions were flown against Kiska and Attu targets. On Kiska, 5,740 bombs (638 tons) were dropped, and 1,341 bombs (154 tons) were released over Attu. No Japanese air opposition came up to defend the installations. One American B-24 bomber and its 11-man crew were lost along with two fighters that went down. One of the latter pilots was a fatality.

For the Japanese on the receiving end of the attacks, life had literally become a nightmare. One diary noted:

> Due to frequent enemy attacks, we dream of enemy planes in our sleep and during our meals. The only peaceful time . . . is when the weather is stormy and then the soldiers have pleasant expressions on their faces and they sing their military songs loudly.

Another described the decrease in effectiveness in stemming the accuracy of the bombers:

> Loss of personnel, installations, air defense arms, fuel and fire-arms influence us considerably, and it is deplorable that even the AAA guns gradually lose their hitting efficiency.

While the bombing proceeded unabated on Attu and Kiska, the U. S. Army's 7th Infantry Division departed from San Francisco on April 23–24, 1943. Desert-trained, the troops were under the impression that they were destined for North Africa, only to be jolted upon the opening of their classified orders to find themselves headed into Arctic terrain.

Concurrently, the two original Alaska PBY seaplane units under Commodore Gehres, VP-41 and VP-42, were decommissioned and the crews became the experienced cadre in new squadrons, VB-135 and VB-136, equipped with PV-1 Ventura medium bombers. The Ventura, along with the Hudson bomber and the C-56 Loadstar passenger plane, was a derivative of the Lockheed Electra commercial airliner. Built by Lockheed's subsidiary, Vega, in Burbank, California, the PV-1 had two 2,000-horsepower Pratt & Whitney R-2800 air-cooled engines, giving it a top speed of 280 knots (322 miles per hour). Its range was 1,660 miles, and it carried a 3,000-pound bomb load. The plane was fitted with four .50-caliber machine guns, two in the nose and two in a top turret. Four .30-caliber guns also were mounted, two in the nose and two under the tail.

The two Ventura squadrons were split between Adak and Amchitka, with fifteen aircraft at each location. VB-135 set down on Amchitka on May 5, 1943, with the more advanced ASD-1 radar-equipped aircraft. Personnel were housed in tents and lived off army field rations. The runway was rough, and a standing joke among the aviators was that the army engineers "wouldn't build a

A PV-1 Ventura from VB-136 operating off Adak Island, Aleutians in 1943. These planes employed their onboard radar to lead bombing missions over Kiska.

runway unless it was ninety degrees to the prevailing wind." The squadron began patrols immediately and, when weather permitted, led B-24D Liberators over Kiska for radar-directed bomb runs.

By May 11, 1943, the forces were fully assembled for the invasion of Attu. For the U.S. Army and for the men of the 7th Infantry Division, it would be their first amphibious operation of the war.

The assault was to be a three-pronged effort, with a primary force of three infantry battalions and three 105-millimeter artillery batteries landing on the deserted southeastern shore, at Massacre Bay. This element was to advance up the valley and seize the passes linking Holtz Bay and Chichagof Harbor. The second prong included an infantry battalion and a supporting artillery battery and was to land at the west arm of Holtz Bay in the north, three miles from the main Japanese camp. This unit was to proceed along the high terrain on Moore Ridge, overlooking the Japanese positions. The third force, a five-hundred-man-strong mix of scout and reconnaissance companies (recons), was to be landed by submarine at Austin Cove, west of Holtz Bay. It was assigned to advance behind the Japanese artillery positions defending Holtz Bay, neutralize them, and link up with the element on Moore Ridge. All three segments were then to combine on an assault over the ridges to Chichagof Harbor and Attu Village. The entire operation was expected to last three days.

Despite high U.S. efforts at secrecy, the Japanese learned about the intended invasion of Attu via a slip in the security system. They even determined that the landings would take place in May. The security lapse was apparent after the decoding of an intercepted message from Admiral Hosogaya's replacement, Vice Admiral Shiro Kawase, to Colonel Yasuyo Yamasaki, who had finally arrived on Attu by submarine in April. Yamasaki was ordered to defend the island at all cost.

The Japanese positioned two companies above Massacre Valley: at Clevesy Pass, where they controlled access to Holtz Bay, and at Chichagof Harbor. The rest of Yamasaki's men were kept busy digging trenches and foxholes from which to bring heavy firepower on any invading force. Hope for reinforcements faded as more and more American bombs fell daily from the sky.

D-Day was set for early morning on May 8, 1943, but surf conditions were forecast to be high, so the execution order was delayed day by day until the eleventh. When the twenty-nine ships of Task Force 16 assembled off their respective beaches, the fog was so thick that the danger of vessels running into one another loomed greater than the threat from the Japanese. During maneuvering, the *Sicard* and the *MacDonough* collided, and the services of these vessels were lost. The *Sicard* was to have been the boat-control ship in the Holtz Bay area.

At 3:09 A.M. the *Narwhal* disembarked her 7th Scout Company detachment west of Holtz Bay. At 5:10 A.M. the *Nautilus* reported that she also had safely landed her scouts at Beach Scarlet. The carrier *Nassau*'s planes then bombed the Holtz Bay area for half an hour (see third map).

Meanwhile, the southern force off Massacre Bay received permission to delay its landings because of dense fog. Finally, at 4:06 P.M. the beach was sighted when visibility suddenly improved to fifteen hundred yards. The landing craft headed in. Fifteen minutes later, word was received that the first two waves had reached shore without resistance. Radio communications with the beachmaster were established. By 4:40 P.M. all the remaining waves had landed: six on Beach Blue, three on Beach Yellow, and one on Beach Rainbow. No opposition had been encountered. In fact, the troops on Beach Yellow met no resistence while pushing two thousand yards inland.

By the end of the second day, however, the ill-equipped and desert-trained men of the 7th Infantry Division were locked in combat with determined Japanese defenders everywhere they came in contact with them. At midnight, the first casualty report reached the task force commander. Forty-four U.S. soldiers had been killed. Progress inland had ceased in the Massacre Bay sector, both battalion combat teams being pinned down. The Japanese, with two infantry companies of fewer than a hundred men each, had spread out along the edge of the fog. Using small-bore artillery, machine guns, hand grenades, and riflemen, they confronted a three-thousand-man task force that was aided by naval air and gunfire support and stopped it cold.

In the northern sector, a U.S. battalion moved forward onto the high ground at Moore Ridge, overlooking the western rim of Holtz Bay. There, despite naval and air support, the advance got bogged down in the face of stiff Japanese resistance.

The Alaska scouts who had come ashore by submarine at Austin Cove became lost and exhausted. They remained out of action as the unit struggled through deep snow on its way to the rear of the Japanese positions.

Above the battle, P-38s came roaring in on the deck, dropping 20-pound fragmentation bombs, then zoomed up to drop five-hundred-pounders at Chichag of Harbor. One P-38, piloted by

Lieutenant Robert A. Baker, was hit by antiaircraft fire. Baker ditched outside Holtz Bay and was picked up by a destroyer. Two days later, on the fourteenth, a B-24 crew was not so lucky. The bomber slammed into the mountain behind Holtz Bay, killing all eleven men aboard.

During the battle of Attu, Dr. Paul Nobuo Tatsuguchi was in charge of a Japanese field hospital at Holtz Bay. He had attended Pacific Union College of California until 1932. Later, he studied at the College of Medical Evangelists (now Loma Linda University), obtaining his California medical license in 1938. Dr. Tatsuguchi then returned to Japan as an Adventist medical missionary. In 1941 he was inducted into the Japanese army as a physician. He kept a diary during the invasion, and his May 16 entry included:

> If Shitagata-Dai is occupied by the enemy, the fate of east arm is decided. So, burnt documents and prepared to destroy the patients by giving them shots in the arm and die painless. At that moment, there was an order from the Headquarters of sector unit to proceed to Chichagof Harbor by way of Unanose. 0100 in the morning, patient from Ind. Infantry was lost, so accompanied the patients. There was an air-raid so took refuge in the former field hospital cave. The guns of the enemy were roaring continuously.

On the ground in the south, the men of the 7th Division continued to struggle uphill against the Japanese, who were dug in using a system of trenches and foxholes that allowed them to maneuver just above the fog line. Trying to pinpoint their positions was almost impossible, thus preventing accurate naval gunfire support. Four F4F Wildcat pilots from the USS *Nassau* headed up Massacre Valley to attempt to support the troops who were battling the Japanese. A strong wind shear swept in from the passes and tossed two of the planes thousands of feet in the air, while the trailing pair were flung into the ground killing pilots Douglas Henderson and Ernest D. Jackson. Another Wildcat went down near Sarana Bay, killing Lieutenant Commander L. V. K. Greenamyer.

The two opposing ground forces continued to slug it out, with both sides determined to prevail. Every yard of tundra was hotly contested by the Japanese as the American force continued to increase in size and pressure day by day.

Aboard the seaplane tender *Casco* just offshore was navy aerographer Paul E. Carrigan. A veteran of the Dutch Harbor attack, he tried to keep abreast of the situation. "We knew without being told that the battle of Attu was not going well. This was especially evident at night because of the fireworks display of tracers crisscrossing the blackness." Carrigan and his shipmate, aerographer, Robert R. Calderon, watched during the day through binoculars, but on one occasion they tried the theodolite scope, a modified surveyor's transit that the weathermen used to track weather balloons. It had high magnification but a narrow field of view. According to Carrigan,

> Calderon had the theodolite's cross hairs on a soldier. This G.I. left the protection of jagged rocks and was angling upward across snow toward another outcropping. Calderon was following the G.I.'s struggles when the man was killed by a Japanese grenade. The soldier was blown backward and momentarily out of Calderon's viewplate. With entrails coming out, the G.I. slid a hundred yards down a precipitous slope before coming to rest in a heap.
>
> "Jesus," said a shaken Calderon.

His face ashen and feeling nauseous, Calderon stepped away from the instrument. Carrigan came forward and put his eye to the lens to have a look at what had upset his friend.

> I followed Calderon's directions and slowly turned the

> control knobs. From where the grenade exploded, a dark streak in the white snow led downward to the still form. For some reason I could not pinpoint, I felt acute embarrassment. Perhaps it was my having exercised a forbidden right, not mine to begin with. Theodolite power had enabled me to be an immune interloper on the killing ground.

The battle continued to rage. Later on the sixteenth, Moore Ridge, separating the eastern and western arms of Holtz Bay, was taken. From its summit, fire could be directed on all of the Holtz Bay area. By the next day, the Japanese had evacuated, moving over the snow-packed ridge into Chichagof Harbor.

To the south, American forces stormed up Gilbert Ridge and fought in close contact with the defending Japanese on Point Able, the last promontory defending the Massacre Valley area. Japanese lieutenant Honna, who along with Lieutenant Goto and their two companies had held up the U.S. advance for six days, was killed. By the twentieth, the strategic heights were secure and the U.S. southern force joined with the men coming over from Holtz Bay for the final drive into Chichagof Harbor.

On the twenty-first, Dr. Tatsuguchi's clinic was strafed while he was attempting to amputate a patient's arm. He retreated to an air raid shelter until the attack ended, then wrote about his commander's attitude that day.:

> Nervousness of our commander is severe, and he has said his last word to his officers and NCOs—that he will die tomorrow—gave all his articles away. Hasty chap, this fellow. The officers on the front are doing a fine job. Everyone heard this became desperate and things became disorderly.

Though being squeezed into a tight corner, the Japanese ignored the surrender leaflets being dropped by overflying American aircraft. Throwing down their weapons was not an option.

On the twenty-fourth, twelve Japanese G4M1 Betty twin-engine bombers were launched from Paramushiro in the northern Kuriles. They came roaring out of the mist to attack the destroyers USS *Phelps* and *Charleston* steaming just outside Chichagof Harbor. After dropping torpedoes, which missed, the bombers then sped over to the mouth of the harbor, where they dropped bundles of supplies to the remaining Japanese troops.

The next day, sixteen more bombers were spotted west of Attu by a patrolling PBY. Word was relayed to a flight of P-38 Lightning fighters from Amchitka that were patrolling over Attu. Lieutenant Colonel James R. Watt and Lieutenants Warren B. Banks, John K. Geddes, Harry C. Higgins, Marshall E. Clyde, and Frederick Moore, Jr. sighted the Betty bombers at fourteen thousand feet over Attu. The P-38s were spotted by the bomber crews, who then dropped their bombs harmlessly and turned for home, with the fighters in hot pursuit. During a running firefight that lasted twenty-five minutes, Colonel Watt's P-38 was damaged while attacking one of the bombers. Then it was Lieutenant Geddes's turn in the crosshairs. The right side of his canopy shattered from a 20-millimeter cannon round fired by one of the Bettys. Lieutenant Higgins made multiple passes at the bombers and watched as one went tumbling into the sea.

Lieutenant Moore, having seen the effects that stern attacks were having on the Lightnings, climbed above and forward of the Bettys, then did a half roll and pulled down to perform the back side of a loop. He bottomed out, wings level, then made head-on passes at the bomber stream, shooting down three Bettys.

Meanwhile, Watt radioed that his controls were vibrating and his right engine was losing coolant, while Geddes had his hands full trying to nurse his damaged plane to safety.

Five Betty bombers went down and seven were seen trailing smoke as the Japanese headed for their home base on Paramushiro.

Geddes ditched his P-38 off the coast of Attu, where he was picked up by a Kingfisher floatplane. Watt disappeared into the bleak North Pacific. He was later awarded credit for downing one bomber.

On the ground at Attu, the troops moving up from Massacre Valley had managed to conquer Point Able and joined forces with their northern element. The Japanese defenders were now trapped in a small pocket near the mouth of Chichagof Harbor.

Dr. Tatsuguchi's entry on the twenty-fifth revealed the desperate situation during the final days of Japanese resistance:

> By Naval gun firing, it felt like the Misumi Barracks blew up tremendously. Consciousness becomes vague. One tent burned down by a hit from an incendiary bomb. Strafing planes hit the next room, 2 hits from a .50 caliber shell, one stopped on the ceiling and the other penetrated. My room looks like an awful mess from the sand and pebbles that come down from the roof. Hirose, 1st Lt. of Medical Corps, is also wounded. There was a ceremony of granting of Imperial Edict. The last line of Umanose [Fish Hook Ridge] was broken through. No hope for reinforcements. Will die for the cause of Imperial Edict.

On the twenty-eighth, surrender leaflets were again dropped on the beleaguered Japanese. Down to fewer than half the twenty-six-hundred men that he started with, Colonel Yamasaki drew up a bold final plan. He decided to attack in hopes of breaking through the American lines to overrun the artillery that had numbed them, then turn it against their tormentors. From Dr. Tatsuguchi's diary entry of May 29:

> Today at 2000 we assembled in front of Headquarters. The field hospital took part too. The last assault is to be carried out. All the patients in the hospital were made to

> commit suicide. Only 33 years of living and I am to die here. I have no regrets. Banzai to the Emperor! I am grateful that I have kept the peace in my soul which Enkist [Christ] bestowed upon me. At 1800, took care of all the patients with grenades. Goodbye, Taeke, my beloved wife who loved me to the last. Until we meet again, grant you God speed. Miseka, who just became 4 years old, will grow up unhindered. I feel sorry for you Tokiko, born February of this year and gone without seeing your father. Well, be good. Matsua, (brother), Kochan, Sukechan, Masachan, Mittichan, goodbye. The number participating in this attack is a little over 1000, to take enemy artillery position. It seems that the enemy is expecting an all out attack tomorrow.

As midnight approached, the Japanese began a forced march up Fish Hook Ridge. In darkness, they slipped undetected past the thin American line. At Lake Cories, they fought through the few troops positioned there, then continued across Sarana Valley to Clevesy Pass, surging through two command posts and a cluster of medical tents on Engineer Hill, killing everyone in their path, including the wounded. The 7th Divison Engineers hastily organized a defensive line and stalled the attack. The Japanese came at the Americans again and again. By the time it was over, Japanese soldiers lay in heaps across a two-mile stretch from Clevesy Pass to Engineer Hill. Colonel Yamasaki, sword in hand, died fighting. His few remaining troops used hand grenades to commit suicide.

As for Dr. Tatsuguchi, he did not die in the suicide charge. According to a GI witness, the following day, the doctor came running out of the field hospital cave at Chichagof Harbor. He was waving a Bible and shouting, "Don't shoot, I'm a Christian." Another American soldier, farther away, did not hear the plea and shot him. The diary was found on the doctor's body.

During the next three days, twenty-nine Japanese soldiers were taken prisoner. Since they had never been schooled on how to deal with capture—in the Japanese military ethic the dishonor of surrender was unthinkable—the Japanese POWs were very open with intelligence information. While the details they provided were gathered, the deadly work of rooting out the few remaining evaders continued for three months. The last known defender was killed by a Seabee road crew in the hills southwest of Casco Cove on September 1, 1943.

The battle for Attu was over.

Chapter 4
The Attu Buildup and Kiska Evacuation

The end for which a soldier [or seaman] *is recruited, clothed, armed, and trained, the whole object of his sleeping, eating, drinking, and marching* [sailing] *is simply that he should fight at the right place and the right time.*

—*Clausewitz,* On War

On the night of May 29, radio operator Toranosuke Ozaki was at his post inside the communications center on Kiska. Suddenly the steady hiss of his receiver was interrupted. A shaky voice from Attu announced that with his perimeter broken through on all sides, Colonel Yamasaki's contingent was about to make its final assault on the American lines. Yamasaki then bid the men of Kiska farewell. The nearly daily bombing, artillery salvos, and strafing attacks on Kiska had taken their toll of lives and morale there as well, but as Ozaki listened to the final words from Attu, a gloom descended. The mood became far darker than that from the incessant noise and shaking of the earth caused by what the Japanese called the "regular delivery by Roosevelt." When the signal from Attu finally went silent, all hope of sustaining Japanese occupation in the Aleutians faded with it.

Once resistance collapsed on Attu and operations to secure the island began their final stages, American plans for the retaking of Kiska were set in motion. A joint directive was issued on May 31, with D-Day set for August 15, 1943. U.S. intelligence overestimated the Japanese force at more than ten thousand, so nearly thirty-five thousand Allied ground troops were to be committed to the assault, supported by more than a hundred warships.

U.S. construction in the Aleutians continued unabated, and by the end of June, two more airfields were usable. At Alexai Point, a spit of land that stuck out into Massacre Bay on Attu, the army air force installed a three-thousand-foot matted runway. The second airstrip, a ten-thousand-foot matted runway on Shemya, was operational, but was being upgraded with a concrete surface. Designed for heavy bombers such as the B-24 Liberator, Shemya was intended to eventually become a B-29 Superfortress base once that plane finished development and reached mass production. A third strip, another matted runway, was under construction by the Seabees at Casco Bay on Attu for use by navy medium bombers.

With Attu back in American hands and new airfields coming on line, Admiral Kinkaid turned his full attention to Kiska. Destroyers *Aylwin* and *Monaghan* moved into position to block the entrance to Kiska Harbor and conduct artillery bombardments of the Japanese shore positions. A cruiser task force was stationed west of Attu to intercept any attempt to reinforce the Japanese garrison. Commodore Gehres focused his PBY patrols west, moving closer and closer to Soviet Kamchatka and the Japanese northern Kurile Islands to detect Japanese resupply efforts.

Admiral Kinkaid wanted bombs dropped on Kiska daily, but weather conditions made that impossible. The Japanese troops on the island, however, continued to relish the fog and cloud cover which meant fewer attacks, but even that would soon change.

On June 1, eight AAF B-25 Mitchell bombers led by five navy PV-1 Venturas from VB-135 launched from Amchitka. The Venturas were equipped with the new ASD-1 radar, which provided a crude ground-map picture on its scope. Though the radar image was slightly distorted, a skilled operator could use it and a handheld map of Kiska to identify Little Kiska Island in the harbor. Ordnance was dropped with some degree of effectiveness from above the clouds. This practice of leading AAF bombers over Kiska became standard practice during the next few weeks. At night, PBY flying boats using their own primitive radar dropped bombs on the island, more to harass the Japanese by keeping them awake than to inflict serious damage.

Releasing bombs above the clouds was one thing, but the planes still had to penetrate the weather to get safely home. The Aleutian fog settled in, so for more than a week only sporadic missions were launched, all led by Venturas using their radars to drop bombs through the undercast. On the eleventh, however, the weather dawned sunny and clear. Every operational plane was launched from Davis Field on Atka and from Amchitka. By noon, however, the fog had rolled back in. A flight of five P-38 Lightnings was unable to recover at Amchitka. Advised to head for Cape and Davis Fields, one was forced to make a crash landing without injury, on Tanaga Island. A second Lightning piloted by Lieutenant Glen B. Martin, one of the more experienced squadron pilots, ran out of fuel with Davis Field in sight. Martin radioed, "Motor conked, landing in water three quarter miles north of runway." His body washed ashore and was found six days later. Martin was the 54th Fighter Squadron's seventeenth fatality in less than a year.

Two squadrons of PBY-5A Catalina flying boats began operations out of Casco Cove in early June, flying monotonous patrols over the North Pacific. To relieve the boredom and determine if the war could be carried to the Japanese home islands, Lieutenant Oliver Glenn from VP-61 got local approval to fly across the Bering Sea all the way to the Kamchatka Peninsula, just north of Japan's Kurile Islands. Glenn sighted landfall, then turned parallel to the coast near Petropavlovsk, the peninsula's capital. Two Polikarpov I-16 fighters took to the air to intercept the intruder. The stocky fighters slid alongside the big flying boat, escorting it until it turned back for the Aleutians. No complaint was ever lodged by the Soviets, and nothing official was recorded by the American unit.

Not to be outdone, Lieutenant Commander Carl H. Amme, commander of VP-45, decided to try his luck in Soviet airspace. He flew his flying boat past the northern side of the Komandorski (Commander) Islands in the Bering Sea, where he spotted construction in progress. The next day he dispatched a squadron pilot in another PBY to take photos of the site. Excellent vertical and oblique photographs were taken, but when Commodore Gehres saw them, he became irate over these unauthorized flights and directed that Amme discipline the pilot for violating Soviet neutrality. Amme, of course, was responsible for the mission, so he took no action against his subordinate, but he did recognize Gehres's sensitivity about unauthorized flights. Attacking the Kuriles was likely a thought already germinating in the commodore's mind, and he wanted no one to torpedo the possibility by causing an international incident.

Several weeks later, another of Amme's pilots ventured too far west and had to make a forced landing on a lake at Bering Island, the largest of the Komandorskis. In 1741, Danish explorer Vitus Bering and several other crewmen died from scurvy there during a long, bleak winter. A cluster of Russian crosses near the mouth of a small stream marks the site of their graves.

While Soviet troops garrisoned at the northern end of the island started toward the downed PBY on foot, Amme decided to try a rescue effort. Without telling headquarters, he sent Roy Evans, another of his pilots, to the island with orders to snatch the stranded crew and any classified documents on board the Catalina, then sink the seaplane. He further ordered Evans to keep radio silence during the mission. The recovery operation came off without a hitch, and the PBY went to the bottom, where it surely remains to this day. Commodore Gehres was kept in the dark about the affair.

Sensing a need to find out what was going on at his westernmost base, Gehres arranged a visit several weeks later. Amme laid out the red carpet, putting the commodore up in a recently completed VIP Quonset hut. A salmon barbecue was held, and drinks were hoisted around in his honor. The Fleet Air Wing 4 commander left Attu a satisfied, if not well-informed, man.

Missions against Kiska resumed on July 2 and 3. Three days later, three heavy cruisers, a light cruiser, and four U.S. destroyers steamed into position just off Kiska Harbor. Vought OS2U Kingfisher floatplanes were launched from the cruisers to spot targets. The ships fired 312 rounds of 8-inch, 250 rounds of 6-inch, and 1,250 rounds of 5-inch high-explosive shells at Japanese bunkers and antiaircraft batteries pinpointed by the orbiting Kingfishers. The Japanese took casualties from the naval shelling, especially from rounds that exploded in the air, showering the ground with shrapnel.

While the pounding of Kiska went on unabated, General Butler's 11th Air Force staff began looking into the possibility of taking the war to the Japanese home islands. Just under seven hundred miles separated the new field at Alexai Point and the northern Kuriles, meaning that the Japanese-held islands were within range of the AAF's B-25 medium and B-24 heavy bombers.

Fearing a possible invasion from the north, the Japanese began to augment their forces in the Kuriles. Located on Shimushu, the northernmost of the island chain, was Kataoka Naval Base, headquarters for Japan's Fifth Fleet. Nineteen light and heavy antiaircraft positions protected its two runways of 5,000-by-250 and 4,000-by-250 feet, a 130-by-165-foot hangar, 13 covered and 34 open aircraft revetments, three 60-foot oil storage tanks, a barracks complex, and ammunition/supply buildings. The facility also included the harbor from which operated H6K2 Mavis flying boats. In the center of the island was Miyoshino Airfield, equipped with B5N2 Kate and Mitsubishi G3M Betty medium bombers and Ki-43 Oscar fighters (see fourth map).

Paramushiro Island, the largest of the Kuriles, was just south of Shimushu. At Kakumabetsu Airfield in the south of Paramushiro, a runway was located from which operated Ki-44 Tojo fighters. The army regimental headquarters was at Kashiwabara Army Staging Area in the north, which was used for assembling invasion ground forces. It contained numerous warehouses that adjoined nine piers, one equipped with a fuel pipeline. Included was a nearby 4,000-by-180-foot airfield at Kitanodai, from which operated the 54th Fighter Regiment, flying Ki-43 Oscars out of forty revetments and fifty-five hardstands. The Kashiwabara area was defended by twenty-one heavy and light antiaircraft positions. Kakumabetsu, on the southwestern side of the island, sported the best harbor. A single hard-surface runway (3,800 by 150 feet) and aircraft revetments were defended by 18 AAA positions and 5 machine-gun pits. On the southeast side, two runways were operational at Suribachi. Farther south was a navy facility at Musashi with an airfield at Kurabu Zaki. It contained two runways (4,300 by 260 feet and 4,200 by 375 feet) and was the most active airfield on the island. The flat cape at Musashi was defended by 8 coastal guns, 20 pillboxes, 44 camouflaged gun positions, and 32 machine-gun pits.

Given their sizes, Paramushiro and Shimushu were heavily fortified, but there was limited intelligence about the island defenses available to U.S. commanders. Even so, General Buckner broached the idea of attacking the Kuriles to Admiral Kinkaid, who liked it. The Joint Chiefs of Staff in Washington, D.C., gave the go-ahead. The first mission was set for July 10, 1943, and included eight B-24s from Davis Field on Adak led by Major Robert E. Speer and eight B-25s from the 77th Bombardment Squadron at Amchitka under the command of Captain James L. Hudelson. The limited-range B-25s would refuel at Alexai Point on Attu before continuing across the North Pacific.

The B-25 Mitchell had already attained a distinguished place of honor among aircraft of World War II. The B model medium bomber was used by General Doolittle during the Tokyo raid on April 18, 1942. The B-25C and B-25D models in the Aleutians had improved armor and self-sealing fuel tanks. Armament included six .50-caliber machine guns: one in the nose operated by the navigator/bombardier, two waist guns, a twin-barreled top turret gun, and one stinger in the tail. The Mitchell could carry 5,200 pounds of bombs and was powered by two Wright R-2600-13s of 1,700 horsepower each. Its maximum speed of only 284 miles per hour made it vulnerable to faster Japanese fighters.

The B-24 Liberator was a four-engine heavy bomber weighing 56,000 pounds fully loaded. Its distinctive elephant-ear twin tails and bulky look made it appear slower than its 303 miles per hour top speed. The D model carried ten Browning .50-caliber machine guns—nose (2), top turret (2), ball turret (2), left and right waist (2), and tail (2)—plus a maximum load of 8,800 pounds of bombs. Four 1,200 horsepower Pratt & Whitney R-1830-43s propelled the Liberator to its 2,850-mile maximum range. It saw heavy use on long, overwater missions, but without fighter cover, its moderate top speed made it, too, vulnerable to enemy fighter attacks.

Whether flying in the B-24 or the B-25, the crews worked inside planes that were noisy and drafty. Neither was designed to be comfortable during cold-weather operations. When not in use, the waist guns could be stowed and a hatch cover placed over the window cutouts. However, in combat the guns remained in place, and the freezing wind made its way into every nook of the unheated aircraft. The Plexiglas and thin aluminum fairings that protected the crew from direct wind blast did little to stop the .50-caliber and larger rounds that the Japanese fighters could pour through them. Movement inside these bombers was difficult given the heavy winter clothing worn by the men and the narrow passageways between crew positions. Parachutes were normally not worn by the crew, and gunners and bombardiers had to slither through tiny openings and hatches to get to where their chutes were located. A hit that put the aircraft out of control often meant death for the entire crew, since few could overcome the g-forces, get to their chutes, get them on, then exit the aircraft before impact.

The crew of a B-25 consisted of five men, while the B-24 carried ten, but crew duties were similar in each. The pilot was the final authority on the operation of the aircraft and was responsible for his men even on the ground. Most crews bunked in Quonset huts together, the officers in one and the enlisted men in another nearby. As aircraft commander, the pilot's ability to do just that—to command—was essential to the smooth functioning of the crew as a team. During the mission, he was charged with either leading the force or keeping his aircraft in tight defensive formation. Pilots did not maintain formation on autopilot, and there was no hydraulic system to lighten the flight control pressures. These multi-ton bombers were flown using nothing more than mechanical linkages and were literally controlled by "brute force and awkwardness" by the man at the yoke.

The copilot backed up the duties of the pilot. Both had to be competent in all aspects of flying—takeoffs, landings, formation, and instrument procedures. If the pilot became a casualty, the copilot, serving as second in the chain of command, took charge. He may have had less combat experience than any other crew member and be of lower military rank than some, yet at a moment's notice he might find himself the leader. The copilot had to be skilled in navigation as well, particularly during long, overwater missions. He also handled the cockpit radio and radar.

The radio operator often served as a gunner, but his primary function was to listen to and report back to base using his low-frequency radio, plus keep track of communications between aircraft. He made position reports provided by the navigator or copilot and relayed results of the mission to include battle damage and casualties. He was responsible for getting out distress, or SOS calls. In addition, he was trained in first aid and was proficient in the operation of handheld camera gear.

The flight engineer usually was the senior enlisted man on the aircraft. On the B-24 he was the top turret gunner in addition to being responsible for proper operation of the aircraft systems. Mission success and the continued survival of the crew depended on the proper functioning of every aspect of the aircraft and therefore on how well he oversaw the maintenance of the bomber. In the air, he monitored fuel status and engine performance. If necessary, he was in charge of emergency handling procedures such as the manual operation of the landing gear in the event of damage during a mission. He also made repairs to malfunctions while in flight.

Without good navigation the target would never be reached, and with poor bombing accuracy it would never be struck. On the B-25, the navigation and bombardier functions were assigned to a single man, while the B-24 had a crewman for each role. The navigator used wind drift taken off the movement across the white-capped sea combined with true airspeed and elapsed time to calculate position. In weather, he used dead reckoning and forecast winds. Ground landmarks aided in clear skies, but when above clouds, the navigator needed his sextant for celestial navigation, using stars or the sun to triangulate an approximate position. In case of a break from formation due to damage or engine loss, the

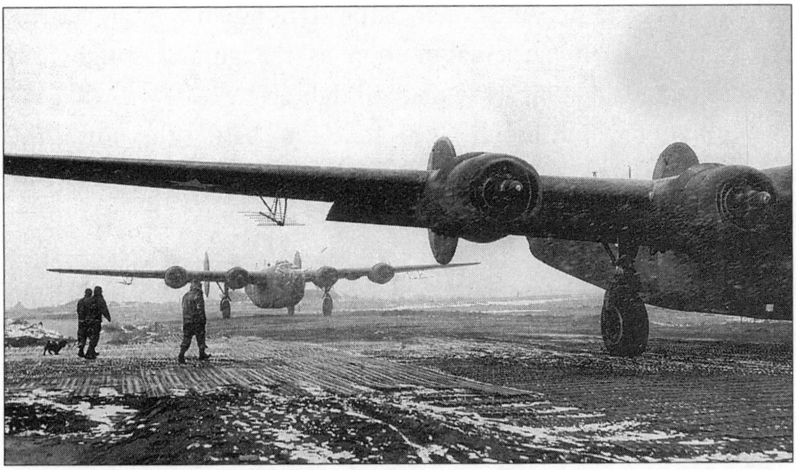

11th Air Force B-24 Liberators taxi out for takeoff in the Aleutians.

navigator had to quickly provide a directional steer for the pilot to take toward safety. A highly skilled navigator was invaluable to success, and his dialogue with the pilot concerning weather, alternates, course, and airspeed was critical.

During the few minutes of the bombing, the bombardier controlled the aircraft in the noisy, drafty nose of the aircraft. While looking through his bombsight, he made minute heading corrections as flak buffeted the air around him, fighters made head-on attacks, and his own gunners rattled the rivets loose as their machine guns fired. Until the "Bombs away" command was given, the bombardier alone flew the plane.

The gunners needed excellent instincts, quick reaction time, and a hunter's eye. The waist gunner was afforded the least protection from the elements, his being the coldest, draftiest spot. With temperatures at fifty-five below zero, grease thickened in the breeches, weapons jammed, electrical systems malfunctioned, and fingers froze, whether in a heated suit or not. The top turret, however, was the one place where temperatures could soar as the sun beamed in through Plexiglas, the greenhouse effect making for a sweltering ride in the cramped space. Turret gunners tended to be smaller men who, as the plane neared the battle zone, left their parachutes behind and squeezed into their battle stations. In the target area, the turret was in perpetual motion as the gunner sought out ground targets to strafe or fended off fighters.

No matter which bomber one rode into battle, the noise, the cold, and the shaking of the aircraft while dodging flak and enemy fighters took a brutal toll on mind and body.

In the Aleutians, the July 10 strike force was about to launch its first mission to Japan's Kurile Islands when word came from a patrolling PBY flying boat that two Japanese transports had been sighted south of Attu, headed in the direction of Kiska. The B-24 force diverted to that area along with five of General Butler's 73rd Squadron B-25s that sat strip alert on Amchitka. The B-25s sank the two transports, but two others were sighted. These were engaged by the B-24s but were not damaged.

Meanwhile, Captain Hudelson's B-25s were ordered to continue with the original mission. They took off at 5:44 A.M. and arrived over the Kuriles five hours later, only to find the target area obscured by clouds. Using a mountain peak that jutted above the clouds, Hudelson's crews used time, distance, and bearing to release the squadron's thirty-two 500-pound bombs. Fortunately for the B-25 crews, no air opposition was encountered during this, the first land-based attack against the Japanese home islands of the war.

That same evening, Fleet Air Wing 4 also entered the fray. Two PBY Catalina flying boats from Adak joined the squadron skipper, Lieutenant Commander Carl Amme, and another of his PBYs out of Attu at 10:15 P.M. The four Catalinas headed west, but the two from Adak got separated in the weather, jettisoned their bombs when fuel ran low, and returned to base. Amme and the crew of the fourth PBY continued on, arriving over Paramushiro in darkness. The island was obscured by clouds, so Amme used his radar to release his bombs in the vicinity of Kashiwabara Bay. The PBYs landed in the Aleutians after some sixteen hours in the air.

Another mission was attempted by the B-24 Liberator squadrons on the eleventh, but it was turned back by weather.

On July 18, Major Speer again led six B-24s, which staged out of Alexai Point on Attu at 6:32 A.M. Each bomber carried six 500-pound general-purpose bombs and was manned by a volunteer crew. Two flights of three planes flew at three thousand feet across the Bering Sea, making landfall along the Kamchatka Peninsula. Lieutenant Billy Wheeler recalled, "We rubbed our eyes at seeing trees, some of us for the first time in a year." The force turned south and began climbing to bombing altitude. Soon the northern shore of Shimushu was sighted, and Major Speer led his flight over Kataoka Naval Base, where bombs were dropped on the runways and hangars. The other flight, led by Major Frederick Ramputi, continued to Paramushiro Strait, where shipping was sighted and attacked. No hits were observed. Flak was light, and though several Japanese planes were seen taking off in pursuit, the bombers were well on their way home at high speed before the fighters reached altitude. The mission was erroneously publicized as the first successful mission against the Kurile Islands.

Bomb damage was minimal, but the Liberator crews took aerial photographs of Shimushu and the northern part of Paramushiro. Two airfields on Shimushu were identified as under construction, and another, on Paramushiro, was estimated as nearly complete. Extensive facilities at Kataoka Naval Base on Shimushu and Kashiwabara Barracks were noted, as was the amount of shipping in Parmushiro Strait and Kashiwabara Bay. AAF intelligence concluded that a major military buildup was under way.

In fact, the setbacks in the Aleutians had alerted the Japanese High Command to increased vulnerability in their northern sector. The AAF bombing mission on July 10 only served to reinforce that concern. With warning of an attack coming only from the sound of planes overhead, the Japanese set up interceptors on strip alert and moved antiaircraft gunners closer to their batteries to reduce response times.

Meanwhile, naval shelling and bombing of the facilities on Kiska continued to increase in intensity as the date for the invasion approached. To weather the barrages, the Japanese had constructed a virtual underground city, with miles of reinforced tunnels, three hospitals, barracks, dental clinics, mess facilities, machine shops, photo labs, and warehouses. But supplies were running out. The troops became so short of food that when American bombs exploded in the harbor, soldiers braved gunfire to rush out in boats and net the dead fish that surfaced. The mess hall menu described the cache as "Roosevelt's Rations."

The Japanese High Command, now well aware that the days of Japanese occupation on the island were numbered, sought a way to extract their six thousand troops. Vice Admiral Shiro Kawase, Fifth

Fleet commander, planned an evacuation by submarine, estimating forty to fifty trips needed to complete the mission. Employing thirteen I Class submarines, the plan had already met with success in May when on the night of the twenty-sixth, a submarine slipped into Kiska Harbor and carried off sixty troops. On June 10, the *I-24* was inbound on a similar run. Brought to the surface by depth charges from *PC-487*, a 170-foot U.S. patrol craft, the submarine was rammed by the steel-hulled ship and sank. The destroyer USS *Frazier* sent *I-9* to the bottom off Kiska on June 13. The *I-7*, on her third trip to Kiska, encountered the destroyers USS *Monaghan* and *Aylwin* and went down near Twin Rocks, south of Kiska, on June 22. Another submarine disappeared on its run to Kiska and three more were damaged.

By late June, Admiral Kinkaid's blockade was even stronger, making the evacuation operation too risky to continue after only 820 construction personnel had been removed. Admiral Kawase decided to commit his surface fleet in a final effort to save the beleaguered garrison. He set out with three light cruisers, an oiler, and eleven destroyers from Rear Admiral Masatomi Kimura's Imperial Destroyer Squadron 1. The Japanese were able to keep the plan a secret by avoiding radio traffic. Admiral Akiyama, the commander on Kiska, sent one of his officers by submarine to Paramushiro to work out the details. The officer returned to Kiska in late June.

On July 2, the Japanese force departed anchorage at Paramushiro, headed south, then swung east beyond the range of patrolling PBYs from the Aleutians. At a point five hundred nautical miles southwest of Kiska, Kawase's ships needed heavy fog but found it too thin to proceed undetected, so the ships turned back. Another attempt was made, on the twelfth, with similar results. Meanwhile, the troops on Kiska were told to be ready for immediate departure. Radio operator Toranosuke Ozaki had luckily escaped from Attu when the island was evacuated in September. Now he manned a radio near Gertrude Cove and waited for orders to move north for an evacuation, wondering if he would again be lucky enough to escape a tightening noose, this one surrounding Kiska.

On July 21, assured they could count on foggy weather, Admirals Kawase and Kimura made another probe north with their fleet. Low on fuel, this would be the last attempt at rescue. The fog was indeed thick, so the ships pushed ahead toward Kiska.

On the twenty-third, a PBY patrol plane reported seven radar contacts two hundred nautical miles southwest of Attu. Thinking the Japanese were attempting to reinforce Kiska, Admiral Kinkaid ordered his naval forces to intercept. Rear Admiral Robert C. "Ike" Giffin swung his cruiser task force from their station west of Attu and headed southwest. Rear Admiral Robert M. Griffin took his two battleships and cruiser from outside Kiska Harbor and steamed toward the Japanese fleet. The destroyers *Monaghan* and *Aylwin*, on station blocking Kiska Harbor, moved in that direction, too, leaving the approach to Kiska wide open.

Eighty nautical miles southwest of Kiska, just after midnight on the twenty-sixth, the radar operator aboard the battleship USS *Mississippi* picked up radar contacts on his scope. The "pips" appeared to show the Japanese fleet headed east. Radar operators aboard the USS *Idaho* and several cruisers in Admiral Giffin's force confirmed the radar returns, but no sightings were possible in the dense fog. Klaxons sounded, and all hands took up battle stations. Using their radars to determine appropriate range, the battleships opened fire, hurling 518 14-inch shells at the contacts. The cruisers sent 487 rounds of 8-inch projectiles at their radar targets.

At dawn, the American ships encountered only the white-capped, heaving swells of the North Pacific. There were no oil slicks, no debris, no lifeboats. Some combination of fog, temperature inversion, or atmospheric disturbance had apparently caused false echoes to appear on the radar scopes. Referred to as the "Battle of the Pips," this diversion provided Admirals Kimura and Kawase with the luck they needed.

As the American flotilla steamed east to join the oiler *Pecos* for refueling 105 nautical miles southeast of Kiska, the Japanese fleet took the opportunity to make their dash through the very area that Admiral Giffen's force had vacated. Though five ships collided in the fog and two destroyers had to be sent back, Admiral Kawase broke radio silence to inform Admiral Akiyama on Kiska that his remaining destroyers and two cruisers were inbound and asked for a weather report. The prevailing conditions and forecast were not as favorable as Kawase had hoped and caused him to rethink his next step. He brought his fleet to a halt fifty miles southwest of Kiska and waited for the fog to thicken.

On the evening of the twenty-sixth at Kiska, the Japanese troops were given two hours' notice to grab what personal belongings they could carry along with their rifles and begin gathering on the beach near the submarine base. Radioman Toranosuke Ozaki, stationed in the south above Gertrude Cove, received word for his unit to destroy anything of use to the Americans, then march to the assembly point. The troops dumped their meager stock of rice on the ground, threw dirt on it, and began a long night march across South Head. Before midnight the men arrived on the beach, only to be told that there was a delay. They waited while overhead PBYs from Patrol Wing 4 used their radar to drop bombs through the undercast. Then, in the early morning hours, the troops were ordered back to their barracks. Ozaki's unit made the round trip to Gertrude Cove, then had to gather soiled rice from the ground and clean it before they could eat breakfast.

After daybreak, Admiral Kawase received another message from Kiska Radio, describing the round-the-clock bombing. It appeared to Admiral Akiyama on the island that the invasion was about to commence. Kawase decided to abandon his wait for thicker weather conditions. Aboard the light cruiser *Tama*, Kawase positioned his flagship twenty miles from Kiska to cover the rear while Admiral Kimura proceeded into the Bering Sea with his destroyer force and two cruisers, then swung toward Kiska Harbor from the northern side.

At midmorning, the troops on Kiska mustered again and were ordered back to the assembly point. To the men who had been on the receiving end of bombs, bullets, and artillery for more than a year, a numb sense of futility descended, yet by noon 5,138 troops had gathered around fires and were shivering in the mist that rolled in off the leaden sea. Suddenly a gray Japanese destroyer, the *Shimakase*, loomed out of the ghostly fog and into the harbor. Other ships followed. Anchors were lowered at 1:40 P.M. With space aboard the ships limited, Admiral Kimura ordered the troops to leave their weapons behind. Hundreds of rifles and automatic weapons were tossed into the sea as the jubilant troops hurriedly scampered onto barges and small boats. The tiny flotilla sped from the beaches, and the troops clambered aboard the destroyers and cruisers as demolition charges set in the camp went off behind them. The barges were then sunk and the ships got under way. In less than an hour, human domination of the island ceased. As the fleet slipped off into the fog, silence on Kiska was broken only by periodic explosions of timed charges set inside empty bunkers and the barking of abandoned dogs.

While the fleet steamed north into the Bering Sea, the *Shimakase's* radar operator detected a contact ahead. The Japanese altered course, passing within fifteen hundred yards of the American submarine *S-33*. In dense fog on the surface, the bridge watch on the radar-less submarine did not see the Japanese fleet steam by less than a mile away. Once clear of Kiska, Kimura swung south and sped to join Admiral Kawase. By dawn the next morning the fleet was two hundred miles from Kiska and safely away.

Toranosuke Ozaki's joy was unbounded. He was headed home after two narrow escapes from near certain death. On deck, he breathed in the cold, damp Pacific air and felt new life. His hardships were far from over, however.

The now thinning fog held for five more days, allowing the Japanese fleet to slip through the American blockade undetected. Vice Admiral Kawase and Rear Admiral Kimura had pulled off one of the most daring rescues of World War II.

On August 1, the weather cleared. Lieutenant Bernard J. O'Donnell from the 21st Bombardment Squadron flew a reconnaissance mission over Kiska and reported "no antiaircraft, no enemy aircraft, or shipping observed." In spite of no signs of Japanese presence, Admiral Kinkaid's forces continued to pound Kiska with artillery and bombs day and night.

Casco Field on Attu became operational on August 10. Navy squadron VB-136 moved onto the base with eight PV-1 Ventura medium bombers. These planes were immediately put into the round-the-clock bombing shuttle over abandoned Kiska.

With the Aleutians seemingly back under American control, a third raid against the Kuriles took to the air on August 11. Six B-24 Liberators from the 404th Bombardment Squadron and three from the 21st Bombardment Squadron left Davis Field on Adak and staged through Alexai Point. The nine B-24s, led by Major Louis Blau, departed Attu at 6:45 A.M., headed westerly. Blau had been on the July 18 strike along with Major Frank T. Gash and Captains Harrell Hoffman and Irvin Wadlington, who also were on this mission. The other five pilots were all lieutenants. For once, the skies over the North Pacific were clear, and the bomber stream made good time, turning left when Blau spotted the Kamchatka coast. As the formation continued south, it passed above a broken layer of clouds, arriving over Shimushu shortly after noon.

Just south at Kitanodai Airfield on Paramushiro, the Japanese pilots were taking it easy in the standby room playing Shogi (Japanese chess) and Go (a Chinese chesslike game). The day's routine patrol activity had been canceled while a portion of the wooden runway was being repaired. Then the roar of engines high above was heard and someone shouted "Air raid!" A hand-operated alarm siren went off. "At that time," former army warrant officer Sei'ichi Yamada recalled, "we didn't have any effective anti-air defense system. When we heard the sound of the enemy bombers, we knew it was an air raid, so we scrambled." The runway repair crew cleared the work area as five Oscars roared down the available runway, while Yamada had to wait. Maintenance had been trying to fix one of his two 12.7-millimeter machine guns. They gave up and began hastily putting several panels back on his plane, a Ki-43 Type 1 Oscar fighter. When they finished, he would take off with only one working machine gun.

At 11,500 feet overhead, Major Gash led his flight of three above the Kataoka Naval Base on Shimushu, where moderate but inaccurate flak rose to greet them. The Liberator crews released twenty-six 500-pound general-purpose bombs and fifteen incendiary cluster bombs. The two other flights continued south to Paramushiro and the Kashiwabara Barracks area.

Members of Major Gash's flight observed hits on buildings near the Kataoka Naval Base, and fires were seen inside the base itself. Gash wheeled his formation for home and spotted fighters approaching. He turned into the attack, lowering his nose to gain airspeed and to give his top turret gunner a chance to open fire on the fighters rapidly closing from below. The Japanese broke off their intercept. In the same flight, the B-24 piloted by Lieutenant James R. Pottenger was not so fortunate. "We made the primary strike on the target and lost an engine on the bomb run," recalled the navigator, Second Lieutenant Charles K. Hanner Jr. The failed engine would not feather. "We had been briefed to [maintain] close formation on withdrawal, but due to lack of power, we were unable to do so." Japanese fighters began making multiple firing passes and a second engine began to run rough, its supercharger on fire. Pottenger informed Gash of his situation, and Gash radioed for him to head for "the alternate." That meant Kamchatka and the airfield at Petropavlovsk, about forty-five minutes' flying time away. Pottenger turned north for Soviet territory while the Japanese continued attacking.

Inside the stricken B-24, the waist gunner, Technical Sergeant Thomas E. Ring, had been a busy man fending off the Japanese attacks. He spotted an Oscar approaching from astern, swung his twin .50-caliber machine guns ahead of the fighter, and opened fire. The Oscar took hits and rolled toward the ground. The other fighters broke off pursuit as the bomber neared Soviet territory.

Back on Miyoshino Airfield, Warrant Officer Yamada's plane was finally ready. He primed the cylinders, fired up his 1150-horsepower Nakajima Ha-115 engine, and taxied toward the runway as nearby antiaircraft batteries peppered the sky with flak bursts.

As the flight led by Captain Wadlington approached their target, Captain Hoffman was seen to turn his bomber away and head for home. The remaining B-24s unloaded forty-five 500-pound bombs and fifteen incendiary cluster bombs on Kashiwabara. Antiaircraft fire was intense but ineffective, since the bombers were above the ten-thousand-foot range of the Japanese 12.7-millimeter guns. Bombs were observed striking the barracks area and the nearby airfield as the two flights turned toward Attu, but Japanese fighters were seen taking off from Kashiwabara Airfield.

Above Shimushu, Major Blau was the first in his group to spot Japanese interceptors. He began turning away to the north along with B-24s piloted by Lieutenants Kemmerer and Lockwood. One Ki-43 Oscar came streaking in from Blau's right front but rolled underneath the bomber and disappeared. Three others made approaches from the rear, one of which came within range of a burst from the B-24's tail gun. The Oscar nosed down into the clouds, trailing smoke. Another Oscar was seen to pull up into a stall, then fall off into a cloud.

Lieutenant Kemmerer's B-24 was jumped by three Japanese fighters. Attacking from behind, one fighter, trailing smoke, was seen going into a cloud after taking a burst from the B-24's tail gunner. Another was driven off by the waist gunner.

Lockwood's crew took on a string of attackers. His gunners blasted away as Japanese planes bore in. In the exchange of fire, two fighters were shot down, while Lockwood's bomber was riddled with bullet holes. In spite of having one engine out, Lockwood decided to try to make it back to Attu.

In the group egressing from Paramushiro, Captain Hoffman's B-24 was now in front of the scattered formation.

To the north, Warrant Officer Yamada was clawing his way to altitude when he "spotted six aircraft on their way back home from bombing." With only one machine gun working, Yamada positioned himself ahead of the bombers. "Then I made a 180-degree turn, and faced the enemy planes. I saw flashes of gunfire aiming at me, but I didn't care about the gunfire, and continued." When a bomber filled Yamada's windscreen, he opened fire at three hundred meters. "I shot no more than fifteen rounds. Bullets tore into part of the wing near the fuselage of the plane. After shooting, I turned again, and saw the enemy plane spraying fuel. I followed it for about five minutes as it flew toward Kamchatka. Then a fellow pilot caught up and started firing from the back at the disabled enemy plane. It blew up into pieces. I saw two or three parachutes. Down below was cold seawater. You wouldn't survive more than ten minutes. I hated to see them going down. I felt very sorry for them." Captain Harrell Hoffman and his entire crew perished.

Captain Wadlington's crew fought both Oscars and Rufe floatplanes in a running battle across Shimushu. After driving off their attackers, claiming one plane destroyed, Wadlington and crew were able to break free for home. In the same flight, Lieutenant Leon A. Smith remained engaged with fighters for more than forty-five minutes, with the Japanese finally breaking contact about a hundred miles northeast of the Kuriles.

Out ahead, Lockwood had his hands full with one engine feathered. Fuel consumption on the other engines was too high, so to lighten the weight, the crew began tossing out everything not bolted down. Suddenly all three remaining engines quit. As the plane glided silently toward the frigid waters below, Lockwood and his copilot frantically managed to transfer fuel and get the engines started again just feet above certain death. They would later barely make it back to Attu.

Lieutenant Pottenger's B-24 remained under attack as it made its way up the Kamchatka coast. The Japanese finally broke off pursuit after Technical Sergeant Thomas E. Ring shot another of the planes down. The rough-running engine finally quit, and Pottenger was unable to hold altitude. He advised the crew to prepare for a crash landing some twenty-five miles south of Petropavlovsk. The bombardier, Second Lieutenant Robert W. Wiles, lifted his Norden bombsight from its mounting and moved from the nose to the waist area, where he tossed the sight overboard. Then he and the waist gunners braced themselves against a bulkhead. When the plane hit the water, the bomb-bay doors were ripped off. A machine gun, torn from its mount, flew at the men inside the compartment. Ring's hip and pelvis were broken, and he was knocked unconscious. Staff Sergeant Donald L. Dimel suffered a ruptured spleen. Corporal Richard T. Varney had a knee injury, and Lieutenant Wiles cracked a shoulder blade.

The crew was soon found and interned by the Soviets. Sergeant Ring, still unconscious, was taken to a hospital, where he subsequently seemed to be recovering when a blood clot induced a fatal stroke. Dimel's spleen was removed by a Soviet doctor. Dimel recovered, thanks in no small part to blood donations by other members of the crew.

The Japanese suffered losses as well. One casualty was that of First Lieutenant Isao Iwase, an Oscar pilot in Warrant Officer Yamada's unit, shot down and killed during the engagement. Japanese records indicate the Kataoka Airfield barracks building was destroyed, with thirty-three troops killed. Overall results of this initial engagement were encouraging for the Japanese, but the realization that the islands were vulnerable to attack spurred them to buttress the islands' defenses even more.

With two of nine AAF B-24s downed by Japanese fighters, and two others heavily damaged, missions to the Kuriles were put on hold until the Kiska issue was settled. Then, after a week of incessant pounding of the island, General Butler's intelligence section released a bomb damage assessment made from analysis of aerial photos taken between July 27, the final day of Japanese occupation, and August 4. Twenty-three buildings in the main compound and nine at the submarine base were considered destroyed. There was no sign of the two radio stations previously identified, and the radar antenna had been dismantled or damaged. No attempt to fill some thirty bomb craters in the runway at North Head had been made. The photo interpreters were bewildered by what they saw, commenting, "It is significant that most of the buildings affected show no evidence of having been bombed and shelled. . . . It is also significant that the photographs of 2 August and 4 August show all the trucks in identical positions and show ten to twelve less barges than usual in the Kiska Harbor area."

Though reports of ground fire and sightings of Japanese troops continued to come in sporadically, these were primarily relayed by "green" pilots, according to Admiral Kinkaid's staff. For another week the bombing and shelling continued, even though no radio communications had been detected from the island. One P-40 pilot landed back at Amchitka after a mission over Kiska and complained, "If there are any Japs on that g-d- island, I'll eat 'em all."

A few days before the August 15 D-Day, four pilots began flying low over the empty positions. No ground fire came up, so Captain George Ruddell decided to check things out firsthand. He made several low and slow passes over the main camp area, then swung past the gun pits on North Head and near Salmon Lagoon. Nothing moved. After circling the cratered runway, he decided to try setting down on a clear section of the North Head strip. Ruddell landed first, and recalled, "All four of us got down OK, although . . . No. 4 almost went off the end of the runway and down a 100-foot drop. We knew there were no Japanese there, and wanted to prove it and get back and say so."

Captain Ruddell and the other pilots shut down their engines and began exploring the area. They came upon a grave site marked with a crude wooden cross and a Shinto marker that read in English, "Sleeping here a brave air hero who lost youth and happiness for his motherland."

When Ruddell and his wingmen returned to Amchitka, they reported what they had seen, and Ruddell got a genuine chewing out because they had no authorization to land on Kiska. Ruddell recalled, "Apparently nothing else came of our information, because the invasion, which I thought was a terrible waste, went ahead as planned."

Even though Admiral Kinkaid was briefed on the indications that Kiska was unoccupied, he believed the Japanese might have retreated into the hills to prepare fighting positions as were encountered on Attu. Regardless, the admiral considered the invasion to be a "super dress rehearsal, good for training purposes."

On D-Day, the fifteen, the assault force, comprised of Canadian and American troops, made a feint toward Kiska Harbor, then swung to landings on the northern and western sides of the island. As they landed, out from under the detritus of war came Explosion, wagging his tail in greeting. The canine mascot of the navy radio station had witnessed two invasions and survived fourteen months dodging an untold number of explosions of the deadly strain.

For the next few days, American and Canadian forces probed deeper into the island's interior and wound up surprising each other in the fog and mist. Seventeen U.S. and 4 Canadian soldiers died in errant exchanges of gunfire. Another 121 men suffered from wounds and sickness. Not a single Japanese soldier was encountered. Offshore, the destroyer USS *Abner Read* struck a floating Japanese mine and sank. Seventy-one seamen went down with her, and 47 others were injured. The cost of the training exercise was indeed high, but the fight for the Aleutians was over.

In the end, the Japanese had deployed 8,500 men and its Fifth Fleet ships and submarines in the Aleutian operation. They managed to divert dozens of U. S. ships, bomber and fighter squadrons, plus 144,000 Americans and Canadians from use in other theaters.

Chapter 5
Ice Station Attu

The engines from Bomber 31 had several large-caliber bullet holes whose angle of penetration indicated they were fired from forward and above the aircraft. Fighters usually latch onto their victim from the six-o'clock position, behind the target. But the holes in the exhaust stacks and the shrapnel inside the propeller spinner were very real. I placed my index finger inside a jagged metal hole and wondered how in the world the damage got there.

—Kamchatka crash site

Before the fighting had ended on Attu in May 1943, army engineers began constructing airfields on the island. Rejecting the Japanese runway at Holtz Bay as unsatisfactory due to nearby mountainous terrain and weather, the engineers began work on Alexai Point, which eventually served both fighters and bombers. Initially the men lived in tents, the floors of which became covered immediately with a "wall-to-wall carpet of that black oily mud obtained from well trampled tundra." Tent poles were placed on pieces of plywood or boards to prevent the tents from sinking into the muck and toppling. Small, potbellied stoves were rigged with exhaust pipes that rose through metal tent-caps. The pipes frequently clogged with soot, and clearing them was an odious task that often resulted in tent fires, personnel injuries, and cracked stoves.

On July 6, 1943, Naval Construction Battalion 22 moved into Casco Bay on Attu. The Seabees' task was to build an airfield for

Alexai Point eventually had two runways and was used by 11th Air Force bombers to launch strikes against the northern Kurile Islands from 1943 until the end of the war.

navy bombers. The effort began on July 16, with shifts working twenty-four hours a day in violent, unpredictable weather. Though midsummer, the weather never got comfortably warm. Attu veteran Frank Davis recalled, "The temperature must have been up to 50 degrees Fahrenheit, and everything was sparkling with dew of sea spray or whatever it was that could resist evaporation in a 30-knot breeze." After eleven days, the first usable section of runway was completed. The Seabees also erected hangers, and put up a score of Quonset huts and a boat dock. They built piers that stretched out into Massacre Bay.

By now, the industrial might of the United States was in full bloom. Clogging the bay were cargo ships filled with everything from Coca-Cola to long-barreled 80-millimeter antiaircraft guns to tons of construction material. As fast as structures went up, problems arose. Fires caused by improper use of stoves and heaters swept through the tent cities. To combat the fires that engulfed the living areas, the Seabees began laying out a high-pressure hydrant system that extended from Casco to Alexai Point.

The ubiquitous Quonset hut, prevalent throughout the Pacific theater, was no more well suited to the weather conditions it would face than in the Aleutians. Quonsets began dotting the landscape like mushrooms sprouting out of the muskeg. The distinctively curved structures of corrugated metal panels were originally called "Butler buildings," named after their manufacturer, Charles Butler. They got their more common moniker from Quonset Point Naval Air Station, Rhode Island, where the first military versions were constructed in 1941. The shape allowed the buildings to withstand heavy snow and the hundred-plus-mile-an-hour winds or *willi-waws*, as the Aleuts called them, that frequently swept the Aleutians. Quonsets became supply warehouses, offices, and provided billeting for troops, airmen, and sailors. Wooden boardwalks connected the huts to reduce the amount of mud tracked inside, but mud penetrated everywhere.

Officers' Quonset huts on Attu. The shape of the structures allowed the buildings to withstand heavy snow and the hundred-plus-mile-an-hour winds that frequently swept the Aleutians.

Within months, whiskey, beer, and Cokes made their way off the supply ships in quantity, and as Attu veteran Frank Davis noticed, "Many other trappings of civilization were rapidly undermining the good-clean pleasures of frontier days."

By the time Kiska was back in American hands, Attu had been transformed into a city of more than five thousand army and navy personnel. Five days before the Kiska invasion "training opportunity," the first squadron of navy PV-1 Venturas moved from Amchitka and set down on the new Marston matting runway at Alexai Point. Surfaced with interconnecting sheets of pierced-steel planking (PSP), the runway was rough and slippery when wet, which was most of the time. Adding to the standing joke that army engineers would not build a runway unless it was ninety degrees to the prevailing wind was that in the Aleutians there was no such thing as a prevailing wind. In fact, another common quip was that on Attu, the wind could be blowing at a hundred miles an hour from every direction at the same time.

The navy's first runway was called Casco Field, named after the seaplane tender that had faithfully served in the Aleutians. The strip was laid out from the mouth of Massacre Bay northwest into a box canyon. The only way to approach the field from the air was from the bay side. Crews descended below the weather out over the water, and homed on the radio beacon at Casco until seeing the island landmass. The pilot then lowered the landing gear and lined up on the runway. Go-arounds in bad weather were a tricky maneuver, since during the initial phase of a missed approach, mountains loomed everywhere except behind the aircraft.

Unlike the Patrol Wing 4 PBY seaplanes that could put down in the open ocean if necessary, the PV-1 Venturas of VB-135 were land-based, twin-engine medium bombers. Their Pratt & Whitney R-2800 power plants generated 2,000 horsepower, which pushed the planes to 322 miles per hour on the deck, considered quite a brisk clip for the time. With two (later five) .50-caliber Browning machine guns in the nose, two more in its top turret,

A squadron of PV-1 Venturas on the ramp at Casco Field, Attu.

and two .30-caliber Brownings under the tail, the PV-1 was a formidable opponent to Japanese fighters.

Initially bivouacked in tents, the crews of VB-135 were immediately put into action over already abandoned Kiska and began patrols in six sectors extending five hundred miles south, west, and northwest of Attu. The patrols served in an effort to spot enemy ship movements and bomber groups launched from the northern Kuriles, as had happened when the flight of Betty bombers attacked U.S. Navy warships operating off Holtz Bay during the Attu invasion. No sightings were made, and these missions soon became weary, boring exercises. Though the unit had lost four aircraft while at Amchitka, none was lost while at Attu.

On September 10, nine B-24 heavy bombers flew from Adak to Attu in preparation for another swipe at Paramushiro and Shimushu, joining a force of B-25 Mitchell medium bombers already in place at Alexai Point. Seven hundred miles to the west, things were being prepared as well.

The Japanese defense of the Kuriles had been the responsibility of the General Defense Army commander until November 1942, when it was transferred to the Northern District Army. On February 11, 1943, the organization was renamed the Northern Army and North Sea Garrison, under Lieutenant General Kiichiro Higuchi. The 1st Air Division, 1st Kurile Garrison, and the Northern Shipping Unit had been placed under his command as well.

As the empire's stronghold in the Aleutians deteriorated, Japanese units began relocating to defend the Kuriles. On July 20, 1943, the 27th Squadron moved with their Nakajima Ki-43 Oscar (Hayabusa) fighters from Obihiro Army Air Base on Hokkaido to the airfield at Kitanodai on Paramushiro. There the Japanese had finished construction of the runway, made of interlocking hardwood planks, each 33 feet long, 18 inches wide, and 4 inches thick. The surface was designed to be operational during wet and snowy weather and was 165 feet wide and 4,000 feet long. This constituted a major expenditure, since material of this nature was a scarce resource in wartime Japan. Karabu Zaki Airfield was another major installation, on the southern cape of Paramushiro at Musashi Naval Base, with its attendant early-warning radar and antiaircraft batteries.

As noted, on July 27, 1943, Admirals Kawase and Kimura brought their fleet out of Kiska Harbor with 5,183 beleaguered remnants of the invasion force aboard. He steamed directly to the Kuriles, where the troops were offloaded on August 1. Navy personnel were dropped off at Kataoka on Shimushu and immediately began work improving the airstrip and defenses. The army troops were taken to an isolated barracks area near the Kashiwabara army base on Paramushiro.

Among the survivors of Kiska taken to Paramushiro was radio operator Toranosuke Ozaki. Upon his arrival, Ozaki recalled, "We were quarantined, not allowed contact even with other military units for three months to prevent word of the Kiska defeat from spreading to the Japanese population."

With the evacuation of the Aleutians, the Japanese plans for northern expansion had collapsed. The Imperial General Headquarters now designated the Kuriles as the first line of defense in the northern sector. On August 8, the headquarters ordered the 1st Kurile Garrison upgraded to division strength.

By September, Japanese searchlight, sound detector, and antiaircraft batteries pockmarked the northern islands. Aircraft were operating from three bases on Paramushiro and two on Shimushu. A radar was up and running on Shimushu's eastern coast, and picket boats ranged to two hundred miles offshore. These boats were armed and carried radar and listening devices to alert them to planes flying overhead. Word of detected aircraft headed toward the Kuriles was then relayed via radio to shore installations.

Assigned to Shimushu was Warrant Officer Kiyomi Katsuki. Born in 1919 in Fukuoka Prefecture, he joined the naval service in June 1938 and graduated from flight training in May 1941. When the Pacific war started, Katsuki was flying from the seaplane tender *Chitose*, and completed a number of reconnaissance and patrol missions over the Philippines and the Dutch East Indies in an F1M2 Pete biplane, a scout aircraft. Then, on January 11, 1942, the Japanese sent a convoy of special landing force marines to invade Kema, in the northern Celebes. Seven Dutch and American PBYs off Menado rose to defend the island. Katsuki and his squadron-mates attacked the flying boats in their biplanes. During the combat Katsuki claimed his first victory, a Dutch PBY (No. Y-58 of GVT-17). In September 1942, Katsuki was transferred to a forward seaplane base in the Shortland Islands and flew patrol missions over Guadalcanal. On October 4, 1942, while flying combat air patrol above the Japanese fleet in his Pete, he spotted four enemy fighters and five B-17s. To prevent the bombers from hitting the seaplane carrier *Nisshin*, Katsuki dove on the leading B-17 (B-17E of the 72nd Bomb Squadron, flown by Lieutenant David C. Everitt, Jr.) and commenced his attack. After making his pass, he rammed the aircraft from below, tearing the right main wing and the vertical stabilizer off the bomber and damaging his own right wing. Together with his observer, Katsuki bailed out of his stricken aircraft. Both were rescued by the destroyer *Akisuki*. The crew of the B-17 perished. Katsuki later returned to Japan and began conversion training on the seaplane fighter Nakajima A6M2-N Rufe at Yokusuka Air Base. In July 1943 he was assigned to the 452nd Air Group and posted to their base at Shimushu, in the Kuriles. By August he and his squadron pilots were ready for action.

The U.S. Army Air Force crews on Attu arose at 5:30 A.M. on the morning of September 11. Among them was Second Lieutenant Vladmir P. Sabich, a B-25 copilot. He put on clean clothes "from head to foot so that I wouldn't operate in Russia in dirty clothes in case we have to land there." Then he went to breakfast and on to the mission briefing, which was held in the chapel.

The plan discussed was for the B-24 heavies to bomb the Kashiwabara staging area on Paramushiro from high altitude and for the B-25 Mitchell medium bombers to come in low and pick shipping targets of opportunity. According to Lieutenant Sabich, "In the event of serious battle damage, we were to try to make it to Russian territory." The briefer told the crews to claim upon landing that they were on a navigation training mission. This "lie" was intended to satisfy the "diplomatic arrangements" made with the Soviets regarding neutrality and the repatriation of interned crews. The Soviets were required to follow the April 1941, Soviet-Japanese Neutrality Pact and the International Hague Rules of Air Warfare, adopted in 1923. The latter mandated that incursions be protested to the offending nation, and combat aircraft forced to land in "neutral" territory were to be interned along with their crews until hostilities ceased. This was consistent with an August 30, 1943, radio report from Moscow on the subject. The announcer mentioned that the crew of a bomber had in fact been interned after landing on Kamchatka on August 12. That report, possibly meant primarily for Japanese ears, was the first acknowledgment of a neutrality violation. The plane involved was Lieutenant Pottenger's B-24, which diverted with battle damage to Petropavlovsk on August 12, 1943.

Earlier in July 1943, the Soviet Union had accomplished a decisive victory over the Germans at Kursk during the most colossal tank battle in history. If Japan determined that Stalin had violated the 1941 agreement, they might attack, diverting Soviet combat divisions needed to defeat Hitler. Thus the men on Attu considered the possibility of quick repatriation as being more of a morale ploy used by the headquarters than a reality. Of real concern was the fact that the Japanese had ample time since the last bombing raid to strengthen defenses. Without fighter escort, the American bomber crews could expect a rough go of it. Lieutenant Sabich wrote of his apprehension, "Have a hunch that all is not going to be well on this deal. In fact, most of us feel that at least half of our flight will be lost."

Following the briefing, eight B-24s and twelve B-25s took to the air well before dawn and crossed the North Pacific at five hundred feet, then once within two hundred miles of Kamchatka the B-24s climbed to eighteen thousand feet, but the approaching aircraft were detected and Japanese fighter pilots were ordered into the air.

As the sun broke above the horizon, the B-24 bombers lined up on their targets on Paramushiro. Japanese defenses opened up. In the B-25 element following behind the Liberators, Lieutenant Sabich's memory of the scene was vivid: "Every time I looked at the water, I swallowed to keep my heart down. The water was just whipped to a froth by machine gun bullets, shell fragments, 20-mm slugs, and big stuff that was throwing up geysers. . . . The tracers were so thick that they looked like Roman candles, and I can't figure out how anybody could have gotten through the barrage."

Major Frank T. Gash, who had survived as one of the flight leaders on the August 11 raid, bore through the clouds of flak to complete his bomb run over the Kashiwabara staging area; then he and the rest of the B-24s came under fighter attack.

B-25 from the 77th Bomb Squadron over the Bering Sea, September 1943.

Warrant Officer Katsuki and a number of combat veterans assigned to the northern Kuriles after the July attacks brought with them experience and proven tactics. Katsuki piloted one of ten Pete seaplanes that teamed with Nakajima Ki-43 Oscars of the 54th Squadron to attack the B-24s.

The Japanese fighters did not approach from the stern. Instead, they sped past the lumbering bombers, well to the side and out of range, until they were several miles ahead. Then they peeled off to make individual head-on passes from out of the rising sun.

Radar operator and second radioman Staff Sergeant Vale W. Wright recalled, "So determined were their attacks that we thought, at first, they intended to ram us. At the last possible second the enemy pilot would stand his plane on one wing. Holding this quarter roll, he would slice through our formation. In doing this, he barely missed the tail of one bomber and the wing of the following one. After each pass, the fighter would fly off to our right out of range, overtake our formation and come at us again."

Wright gained respect for the skill of Katsuki and his Rufe-flying comrades. "Oddly, it was the slightly slower half dozen or so float fighters that raised a lot of hell. After they broke through our formation they went into a tight banking turn. With guns blazing wide open they flew a circle inside our formation. Our gunners could not get off many bursts because our planes were in line of fire."

As one fighter came at Wright's plane out of the sun, his pilot, Captain Jerome J. Jones, spotted the Oscar boring in at high speed. At the last second, Jones pulled the bomber's nose toward the fighter and opened fire with his .50-caliber machine guns. The Oscar was hit and began shedding parts, then rolled over and disintegrated as it slammed into the ocean, creating a tremendous splash behind the bomber.

Wright was flying in the B-24 formation trailing Major Gash. He saw the Japanese make repeated passes on Gash's aircraft.

First, Gash lost his number one engine; then number three was hit, and its propeller unwound to a stop. The bomber was seen to nose up, then fall into a shallow dive. Wright could see the tail

A Japanese Oscar slices past two 11th Air Force B-25 Mitchell bombers. After numerous hits from the B-25 gunners, the fighter's landing gear is just starting to appear coming down out of the lower wheel well. The Oscar crashed.

gunner still firing at the Japanese as the B-24 hit the water. The tail section broke off, and the plane began to sink.

Captain Jones broke out of formation and circled the wreckage, intending to prevent any attempt by the Japanese to strafe survivors who might appear in the water. "This was when we really got it," Wright recalled.

The other four flyable B-24s continued toward Attu, and Jones and crew found themselves alone. While banking over the crash, a cannon round came through the bomb bay and exploded against the radio panel. Fragments ruptured the deicing tank, and fluid sprayed into the bomb bay. An insulation fire began smoldering in the radio compartment. As another fighter made his run, the life rafts were riddled with bullet holes. The vertical tails were sieved, and bullet fragments rattled around inside the fuselage.

Crew members scrambled forward to extinguish the blaze in the radio compartment. Amid shouting and confusion, pilot Jones did not see the next fighter approach until it opened fire from head-on. Though close to the water now, Jones dipped the nose to spoil the attacker's aim. A cannon round struck just in front of the windscreen and exploded. The Plexiglas on the right side shattered. The copilot, Lieutenant Raymond K. Underwood, took the brunt of the explosion in the face. The flight engineer, Technical Sergeant Dwight C. Lambe, standing right behind Underwood, was struck in the face by flying Plexiglas. In the pilot seat, Jones had his face peppered with fragments and also was hit in the right arm and hand as he held the throttles. The shock shoved his hand backward, pulling power off the engines. The plane dipped toward the water, but Jones was able to shove the levers forward. The engines surged back to power, and the nose came level. Lambe, though wounded, helped the copilot out of his seat and onto the cockpit floor. Underwood's face was a bloody mass, and he was bleeding profusely from a deep gash in the neck. Meanwhile, Jones's arm went numb. It hung bleeding and useless at his side. The cameraman, Technical Sergeant Alex D. Ciurczak, came forward to help Lambe treat Underwood.

The flow of blood from the neck wound was stopped, and Ciurczak gave him a shot of morphine.

Technical Sergeant John Stroo, whose radios were knocked out, came forward and took the copilot's seat. Jones gave Stroo instructions on how to keep the bomber level, while Lambe helped Jones out of his seat so his wounds could be treated. With the plane stabilized, Stroo looked outside and saw no more fighters. The Japanese had turned for home.

As five B-24s struggled toward Attu and two others headed to Kamchatka, the B-25 crews led by Major Richard D. Salter came barreling in on the deck, looking for ships at anchor in the strait between Shimushu and Paramushiro. When the Mitchell bombers came off their targets, they were immediately engaged by Japanese navy Zeros and army Oscar fighters. Three B-25s were shot down, adding to the loss of Major Gash's B-24. Five B-25s with battle damage headed for Kamchatka behind two B-24s already struggling to make it to safe haven. Another B-25, battered and battle-scarred, headed for home, where it eventually crash-landed, killing all but two crew members.

One of the B-24s ahead of the string of Mitchells en route to Kamchatka was piloted by Second Lieutenant Roger K. Putnam. His bomber had developed an engine problem, and the prop could not be feathered. The high drag made recovery at Attu impossible, so Putnam had elected to divert to Petropavlovsk. On arrival, he found a long, concrete runway just south of the city and landed safely.

At the same time, five B-25 bombers and the second B-24 continued to battle their way up the Kamchatka coast with the Japanese in hot pursuit. As each plane neared the capital, the fighters broke off the chase. B-25s flown by Second Lieutenant Norman R. Savignac and First Lieutenant John T. Rodger approached the same field Putnam's B-24 had landed on. Both touched down safely, but Rodger's B-25 was unable to taxi because of damage to his landing gear.

Major Salter's B-25 had been riddled by antiaircraft fire during his bomb run, and when his left engine began losing power, he took up a heading for Kamchatka. "We approached Petropavlovsk across Avacha Bay from the southeast [and] were greeted by machine gun fire with tracers plainly visible." Two Soviet fighters pulled alongside but did not shoot. "Instead," Salter reported, "the pilot of the lead plane dipped his wing to indicate the direction we should fly." The heading led to the field.

Back over Paramushiro, Second Lieutenant Wayne A. Marrier began his run through streams of tracers and exploding flak. The plane shuddered from one impact after another. After releasing his bombs, the copilot, Second Lieutenant Sabich, discovered that his bomb bay doors were not closing. The hydraulic system had been damaged, and the doors refused to budge. The increase in drag would prevent return to Attu, so Marrier swung the nose in the direction of Petropavlovsk. Another damaged B-25, flown by Lieutenant Albert Berecz and crew, in front of Marrier and Sabich, also was struggling to make it to safety. Sabich watched the bomber ahead as it rolled out on its new course: "We could see the flames starting up. Shortly thereafter [the B-25] landed in the water. He made a swell landing. The flames on his left wing were really going then. It sure was a helpless feeling to see those boys hit the water and not be able to help them in any way."

Soviet soldiers stationed on Cape Lopatka had front-seat views as the drama unfolded. Then, after Berecz ditched his B-25, they watched the crew attempt to launch a life raft. According to the Soviets, the Japanese fighters machine-gunned the struggling airmen. None survived.

Marrier and Sabich continued north along the coast of the peninsula until about twenty miles south of Petropavlovsk, where they sighted another damaged B-25, flown by Second Lieutenant Russell K. Hurst. The two joined and headed inland when they reached Avacha Bay. As they overflew five Soviet naval vessels, the B-25s drew heavy antiaircraft fire from the ships, even though Hurst had extended his landing gear to signal his intent to land.

Hurst retracted his wheels and the two planes swung east, out beyond the bay, to discuss a course of action. Hurst elected to try approaching the field from the southern side of the bay, so he headed off alone in that direction. While waiting to hear how it went from Hurst, Marrier and Sabich watched as the second of two diverting B-24s, this one flown by Major Carl G. "Whitey" Wagner, came into view. Two engines were out, but Wagner flew directly across the harbor and through intense naval gunfire. Unscathed and undaunted, Wagner bore straight ahead until he spotted the field and lowered his wheels for landing.

Lieutenant Marrier and copilot Sabich continued to listen for a report from Hurst but heard nothing. Marrier eventually decided to follow Hurst's southern route and flew directly over a submarine base on the way but received no ground fire. Two Soviet fighters suddenly appeared and escorted the B-25 to a landing at the same field the others had used.

The Soviets were thrust into a tight situation over what was clearly a violation of their neutrality. They were certain the Japanese pilots would report these breaches during their debriefings. As Marrier and Sabich taxied their B-25 to parking, they passed camouflaged revetments, each harboring a Soviet fighter with its pilot sitting cockpit alert. The scene was tense as the Russians scanned the skies, looking for Japanese planes.

An hour passed. Nothing happened.

Above the cold North Pacific, though, tense times were not yet over as the remnants of the strike force made their way toward Attu.

Inside Captain Jones's battered B-24, Technical Sergeant Stroo, who had never flown a plane before, continued to fly the big bomber for three hours before flight engineer Lambe took the pilot seat to give him a breather. Neither man had any flight training, nor did any of the other crew members except Jones and Underwood. With coaching from Jones, both Stroo, then Lambe were able to keep the plane level and on the heading determined by the navigator, Captain James S. Eliot.

As the plane neared the Aleutians, not only battle damage, but also loss of fuel became a problem. A faulty transfer pump had dumped a considerable amount of gas overboard before the problem was discovered and corrected. Because of the difficult approach into the box canyon at Attu, the decision was made to land on the longer runway under construction at nearby Shemya Island. With the fuel gauges approaching empty, Captain Jones was assisted back into the pilot's seat. Keeping the plane airborne was one thing; landing was a whole different matter. Only Jones would be able to bring the stricken bomber in. Lambe helped by holding Jones's right hand on the throttles. Though the runway was not yet operational, Jones lined up on the lengthy strip. He came in barely above the crashing surf, rotated the nose, touched down on the matted surface, and hit the brakes. The B-24 came to a stop just short of the end of the completed portion.

In one day, twelve of twenty American planes (nine B-25s and three B-24s) and crews were lost or knocked out of action, more than half of the available Eleventh Air Force bomber force. Lieutenant Sabich's hunch had been right. Damage to the Japanese, according to their records, included hits on navy transports *Masajima Maru* and *Toei Maru* by B-25 Mitchells in the Paramushiro strait. Thirteen Japanese fighters were claimed by the bomber crew, with two more listed as probables.

When Admiral Nimitz was informed of the strike and the high losses, he wrote about his satisfaction with the attack and his feelings about the cost: "Please express my gratification to those concerned." Army air force headquarters, however, was clearly *dissatisfied* as two days later, Eleventh Air Force Commander, Major General William O. Butler was replaced by Major General Davenport Johnson.

The army air force leadership in Washington doubted the wisdom of continued daylight strikes against the now well-defended Kuriles and for the time being withdrew all but two squadrons of bombers to fight in the South Pacific. Meanwhile, the navy men of VB-135 continued to settle in on Attu. The squadron flew their PV-1 Venturas in routine sector patrols in search of Japanese aircraft and shipping. For the most part, these flights quickly turned into boring, tiresome cycles where no Japanese forces were sighted.

VB-136 arrived at Attu on October 1, 1943, and immediately began patrols. Lieutenant "Sandy" Dinsmore encountered a Japanese Betty on one of his missions. He chased the bomber toward Paramushiro and began closing the distance. After trading gunfire, Dinsmore realized that the Betty's 20-millimeter tail cannon had a more potent sting than his .50-caliber machine guns, so he broke off pursuit. That was the only engagement of note during the period.

On November 5, 1943, VB-135 was relieved and departed for its home base at Whidbey Island, Washington. VB-136 took over the full mission schedule.

Life on Attu assumed a dull routine, especially for the men who were not fliers. To them, life on the gray, fog-shrouded island made many of them feel more like exiles than American servicemen. Most men spent their idle hours, of which there were many, sleeping or playing card games. Time moved slowly, meals becoming the only thing that broke up the day. Tempers got short. Letter writing became more and more difficult, since there was little news to write about. The men were captivated, however, by the nightly radio broadcasts from Japan.

Tokyo Rose, her sultry voice the only personal contact most of the men stationed on Attu had with the Japanese, established a presence. The troops and sailors huddled around shortwave radios in their barracks huts, mesmerized by this very "American- sounding" female.

Aerographer Second Class Carrigan recalled, "We discussed her personally much more than her propaganda. . . . There was unanimous agreement that her voice, the only female voice we heard nightly, was the sexiest, most seductive sound to caress our ears in endless months."

In October, Tokyo Rose made renewed comments about Attu, noting that the last American attempt to bomb the Kuriles from the Aleutians had been repulsed with such heavy losses that no more foolish attempts had been made since the second week in September. The men of Attu knew this to be accurate. For the first time, she went on to forecast another invasion of Attu by the Imperial Japanese Army, this time conducted at night by elite paratroopers. That she publicized the plan made it highly improbable, but did not, however, diminish its impact on morale. The men on Attu had seen the bones of the dead Japanese soldiers who had charged up Henderson Ridge. They well knew the penchant for the Japanese to embrace suicide missions.

"Hundreds of innocent, young American boys would be killed silently and quickly before they knew what was happening," Tokyo Rose predicted. She went on to describe the paratroopers descending out of the darkness and overrunning American defenses.

For the men who worked after dark in well-lit areas, this type of propaganda had little impact. But for those trying to make it through the night zipped inside sleeping bags in damp, gloomy barracks, some of which were on the periphery of the bases, it was a different matter altogether. Thoughts of being killed in one's sleep coupled with the knowledge that U.S. ground troops were no longer stationed on the island made some conclude that this might not be a bad plan by the Japanese. Many a fitful night was spent awake wondering if a faraway disturbance was in fact the start of the slaughter.

In the early evening of October 18, the routine on Attu was broken by the sound of 90-millimeter antiaircraft fire. Men poured out of their huts and looked at the darkening sky. A "V" formation of ten twin-engine bombers was high overhead. Flak burst below and behind the formation. Men grabbed their helmets, rifles, and submachine guns and began firing into the air as the bombers, now identified as Japanese G4M Type 97 Bettys, opened their bomb bays and released their weapons above the runway and the approximately twenty cargo ships anchored in Massacre Bay.

Aerographer Paul V. Carrigan scrambled out of the navy weather shack near the runway and peered up. "Strings of bombs came raining down. I was looking directly overhead and could see the enemy planes amid black blossoms of ack-ack. The first bombs hit and exploded. I was conscious of four erupting across the runway from us and between it and Massacre Bay."

In the midst of the attack, P-40 Warhawk fighters took to the air from Alexai Point. They swung out over the bay and began clawing their way to altitude as the bombers reversed course for the Kuriles and sped homeward. None was engaged or shot down.

Damage from the attack was minimal, no aircraft or facilities were hit, but it served to reinforce the thought that the Japanese just might try that airborne invasion Tokyo Rose was so certain was coming. Four days later, the Japanese came again. Twelve bombers were intercepted by Alexai Point P-40s thirty miles before reaching Attu. The Bettys scattered and returned to Shimushu. The excitement over, days drifted into weeks and though several Japanese reconnaissance aircraft were encountered, no more bombers were seen over Attu.

As the island's weather pattern slid into the winter fog season, local patrol missions continued. Then in November Lieutenant "Hap" K. Mantius of VB-136 was assigned to calculate the useful operating range of the PV-1 aircraft. He kept fuel consumption records of all the unit aircraft and experimented with power and mixture settings to determine the best profile for maximum range. Using a combination of rpm, manifold pressure, and manual leaning of the fuel from the carburetors, he established parameters that extended the range of the PV-1 significantly. On November 16, 1943, Mantius flew his Ventura profile to within thirty miles of the southern tip of Paramushiro before turning back. He landed on Attu after nine hours and thirty-five minutes and had 135 gallons of fuel remaining (one hour and twenty minutes' endurance). The flight had great significance. It was the longest patrol flown in a PV-1 and demonstrated that the Ventura could fly missions over Japanese territory. But after the disastrous missions in August and September, could approval be gotten from naval headquarters?

At this point, Commodore Gehres, wing commander of Fleet Air Wing 4, reentered the scene. Ordered by Admiral Chester W. Nimitz, commander in chief, Pacific (CINCPAC), to obtain photographic intelligence of Japanese military strength in the Kuriles, Gehres jumped on the opportunity to get his Ventura units involved in something more productive than routine patrols.

Suddenly, navy missions out of Attu were to become anything but routine.

Chapter 6

The Empire Express: On Wings of Fire and Ice

The propellers were to me an enigma. I checked the tips: all smooth and without serious nicks. The shafts were bent backwards, but not severely. How was it possible for a plane to slam into the side of a mountain without badly damaging the propellers?

—Kamchatka crash site

Though VB-136 had proved the feasibility of flying PV-1 sorties over the Kuriles, weather precluded long-range combat missions, and the squadron rotated back to the naval air station at Whidbey Island in time for Christmas leave, 1943.

They were replaced by the "Bats" of VB-139, who moved from Amchitka. The fifteen Venturas they brought with them had been modified after manufacture to include a full set of instruments on the copilot side of the cockpit. The need for this improvement had been identified by previous Aleutian veterans of long, overwater missions.

Three crews and two training aircraft of VB-139 went to Adak, while thirteen planes and crews landed at Casco Field, the navy runway on Attu, on December 10, 1943. The squadron included thirty-six flying officers, seventy-two enlisted crewmen, a personnel officer, an intelligence officer, two chiefs, and a yeoman.

Casco Field in winter. Beyond the mountains, 700 miles west, lay the Kuriles.

The Bat's skipper was Lieutenant Commander William R. "Steve" Stevens, a Naval Academy graduate. Sporting a rakish mustache, Stevens at thirty-four was the cocky "Old Man" of the outfit. Small in stature, with a dark complexion, he had spent several tours in staff positions and consequently had less flying time than many of his junior plane commanders. To the experienced squadron pilots, he had yet to prove himself.

Commodore Gehres sent the three crews to Adak to test the Venturas that were being further modified there for long-range missions. Lieutenants Robert A. MacGregor, Thomas H. McKelvey, and Douglas M. Birdsall had volunteered themselves and their crews. The two aircraft at Adak and one of the planes at Attu were each fitted with a bomb bay fuel tank for additional range. The test planes at Adak also were configured for reconnaissance missions with new K-19A cameras mounted in the nose. The camera shutters were activated when million-candlepower photo-flash bombs ignited beneath the plane and were detected by a light-sensitive triggering mechanism on the camera. The photo-flash bombs were

Austin's plane after crash landing on Agattu Island.

Lieutenant (j.g.) V.C. Austin's crew was saved by the quick action by squadron commander Lieutenant Commander William R. Stevens after the crew became lost while trying to recover on Attu after a mission on December 30, 1943. Left to right, standing: Austin, pilot; Ensign J.J. Cooper, navigator; Lieutenant (j.g.) H.M. Jack, copilot. Left to right, front: ARM3c L.P. Russo, radioman; AMM2c W. Dean, gunner; AMM2c J.N. Miller, plane captain; AMM2c A.J. Ferranti, navigator/cameraman.

carried internally and tossed out by a crewman on command from the pilot. A flat plate was fitted across the back of the tail fins to slow the bomb so the flash would not appear in the picture. By carefully spacing the release of the bombs, an overlapping sequence of pictures could be obtained.

Meanwhile, on Attu on December 30, a Ventura that did not have the extra fuel tank was flown by Lieutenant V. C. Austin and crew on a search mission in Sector 8, over the Bering Sea. Upon return, Austin ran into thick weather and got low on fuel. He radioed to Attu requesting a "steer," saying he "had no idea whether I am north or south of the chain." He had actually overflown the island and was south. Commander Stevens was supervising right beside the communications operator in the Attu radio room. Stevens "took what I had, one out-of-range blip on the Agattu radar and one unreliable bearing from the DF station at Imperial Beach, California, and told him to steer due north."

Minutes later, Austin's radioman reported that they were out of gas and going down through the overcast. He then formally signed off.

The men hovered over the radio and "were stricken with grief," according to Stevens, but after a few minutes, a call came in. The Attu radio operator shouted, "They're down safely on Agattu!"

Stevens recalled, "All hell broke loose. We cheered like college kids!" Whether luck played a role in Stevens's radio call to Austin or not, the "skipper" had proven his worth.

The plane had crash-landed on a frozen lake and had skidded onto the shore. Injuries were minor, and the crew was soon rescued. The loss of the plane reinforced the need to have sufficient fuel on missions to enable holding or diverting for weather upon return from combat.

On the night of January 9 and 10, MacGregor, with Birdsall as copilot, flew a nine-hour "dummy" mission from Adak to Umnak to Agattu, where they photographed the islands and dropped practice bombs, then recovered at Amchitka. "Mac," an aeronautical engineer and highly respected pilot, gathered data from the aircraft that utilized the new bomb bay fuel tank. On January 12 the three crews rejoined the squadron on Attu.

Living conditions on Attu were somewhat improved over the more easterly island bases. Six officers were billeted to each Quonset hut, each having his own room. An officers' bar was opened, and a theater served as both movie house and gym. The planes, however, were all parked in open revetments, where most maintenance was conducted, fog, snow, rain, or shine.

On a rise overlooking the runway at Murder Point, Commodore Gehres had the Seabees build a headquarters befitting his stature. Sometime in January—no one seems to know exactly when—Gehres installed himself and his staff into these relatively lavish quarters, which the navy men dubbed "The Palace" or "Sweat Hill," the latter referring to how the men reacted to orders emanating from the heights.

Gehres enjoyed his perks and was particularly put off by the taste of the powdered milk available in the mess. He relished the real thing, so he solicited contributions from his staff, then sent one of his aides to Seattle aboard the USS *Avocet*, a seaplane tender. While the ship sailed to Washington, the commodore had the Seabees erect a barn complete with electric light and heat. It was built at the base of a hill near the PV squadron Quonset huts.

Soon the tender had accomplished its resupply mission down south and steamed out of Puget Sound, a cow tied on her fantail and her hangar full of hay. The animal arrived in good shape—no word is available regarding any propensity toward seasickness—and was immediately put to task. Happily back on solid ground, her milk output exceeded the demands of the staff, so the admiral prevailed upon the officers' mess to utilize the excess.

That same January 1944, a Japanese infantry battalion and the 11th Tank Regiment were moved from Manchuria to Shimushu. The 1st Garrison was upgraded to nine infantry battalions, nine field artillery batteries, and two heavy artillery batteries.

At Kagenoma, on the southeastern coast of Shimushu, the radar was performing well and was defended by six gun batteries, part of three antiaircraft battalions assigned to defend the island. Kataoka Naval Base also had a well-functioning radar and nineteen light and heavy antiaircraft positions to protect its two runways, maintenance hangar, aircraft revetments, oil storage tanks, barracks complex, and ammunition/supply buildings.

Miyoshino Airfield, an army installation, in the center of the island, and Numajiki on the eastern coast were equipped with B5N2 Kate and Mitsubishi G3M Betty medium bombers plus Ki-43 Oscar fighters. Both fields bristled with antiaircraft batteries. Shimushu had become a veritable fortress.

The Japanese navy continued to position 20 to 30 picket boats a hundred to two hundred miles northeast of the Kuriles. The slow-moving vessels used lookouts and listening devices and had a small directional radar to detect bombers overhead. Equipped with shortwave radios, they relayed early warning to the northern islands. The pickets carried three- and four-inch guns, light automatic cannons, and heavy machine guns, but their most effective defensive measure was to hide in fog banks.

By mid-January, the U.S. Navy VB-139 crews had been flying routine patrols for more than a month above the North Pacific and the Bering Sea while they waited for completion of the endurance testing at Adak. There, the normal crew of five men had been increased by one, adding a navigator, a job previously done by the copilot. In addition, on board was a plane captain, whose job was to get the plane ready for flight, similar to that of the engineer on the B-24 and B-25. While airborne he monitored the engines and tended to other maintenance duties. A radioman saw to communications, while an ordnance man operated the twin .50-caliber-gun turret. The small-caliber tail gun was removed to save weight.

Birdsall made a weather reconnaissance flight on the sixteenth, during which he did more checks of the fuel system. The PV-1 now had eleven different tanks, with no crossfeed capability. Each tank was plumbed to feed directly to its associated engine.

After takeoff Birdsall switched from the two rear mains to the bomb bay tank, and when it went dry, purged the fumes with CO_2 from a bottle that had been fitted for the purpose. The next tanks used were two external drop tanks, then two fuselage tanks, left and right auxiliary tanks, left and right front mains, and then back to the left and right rear mains. The pilot waited for a drop in fuel pressure before switching tanks to be sure that every drop of fuel was used. Frequently they would be distracted and miss the drop in pressure and the engine would sputter and sometimes quit. Engine failure over the Bering Sea was not a minor issue, so crews never had both engines running on nearly empty tanks. Tense moments were experienced whenever crews had to switch tanks and restart a failed engine.

The lead crew during the first offical "Empire Express" mission flown on January 20, 1944. Left to right, standing: Lieutenant R.A. MacGregor, pilot; Lieutenant R.A. Watson, copilot; ARM2c H.G. Grabowski, radioman. Left to right, front: AMM3c W.C. Dehnel, nav; AMM2c R.G. Oliphant, plane captain; AOM2c F.A. Gullstad, gunner.

Birdsall flew the practice mission at 8,000 feet and set his cruise to maintain 142 knots indicated (160 knots true airspeed). Four hours later and about 100 miles from Paramushiro, he turned for home, satisfied that the weather and fuel system were manageable for night raids. With less than six hours of daylight in January, Birdsall had flown the entire mission in the dark. For the next three days the squadron honed their bombing and navigation skills.

The fuel tank fitted in the aft section of the bomb bay left room for only three 500-pound general-purpose bombs. Twenty-pound incendiary bombs, carried in boxes, were to be thrown out an open hatch. Armor plating aft of the wings and the lower turret guns

This crew flew in the number two position on the first official "Empire Express" mission on January 20, 1944. Left to right, standing: Lieutenant T.R. McKelvey, pilot; Ensign H.R. Towle, navigator; Lieutenant (j.g.) L. Bradbury, Jr., copilot. Front row: AMM2c D. L. Montoya, navigator/bombadier; AMM2c D.T. Becnel, plane captain; ARM2c H.L. Sutton, radioman; AOM2c R.E. Jenkins, gunner.

were removed. Even so, the modified PV-1 at takeoff was three thousand pounds over the maximum allowable gross weight published by Lockheed.

On January 19, 1944, Commodore Gehres authorized resumption of strikes against the Kuriles. Three crews reported to the operations Quonset at 8:00 P.M. to get intelligence and weather briefings for their target: the Kashiwabara staging area. Birdsall recalled that the briefing "placed a lot of emphasis on expected winds and weather over the target and at base for our return. We were assigned primary and secondary targets and procedures to divert to Petropavlovsk if we didn't think we could make it back to Attu." Armament included three 500-pound bombs and boxes of 20-pound fragmentation

Birdsall's nervous crew was third on the January 20, 1944, mission that inaugurated the Empire Express. Photo was taken prior to the mission: Standing, left to right: Ensign, William Plassey, navigator; Lieutenant Douglas Birdsall, pilot; Ensign Al Fred (Fritz) Daniel, co-pilot. Front row, left to right : ARM3c Oleen Hess, radio-radar operator; AMM2c Frank Dixon, plane captain; AOM3c Lee Rindlisbacher, gunner.

This picture was taken on return from the crew's first mission. Note the smiles of relief upon safe return. Standing, left to right: Ensign Al Fred (Fritz) Daniel; Lieutenant Douglas Birdsall; Ensign William Plassey. Front row, left to right: ARM3c Oleen Hess; AMM2c Frank Dixon; AOM3c Lee Rindlisbacher.

bombs. The two lead aircraft had the K-19A camera in the nose and photo-flash bombs mounted on the rack by the hatch.

This first strike since the disastrous September 11 mission was led by Lieutenant MacGregor. Lieutenants McKelvey and Birdsall were in command of the other two aircraft. The crews donned cold-weather gear, climbed aboard their planes, and began starting engines for the thirty-minute warm-up. While they waited, systems checks were completed.

At Birdsall's plane, the left engine starter would not engage. Meanwhile, his squadron mates MacGregor and McKelvey finished their preparations and began taxiing over snow and ice down the length of the taxiway. At runway's end, a fuel truck waited. Once on the runway, MacGregor and McKelvey shut down so their tanks could be topped off to replenish fuel used for warm-up. A few extra gallons might be the difference in making it back safely or going in the drink.

VB-139 squadron skipper Lieutenant Commander William R. Stevens approached the third aircraft after noting that only one engine was running. A short discussion ensued. Stevens agreed to let Birdsall attempt to get the engine started manually. If successful, Birdsall could launch without topping off, to preclude another delay restarting the balky engine at the end of the runway. Birdsall got out of the Ventura and used a hand crank to turn the engine over. On the fifth try the engine caught. Birdsall reboarded, had the chocks pulled, and started down the taxiway.

Waiting in the bitter cold to see the planes off was Commodore Gehres. MacGregor completed his refueling, then, restarted engines and took off at 1:35 A.M. January 20. The commodore bade MacGregor and crew bon voyage and was soon joined by Stevens.

Lieutenant Commander William R. "Steve" Stevens (left) and Commodore Leslie M. Gehres. Stevens, though small of stature, was able to stand up to the imposing nature of the "Commodore."

Minutes later, McKelvey was ready, began his departure, and received the same send-off.

Approaching the runway now, Birdsall simply added full power and swung his nose to begin a rolling takeoff. The prop wash kicked up a flurry of loose snow and gravel that dusted off the commodore as Birdsall's plane swept onto the snow-covered matting that formed the runway. Gehres was livid, but Stevens was good at handling people both senior and subordinate. The commodore calmed down as soon as Stevens explained the starter problem.

Inside the still-rolling Ventura, the crew tensed as the plane surged ahead and Birdsall eased the yoke forward to lift the tail. A dip in the runway was used to check acceleration. Birdsall felt a jolt as the plane hit the depression and looked to ensure that he had 60 knots minimum. He did, but the thirty-four-thousand-pound plane seemed to take an eternity to reach 80-knots flying speed. Birdsall pulled the yoke aft and the Ventura lifted off a few hundred feet before the end of the runway. He snatched up the landing gear handle and skimmed the plane above Massacre Bay as the PV-1 gradually picked up speed. Then a shallow climb was begun as the crew took a deep breath of relief. Up ahead, Birdsall caught sight of McKelvey's tail light and joined in a loose formation.

There was no insulation along the sides of the fuselage, so at cruising altitude, biting cold soaked through the planes. The aircraft heater was ineffective, but the crews had bummed electrically heated flying suits from the army air corps. These suits kept the torso warm, but hands and feet stayed cold. Birdsell's radioman, Oleen Hess, wired his slippers and gloves so feet and hands would get heat. The PV-1 electrical system would allow only one man plugged in at a time, so they took turns keeping warm.

Out over the leaden North Pacific they flew hour after hour, the droning of the propellers becoming hypnotic, the roar and vibration numbing the senses. The planes entered a frontal system, and the men held on as the airframes rocked from turbulence. Birdsall tried to use the autopilot, but it was inoperative, so he and copilot Lieutenant (j.g.) Alfred F. "Fritz" Daniel took turns at the controls, Daniel greatly aided by the new instruments on his side. Radio silence was mandatory from start-up until each plane was off-target, meaning all changes and directions had to be received before takeoff. Any aborts en route were to be done in silence as well, so no one knew what was happening ahead or behind a particular aircraft, especially now that they were in weather. Each plane was on its own as pilot and copilot spelled each other flying into the black night. The waning moon had not yet come up. An hour later, MacGregor's plane came out of the frontal system into the clear.

Nearing Kamchatka, the running lights were turned off and the radar was switched on. The Soviets operated a marine radio beacon on the southern tip of Kamchatka Peninsula and broadcast every half hour. MacGregor's copilot tuned it in, and the navigator used it to get a bearing. MacGregor homed the beacon, then turned south.

Ahead, the target islands loomed out of the darkness. Covered with snow and illuminated only by starlight, the features of Shimushu and Paramushiro were easily identified.

As MacGregor's plane got over Paramushiro, he had his ordnance man toss out the first photo-flash bomb. Within seconds of its ignition, MacGregor's Ventura was held in three different Japanese searchlight beams at the same time. Tracers immediately rose into the air from antiaircraft fire in the Kashiwabara complex as the gunners sought out MacGregor's plane. Flak bursts sparkled against the black background.

McKelvey was next over Shimushu. As he began taking photo-flash pictures, two searchlights from Kataoka and three from Kashiwabara illuminated the plane for two minutes on the first run. Again tracers and detonating flak lit up the sky, but the rounds exploded behind the aircraft. McKelvey made another pass, this time south to north. Searchlights captured his Ventura again throughout this run. At least ten antiaircraft batteries fired on the plane.

Though the crews had not broken radio silence, the men in Birdsall's Ventura could see the photo-flash ignitions from the two aircraft ahead and the withering ground fire that surged up from the islands. Inside Birdsall's plane, mouths got dry, heart rates jumped. Then it was their turn as Birdsall approached his target, Banjo Zaki on Paramushiro. Using the same crude radar system that had been used to bomb Kiska six months earlier, he lined up on the target area on the northern end of the island. Birdsall's plane had no camera, hence no photo flashes to give his position away, but even so, the cockpit suddenly filled with light as Japanese searchlights found their target. The sky came alive with streaking tracers and exploding flak from the Kashiwabara Wan Harbor area. Birdsall pressed ahead, made the bomb release, and swung the bomber northeast, toward Attu and home.

For the next thirty minutes the crew kept a wary eye aft to make sure no Japanese night fighters had come sneaking up from behind.

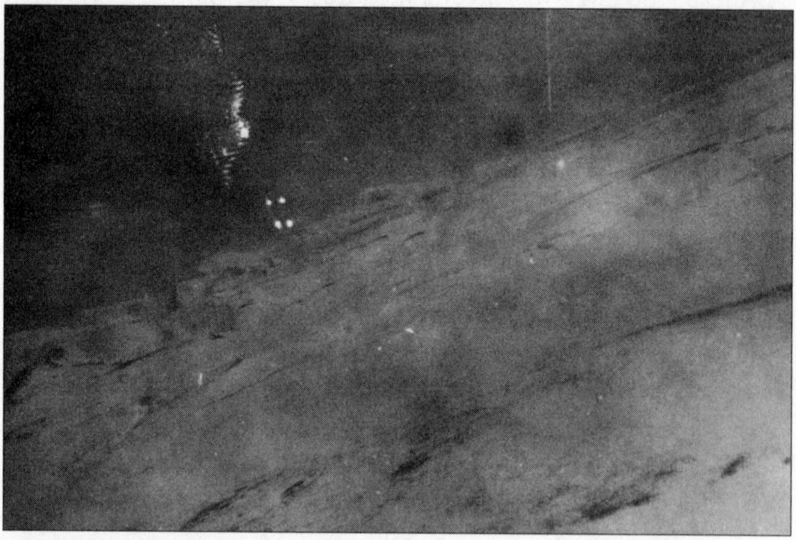

The white specks in the photo are heavy-weapons tracers rising from Paramushiro in the Northern Kuriles. This photo was taken as a PV-1 Ventura pulls off target.

Once the crew was sure they were beyond reach of the fighters, direful thoughts entered their minds. Had one of the Japanese anti-aircraft rounds found its mark in some unseen part of the plane, only to manifest itself in some dismal manner well out over the North Pacific? Odd sounds that would otherwise be ignored caught everyone's attention. A slight change in the prop setting or mixture woke anyone napping. After another four hours of noise, freezing temperatures, and bone-shaking vibrations, the crews now had to concentrate on finding their base. Fingers, numbed from the cold, tuned in the frequency of the radio beacon at Casco.

When Birdsall was fifty miles out, the needle swung dead ahead, right on course. He dropped the nose for descent while all eyes sought that first glimpse of runway. Clouds streaked by the windscreen. Ice built up on the wings. Out of the murk, the runway lights popped into view, like two strings of Christmas bulbs, and never a more welcome sight. The landing gear flopped down with a solid *clunk*, followed by the flaps, which seemed to buoy the plane as though cradled in some sure hand. Everyone tensed as Birdsall flared the nose, feeling for that icy surface, then finding it as rubber kissed metal. On the rollout, everyone seemed to collapse within themselves, cold, weary, exhausted, but alive. With the other two Venturas already safely on the ground, the navy's first official Empire Express combat mission had been flown.

The Japanese had not been caught off guard and could be expected to increase their defenses in the future. Two days later, a second successful mission was flown against the Kuriles with similar results and similar response by the defenders. Sorties continued sporadically, cancellations being caused by home-station weather.

Starting in February, however, strikes were launched four nights in a row, culminating on the fourth when six PV-1s and three PBYs were launched in three waves separated by two hours each. The mission was coordinated with U.S. Navy rear admiral Wilder D. Baker's TG-94.6 cruisers and destroyers operating off Paramushiro.

Fleet Air Wing 4 bombers took reconnaissance photos using photoflash flares and K-19A cameras in February 1944, which revealed the extensive defenses established throughout the northern Kurile Islands. This photo shows the runway at Suribachi Bay, revetments, antiaircraft gun positions and port facilities.

The ships bombarded island targets and damaged the cargo ship *Kokai Maru*. Assessment of the aerial bombardment was less clear, since the bombs were released using the radar. Regardless, Commodore Gehres was delighted with these initial efforts. No aircraft had been lost, and the fight was being taken to the Japanese homeland. When asked the next week by reporter Mel Meadows of the

Seattle Post-Intelligencer about the effectiveness of the missions, Gehres was quick to reply, "What would you think if the Japs bombed Sitka [Alaska] four nights in a row? You'd be demanding planes, troops, battleships—everything we had to defend the mainland. Well, that's what the Japs are faced with at Paramushiro." Gehres went on, "After sitting, sometimes for hours, waiting for 50-knot winds to clear the field, the pilots take off, bucking turbulence, icing and below-zero weather for 13 hours. Sometimes over Paramushiro they run into heavy flak, and occasionally night fighters come up. The first plane may draw twenty bursts from the ground guns, the second plane may be bounced around by 200 bursts. It's a tough flight." Gehres had come to demand the utmost from his men, though he understood the hardships they faced.

The opinion of the commodore among the navy men he led was typified by the comment of one of his officers. Gehres "was the toughest, most ornery SOB that I ever encountered during my many years in the navy, but I respected him. He had a war on his hands, and he would sacrifice people and equipment without a second thought if it meant keeping the upper hand on the enemy." All too soon, the commodore would prove the accuracy of that opinion.

Later in February, Lockheed service representatives came from Burbank with conversion kits and installed crossfeed provisions in the fuel tanks of all the airplanes to ease the workload of the flight crews.

Photographic intelligence of the bay at Otomae Wan gathered on February 4 by VP-139 indeed showed that Japanese activity around Paramushiro was intensifying. As a result, missions to the islands continued at night during the remainder of February and into March against these targets, without losses.

On Shimushu, the main military installation was at Kataoka Naval Base. Petty officer Trueman Shinya Fukuno was assigned there to monitor U.S. radio communications. Born in San Diego in 1923,

Fukuno was the son of a Japanese oceanographer who had come to San Diego and established a fishing business in California and Mexico. Fukuno had two brothers and four sisters and grew up as he described, "an all-around American." He was a Cub Scout and Boy Scout, a high school football player, and a member of the school's ROTC detachment. Early in 1940 his father passed away, and in November his mother died. With no family members in America, the decision was made for the seven children to join relatives in Japan. Fukuno was well aware of the friction between the two countries, and decided "if America was going to war, I was going to fight on her side." Planning to return Stateside if hostilities broke out, Fukuno sailed with his siblings on the *Asania Maru* from Los Angeles through San Francisco, Hawaii, and on to Yokohama. He began schooling, taking lessons in Japanese, and after the Pearl Harbor attack, he learned that leaving Japan for the United States was not an option. Fukuno's uncle, Dr. Terasaka, was staunchly patriotic about the war, but Fukuno knew better. "How can you win against a country that mass-produces cars? Japan mass-produces bicycles!" His uncle was unswayed in his belief of

Japanese servicemen dig out from under heavy snow on Shimushu, Northern Kuriles.

Japanese invincibility, but helped arrange for Fukuno to enlist in the naval reserves in hope that Fukuno would remain out of the fighting until the war ended. "In Japan," Fukuno recalled with irony, "the food was strange, I couldn't speak the language, and I wound up in the wrong navy!" He reported to a downtown Tokyo office, where he and five other linguists were trained to listen to foreign radio broadcasts on shortwave radios. The linguists attempted to intercept American and Soviet radio transmissions. Fukuno overheard a number of historic naval engagements of World War II, and as losses mounted during and after the Battle of Midway and the invasion of Guadalcanal, he was called to active duty. Fukuno received no basic training. "I never fired a gun." He was promoted to chief petty officer along with his five companions. The others "all received jungle clothing, while I was the only one to get cold-weather gear. None of them survived the war."

Fukuno was sent to Shimushu. He lived in a 20-man barracks at Kataoka Naval Base and worked in an L-shaped building which was divided into the American and Soviet monitoring sections. While on Shimushu he began listening to incoming bombing raid communications while on watch for up to twenty hours a day. "[The Americans] spoke in the open when in tight conditions," he noticed. He would write down all the radio calls he heard and turn them over to his supervisor.

With defenses being reinforced, the Japanese made ready for the coming invasions of their main islands. Things began heating up over the Kuriles as the U.S. Navy pilots continued their heavy schedule while the Aleutian spring unfolded in 1944.

Chapter 7
Missing-in-Action

Bombs were scattered all around the crash site. Was Bomber 31 on its way to the target when it ran into the side of the mountain? The impact was on the west side of the volcano, away from the inbound route the planes would have used to reach targets in the Kuriles. Why was that plane headed the wrong way at two thousand feet altitude in mountainous terrain?

—Kamchatka crash site

She was built in the spring of 1942, one of sixteen hundred assembled at the Vega plant in Burbank, California. She looked ungainly, a bit pudgy for a swift combat aircraft. Navy Bureau No. 34641 rolled off the navy production line two-tone gray and seemed almost to squat on the tarmac. Aft by the .30-caliber belly guns, her fuselage dipped to barely a foot off the ground. But looks can fool. The PV-1 was the fastest of the medium bombers of the period, able to outrun many fighters of the era such as the American P-40 Warhawk. At low altitude, Japanese Zeros or Oscars had trouble keeping up with her in a full-power dash. Closing from behind with little overtake made the Japanese fighters easy targets for the Ventura's turret gunner. The PV-1's powerful engines were mounted on short, stubby wings, the whole package made for speed. The downside was her high wing loading—56 pounds per square foot—which made landing "an experience" for those learning to handle her. She had Fowler flaps for landing, though. When extended behind the wings, the flaps reduced the 91-knot stall speed to 78 knots (90 miles per hour) in level flight. But it was when she lost an engine that things got dicey. Let her slow below the critical engine speed, and she would roll toward a dead engine. The pilot then had to pull power off the good engine while lowering the nose to regain airspeed and control, an unnatural procedure. A temperamental handful she could be at times.

Bureau No. 34641 was flown to Ault Field on Whidbey Island near Seattle, Washington, where squadron number 31 was stenciled on her nose, fuselage, and tail. She was used in the training program for pilots and crews in VP-139, many of whom were switching from seaplane to land-based bomber operations. The squadron moved south in July 1943 to the naval air station at Alameda, where the crews continued training while the plane returned to the Lockheed plant at Burbank to be modified with a full instrument panel for the copilot. In August she was back at Ault Field until deployment with the Bats of VB-139 on October 1, 1943, to Amchitka Island in the Aleutians. By the time she arrived on Attu in November 1943, she was well broken in. At Attu, she liked the pilot to hold her on the runway until 90 knots was reached. Even so, hauling three thousand pounds more than recommended gross overload into the air took nearly all of the forty-five hundred feet of runway available at Casco Field. But by March 1944, she had lifted above the snowy confines of Attu often, her guns had fired in anger, and her racks had released many a bomb over Japanese targets in the Kuriles. She had flown through fog and ice, flak and turbulence, and had always brought her crews safely home.

On the moonless night of March 24, U.S. Navy lieutenant Walt S. Whitman, who had joined the navy while living in Cincinnati, Ohio, and his copilot, Lieutenant (jg) John W. Hanlon of Worcester, Massachusetts, stood beneath a dark, overcast sky. The two men looked over their bomb-laden PV-1 Ventura with its weathered number 31 still emblazoned on her.

Bomber 31 and Bomber 28 sit together on the ramp at Attu on March 1, 1944, a little over three weeks before their fateful missions. Note number designation on the left drop tank of the aircraft in the background. Bomber 28 was flown by Lieutenant Moore and Bomber 31 was flown by Lieutenant Whitman on March 25, 1944.

The snow crunched beneath their feet as they continued their walk-around inspection, but it was the damp, cold air, driven through the best of parkas by the relentless wind, that got to Whitman and the others in his six-man crew. In addition to copilot Hanlon were aviation metalsmith/navigator Petty Officer Second Class Donald G. Lewallen of Omaha, Nebraska; aviation radioman Petty Officer Third Class Samuel L. Crown Jr., of Columbus, Ohio; aviation machinist's mate Petty Officer Second Class Clarence C. "Digs" Fridley of Manhattan, Montana; and aviation ordnanceman Petty Officer Third Class James S. Palko from Superior, Wisconsin.

This night, the familiar six were augmented by 22-year-old aerographer Petty Officer Second Class Jack J. Parlier from Decatur, Illinois, who was on his first combat mission, having just been placed on flight orders after a more senior NCO returned to the States. Weatherman/Aerographer's Mate Second Class Elzie B. "Bones" Carey and Parlier had both been assigned to fly that night.

Aerographer AERM2c Jack J. Parlier.

Metalsmith/navigator AM2c Donald G. Lewallen.

Inside "Chez Glue," VB-139's leisure Quonset Hut (all left to right): On the couch—ENS John Bratten; LT Mel Rehill; LTjg Al Hart, Admin Officer, not a pilot; ENS. Don MacMillan, Dudley Dexter's Co-pilot. Front: LT Quenton Norem, ENS Cliff Tambs, LTjg Walt Whitman.

Tambs would lose his life on a mission with Norem. Whitman would pilot Bomber 31 on its last mission.

Scheduled missions included a local search patrol and a bombing run over Paramushiro. The weather section's warrant officer, Jack Ingram, flipped a nickle to see who flew where. Jack Parlier got the Kurile combat assignment. All smiles at the result, Parlier tugged on his heavy, fleece-lined flight gear, then made his way to the flight line and climbed aboard Bomber 31. His role would be to take observations of weather fronts and photograph cloud formations along the route. These would be used to forecast the conditions headed toward Attu. Since it was his first mission, he also

Casco Field on Attu. Massacre Bay is in the foreground and Casco Cove is left center. Approaches to the runway were made from the direction shown. Aircraft that had to execute a missed approach due to weather were faced with mountains on three sides during maneuvering.

would get a feel for the quirky weather the crews faced. Even though by March a small AVP ship had been deployed 200 to 250 miles out along the route to relay cloud cover observations and wind direction, these factors could change rapidly, and fog often made the ships useless. Weather was the principal operational problem, and Parlier needed to have a solid grasp of the various conditions encountered aloft, since his primary job was to brief crews back at Attu before launches.

Whitman, his face greased to protect it from frostbite, warmed his engines on the tarmac, then followed his skipper, Lieutenant Commander "Steve" Stevens, and squadron mates Lieutenants James H. Moore, A. G. Neal, and Quentin E. Norem as their Venturas lumbered onto the runway and shut down beside the fuel truck.

The launch evolution now mirrored carrier deck operations. A duty officer went from plane to plane, giving last-minute updates. After a number of weather delays while topping off tanks and deicing, the hour had slipped to well past midnight, the normally scheduled departure time.

Stevens finally received the visual signal to launch and released breaks on Bomber 25 at 2:04 A.M., got airborne, and went into the overcast at two thousand feet. He set his engines at 2,300 rpm with 34 inches of manifold pressure as he groped for altitude in the murk.

Moore restarted his engines on Bomber 28 and released brakes at 2:08 A.M. His props churned loose snow into a billowing cloud as the PV-1 swept down the runway. But instead of climbing, the plane stayed level. Heavy with wing icing, the Ventura skipped like a flat stone on the sea, becoming airborne again, then plunged into the frigid waters of Massacre Bay. It broke in half and was engulfed in flames.

"Water was coming in," Moore recalled. "I had flight boots on. One was jammed under the rudder [pedal]. I pulled my foot out of the boot without unzipping it! I surfaced and started yelling, 'Let's get to the life raft.'" Moore swam through the icy water with ammunition exploding and fuel burning on the ocean surface nearby. Three of the seven men made it to the raft. "Everyone aft of the cockpit was killed."

Neal, Norem, Whitman, and their crews watched in horror from the runway as Bomber 28 sank, then wondered if the mission would be scrubbed.

Inside Norem's Bomber 33 were crewman Bert Burnham and

gunner Don Chenoweth, who recalled, "We had gotten to the end of the runway and deiced. We sat there and sat there, so we had to deice again with alcohol. We thought they were going to cancel the flight."

Minutes later, from his observation point on Sweat Hill, Commodore Gehres made his decision. Crewman Bert Burnham recalled, "He was sitting up there in that nice warm building and he sent word to 'Get 'em airborne.' We went rolling down that runway and it was 30 or 40 below out and the sweat was rolling off my face. We went all the way to the end and got her off then dropped about five feet. Scared the hell out of us. I thought we were going down. The [rescue] boat was just coming in through the flames as we went over the top of them."

Lieutenant Whitman and his copilot, John Hanlon, watched the proceedings from their cold-soaked cockpit. Whitman was well thought of in the squadron—"a good pilot," Doug Birdsall recalled. Whitman was born in Philadelphia, and his parents divorced when he was three years old. He went with his mother to Texas, where she married R. Walter Lewis. After high school Whitman moved in with

Sweat Hill.

Bomber 31 takes to the air with snow billowing behind and the enemy 700 miles ahead.

his grandparents in St. Louis for a period after his mother's death, then relocated to his Aunt Frances's home on Peoples Street in Cincinnati while attending the University of Cincinnati. There he joined the ROTC and eventually entered the navy on May 30, 1941.

Lieutenant (j.g.) "Moose" Hanlon grew up in Worcester, Massachusetts, graduating in 1936 from South High School. He attended Worcester Academy the following year, then was accepted into the College of the Holy Cross. "Moose" was a good athlete, cocaptain of the baseball team in 1941, the year he graduated.

Now it was Whitman's turn to take off, at 3:06 A.M., three hours later than scheduled. He lined up on the runway and shoved the throttles forward. Bomber 31 rumbled into the air and skimmed above the crash boat still circling the area where Moore's plane had gone down. Out over Massacre Bay the Ventura sped, past Murder Point, clawing skyward toward the Japanese nearly seven hundred cold, leaden sea miles west across the international date line and into the next day.

Stevens had already reached clear air at seven thousand feet and leveled off at nine thousand feet between thick stratus decks. He set his rpm at 1865 with 30 inches of manifold pressure, giving him 160 knots true airspeed. Two hours later, the cloud layers merged, and Stevens went back into the soup. He flew solely on instrument readings while fighting vertigo. Fatigue in the freezing cockpit was a real problem. His copilot took over periodically, but both men still had to keep their eyes on the gauges in case a partial instrument failure combined with vertigo might insidiously cause one of them to lose his sense of equilibrium. Above the pilots' shoulders leaned Clarence C. "Digs" Fridley, the plane captain or engineer, who kept a wary eye on the engine gauges to make sure the cylinder head temperatures stayed within limits while manifold and oil pressures held steady. Raised in Manhattan, Montana, Clarence came by his nickname because according to a neighbor, he "liked to go out and dig in the dirt." Things were running smoothly now, but in a few hours things would become hectic during Whitman's jinxing maneuvers over the target. Fridley would be back aft then, by the rear hatch, where he would toss incendiary bombs outside while trying to maintain his balance.

Sitting next to Fridley was Samuel L. Crown, the radio operator. For now, he had little to do except monitor the squadron frequency for messages from Attu, since radio silence while airborne was being enforced.

Behind Crown, Donald Lewallen worked at his navigation table on the left side of the crew cabin. Navigators were often officers, but Lewallen was an enlisted man whose aptitude was recognized early, so when asked, he volunteered to be trained to navigate. Though he missed his wife and two-and-a-half-year-old daughter back in the "lower forty-eight," there was little time to dwell on his personal situation. He was busy using dead reckoning to plot the plane's position, since he could see neither stars to use for a sextant shot nor ground references for a bearing on this moonless night. No icing was encountered, but static from the clouds blotted out the ability to get a bearing on the Cape Lopatka radio beacon. Located on the tip of Kamchatka, it transmitted a brief homing signal along with a weather report every thirty minutes. Farthest aft sat James Palko, the gunner. He, too, had little to do at the moment except try his best to keep warm. With him was Parlier, who from time to time popped his head into the astro-bubble or gun turret, when either was not occupied, to take a look at the weather situation and record the data.

Well out in front of the other three planes, Stevens noticed that his port engine had been consuming more fuel than normally needed to maintain airspeed. He continued to fly westward for another hour and a half in weather until he realized he was below the line on what crews referred to as the "how-goes-it chart," a matrix that showed how much remaining fuel was needed at specific points along the route. It accounted for the plane reaching the target and safely returning home with enough reserves to divert for weather to Shemya. If fuel on board did not total above the curve minimum at these points, the pilot had to turn back or risk having to ditch in the open ocean. With only 750 gallons left, and estimating another 180 miles to go before reaching Kamchatka, Stevens was below the amount needed to continue to the target and return to Attu with adequate reserves. Keeping radio silence, he swung east for home without transmitting a word.

Lieutenant Neal was having better luck with his fuel consumption, so he continued. Because of the weather, he, too, had to rely on dead reckoning navigation. At 6:40 A.M. he spotted four ground lights through thick haze. He had made landfall, early, on the Kamchatka Peninsula well north of the intended spot. Neal turned south and tried to make his way down the peninsula on radar. Ice began to build up on the wings. More than twenty active volcanoes lined the route down the southeastern coast. The cinder cones of many reach more than eight thousand feet and expel huge volumes of hot gases. A sudden updraft struck Neal's plane. It carried the Ventura on a bone-jarring ride from nine thousand to fourteen thousand feet at the rate of three thousand feet per minute. Half an hour later, radar indications showed that he was approaching Cape Lopatka, so Neal flew south, toward Shimushu. The sun came up at 7:22 A.M., and he released his bombs three minutes later. Neal turned outbound for home with 650 gallons of fuel remaining for the nearly seven-hundred-mile return trip.

Down below, the Japanese were no doubt surprised to find themselves under attack in daylight, something that had not occurred since the September 1943 raid. They had successfully defended the islands then, inflicting heavy losses on American Mitchell and Liberator bombers. But recently they had experienced only night raids, coming in waves spaced several minutes apart. After the first bombs were dropped, they knew more were inbound. Antiaircraft gunners, startled out of an otherwise quiet dawn, ran for their weapons. In the aircraft revetments, planes were being readied for scramble.

Norem approached the target area next. He estimated reaching Cape Lopatka at 7:30 A.M. With thirty minutes to go and reading no beacon signal from the cape because of static, he turned on his radar. Norem could find no land indication on the scope, but at 7:30 he was able to get a bearing from the cape. To his surprise, the bearing needle swung to the bottom, or six-o'clock position. The Lopatka beacon was behind the aircraft! Rogue winds had blown him west of Kamchatka and out over the Sea of Okhotsk. With fuel running low, he used his radar to determine when he was still over water, jettisoned his bombs, then took up a heading for Attu.

Whitman's plane arrived over Cape Lopatka last, and by now the Kuriles were bathed in full daylight. The element of surprise was no longer available, and the Japanese would have by then launched planes to defend the islands. Minutes later, Whitman made his final transmission: "Down! Down!"

Stevens landed on Attu after 6 hours, 37 minutes of his aborted

One of the three surviving bombers of the five launched on March 25, 1944, lands safely back at Attu after over ten hours in the air.

flight. Neal was airborne for 10 hours, 38 minutes and Norem landed after 10 hours, 53 minutes. Whitman's plane never returned.

That afternoon, six aircraft were launched to search for Bomber 31 survivors. They prowled above the icy waters of the Bering Sea and North Pacific for hours, but results were negative. Within days, Tokyo Rose was reported to have announced on the radio that the entire crew had been captured. According to several members of the squadron, she even read off the names of the crew, using the copilot's nickname, "Moose" Hanlon.

We now know that the radio announcement from Tokyo Rose was fabricated. How she obtained the names of the crew remains a mystery, but at least some members of the crew never set foot on Japanese soil. The aircraft was certainly not shot down over the Kuriles. Was it possible that one or more of the crew members bailed out over the islands after their Ventura was attacked and damaged? Had one of the crew been captured, he might have been forced to reveal the names of the other men in the plane, which had managed to escape toward Kamchatka.

Chapter 8
Death in the Archipelagoes

If Bomber 31 had run into difficulty over the Kuriles and tried to reach Petropavlovsk, could the Russians have shot them down by mistake? There were instances when their antiaircraft guns had fired on American planes, but had Soviet fighters shown a propensity to do so as well?

—Kamchatka crash site

The crews on Attu continued the bombing campaign, but subsequent attacks were completed only under cover of darkness. Not that darkness made them undetectable. The Japanese could fly above the medium altitudes used by the Venturas, then use moonlight and the reflective snow background below to silhouette the bombers. They could watch as searchlights swept the skies from the ground, looking for the telltale shadow of a bomber. Then they would roll in for the kill.

By April 1944, the Japanese believed that an attack on the Philippines was imminent and that the United States was planning an offensive operation in the Kuriles to support that effort. Much-needed men, machines, and war-making matériel had to be divided between the two theaters. Japanese northern airfields were continually being built up. The 5th, 20th, and 25th Air Brigades were transferred from Manchuria, Honshu, and Kyushu to the Kuriles.

Kitanodai Airfield on Paramushiro was fully operational and included the 20th Air Brigade headquarters, the 54th Air Regiment, with approximately twenty fighters, and the 3rd Air Regiment, with approximately twenty medium bombers.

Two years earlier, the Japanese had employed eighty-five-hundred men and its Fifth Fleet ships and submarines in the Aleutian operation. That effort tied up 144,000 Americans and Canadians. Now the roles were reversed as a small number of planes flown by U.S. Navy crews forced a large number of Japanese troops to be stationed in the Kuriles. Had it not been for the continuing attacks from the Aleutians, it is reasonable to conclude that these buildups, reinforcements, and construction efforts would have been expended against MacArthur's forces in the South Pacific instead.

Once the Kuriles were reinforced, the major difficulty faced by the Japanese pilots—besides being shot down by Ventura crews, or by their own people—was the weather. Taking off was one thing. Getting back on the ground was another problem altogether. With primitive instrument aids and foul weather the norm in winter, Japanese pilots had little recourse should conditions turn sour. If the bases on Paramushiro got socked in by fog, the ceiling and visibility were likely to be bad everywhere nearby. Emergency landings in Kamchatka were forbidden by the Japanese commanders, and many a plane and pilot were lost purely due to operational matters, without ever firing a shot.

At Kitanodai Airfield on Paramushiro, the ground crew had cleared a hundred-foot-by-two-thousand-foot section of the wooden runway. Called a "snow box" by the fliers, it was their primary launch field during winter. Even though a pilot might get airborne and safely down again, the planes on the ground were still vulnerable to the violent weather. During one stormy period, Oscar pilot Warrant Officer Sei'ichi Yamada recalled, "a hundred-mile-an-hour wind flipped over six planes." Spare parts were not easy to come by due to scarcity and difficulty getting supply ships past American submarines and marauding task forces. During a month-long stretch during the winter of 1943–44, no planes were available for flight at Kitanodai.

Nearly seven hundred miles away—and a day back in time—the men in the Aleutians faced much the same conditions at their fields. To prepare replacement crews, Commodore Gehres flew to Whidbey Island to brief the Blue Foxes of VB-135 on his evolving plans for reconnaissance and bombing of the Kuriles. The squadron began moving north in April 1944. Led by Lieutenant Commander P. L. Stahl and his executive officer, Lieutenant M. A. "Butch" Mason, their unit emblem was a fox riding a gas tank, eyes blindfolded, bombs and guns tucked under forelegs. The squadron flew up the Strait of Juan de Fuca, along the Inside Passage, landing at Yakutak, Alaska. Two crews stayed behind overnight because of engine problems. Their planes were destroyed in a hangar fire that evening. It was considered a bad omen for the squadron.

The Blue Foxes next landed at Adak to begin Aleutian training using newly installed Loran (long-range radio aid to navigation) gear. The system included a scope with a complex arrangement of knobs and dials at the receiving end of transmissions from fixed locations carefully spaced throughout the region. A master station emitted a low-frequency radio signal. Nanoseconds later, "slave stations" transmitted from separate sites in the Pacific Northwest and Alaska. The scope screen was green, and these signals showed up as lines, dubbed "grass." The operator had to isolate the spot where the signals crossed, then use a readout to calculate the plane's longitude and latitude.

While undergoing Loran orientation on April 26, 1944, a VB-135 Ventura flown by J. J. McNulty went missing on a routine training patrol out of Adak.

Ensign Byron Morgan was one of the new pilot-navigators aboard the search aircraft that, for days, went out looking for McNulty and his crew. The planes flew at low level over the water, trying to spot, as Morgan related, "a life raft, a yellow Mae West, an oil slick, anything the cold water would give up which could tell the story."

Morgan wrote of the experience, "I had flown over a lot of ocean, but these flights, looking at every whitecap, every cloud shadow on the water, watching each sea bird and heavy, glassy swell as the Pacific moved into the Bering, left a dull, senseless dread that the sea would always win this one; there was no possibility, no hope, no recourse nor cry that you could let out that would pierce the impassive, heavy being of this dead water."

Each time the crews came back from their searches the tale was the same: no trace.

Despite this setback, VB-135 made final preparations to deploy west, to Attu. While that was in progress, sister squadron VB-139, at Attu, lost another aircraft on May 1, 1944 when PV-1, tail no. 29749, failed to return from a mission. Three days later, VB-135 moved into Casco Field to join the Bats. From this point on, two squadrons of Venturas would pound the northern Kuriles.

Ensign Morgan arrived in a Ventura with a Labrador retriever named Peter Victor, or "PV," tucked under his arm. He had picked up the pup while overnighting at Kodiak and stowed him away aboard the plane. Morgan moved into one of the six-man Quonsets.

Two days later, VB-135 suffered their next casualties. Flown by Lieutenant (j.g.) A. A. Wheat and manned by seven others, the Ventura and crew were lost when the plane blew up shortly after takeoff.

Then on May 13, 1944, a nine-plane strike using planes from both squadrons was launched against targets on Shimushu and Paramushiro. Byron Morgan was on the mission. Two hours out of Attu, his Loran quit working. His plane was between cloud layers, so he could get neither a celestial fix nor a drift estimate over the water. Morgan used dead reckoning and forecast winds to navigate. The plane went through two cold fronts, where heavy turbulence was encountered. Nearing the target area, land was finally sighted. Morgan fixed his position, checked his "how-goes-it curve," and determined that unexpected headwinds had delayed

Battle damage caused by flak. The round blew through the right wing root on a PV-1 Ventura.

their arrival and they were now below the minimum fuel level needed to make it safely back to Attu.

Lieutenant Howard P. Schuette, the plane commander, jettisoned the bombs and turned for home. He asked for another check of the

Heading in! PV-1 Venturas on their way to the Northern Kuriles without fighter escort. Many would not return.

fuel status before committing to Kamchatka (for which there was plenty of fuel). Copilot Lieutenant (j.g.) John E. Brassil and the navigator, Ensign Byron A. Morgan, ran the numbers again, applying the now more favorable tailwind going home. They wound up with a profile above the curve that showed the possibility of making it to Attu, but it would require some creative cruise control. Schuette switched from auto-lean to manual-lean on the engines, running them hotter than recommended to get the maximum range from each drop of fuel. The crew threw every loose item overboard, including parts from the twin .50-caliber machine gun, the navigation octant, books, and a divider. The bomber banged its way through the weather fronts and finally picked up the radio beacon fifty miles from Casco Field. Schuette landed with ten minutes of fuel remaining.

One of the other Venturas on the mission was not so lucky.

Tail no. 48934, flown by H. V. Logan and a crew of six from VB-139, went missing.

The Japanese did not come away unscathed either. Records indicate that American twin-engine aircraft dropped bombs on Shimushu and Paramushiro and one of the Japanese navy fighters failed to return to base.

On May 18, 1944, Lieutenants Quentin Norem and Ralph J. Lowe from VB-139 were scheduled for on a two-plane mission to take out picket ships a hundred miles from Paramushiro. The vessels had been tipping off the Japanese as night missions flew overhead. Norem took off, and because it was their first daylight takeoff in many weeks, copilot Lieutenant (j.g.) Phil Brady was given the yoke as Lowe's plane took the runway. Brady wanted to try letting the plane bounce softly into the air when they hit the "check bump," a depression and rise halfway down the runway where airspeed needed to be 60 knots or better for a safe takeoff in the remaining runway. Lowe gave permission, but most of the pilots preferred to stiff-arm the yoke forward to keep the plane on the ground until well past minimum flying speed. The Ventura never

The Ventura flown by Lieutenant Ralph J. Lowe and his copilot Lieutenant (j.g.) Phil Brady from VB-139 bursts into flames after crashing on takeoff, May 18, 1944. The crew escaped with minor injuries but the plane was destroyed.

Wreckage of Bomber 32, which crashed on takeoff on May 18, 1944. Lieutenant Ralph J. Lowe and crew survived. The plane's logo read, "They don't make them any tougher than us."

bounced very high when it encountered the bump and usually settled back down on the runway, but this time the port engine quit just as the plane lifted into the air. The resulting torque threw the Ventura into a cartwheel. It slammed back onto the matted runway and skidded to a flaming halt. The crew scampered from the burning machine without injury just before the bombs and ammunition cooked off.

Norem continued on the mission and came upon two picket ships, where his plane was fired upon and hit as he made his second run. His copilot, Lieutenant (j.g.) Clifford M. Tambs, was struck in the chest by a round that pierced the fuselage, just below the windscreen. He slumped over in his seat as antiaircraft shells riddled the aircraft, knocking out the hydraulics, jamming the fuel mixture on one engine in full rich, and damaging the up lock on the starboard landing gear. Crew members lifted Tambs out of the cockpit and ministered to him as Norem struggled to keep the plane flying. Two hours later he tried to lower the landing gear, but the hydraulic

Lieutenant Q. Norem touches down gear-up in a "beautiful landing" on Attu after his aircraft was heavily damaged while attacking Japanese shipping.

When the aircraft came to a stop, the props show typical damage, tip bending and shearing that occurs when propellers are under power when they strike solid objects such as the runway surface.

The point of entry of the heavy machine gun round that penetrated the fuselage and killed lieutenant C. M. Tambs.

system had failed. One wheel hung dangling into the slipstream. With his landing gear not fully extended and windshield shattered by gunfire, Norem approached the runway at Attu. The entire squadron had been alerted and stood near the matted runway, watching. Norem made "a beautiful landing" according to Lieutenant Douglas Birdsall, and the plane came skidding to an uneventful stop. There was no fire, but unbeknownst to Norem at the time, Tambs had died on the way home.

On May 23, 1944, tail no. 48889 from VB-135, flown by Lieutenant (j.g.) Carl E. Clark, crashed on takeoff with the loss of all hands.

These deaths were especially hard on the maintenance crews, who often felt responsible for noncombat losses. Working in sub zero temperatures at night with only a piece of wind-whipped canvas for protection against the driven snow, they tried their best to keep the planes ready for flight. The idea of a well-lit, heated hangar with shelves of spare parts was something they could only

Maintenance men had to work under the grimmest of conditions. Work was done outside in temperatures that reached 40 below zero.

fantasize about. But deliver the aircraft the maintenance men did, and the Bats and the Blue Foxes continued patrols out of Attu.

On June 11, Lieutenant John P. Vivian from VB-135 launched on a weather reconnaissance hop. As he approached the Kurile area, he noticed that the sky was relatively clear over Shimushu. He pressed ahead and spotted Miyoshino Airfield crowded with Mitsubishi GM-4 Betty bombers. He used a K-20 camera to photograph the installation and returned unscathed to Attu. When the prints were developed, the photo interpreter noticed twenty-nine Bettys being armed with torpedoes. Rear Admiral Ernest G. Small's Task Force 94 was at the time moving into the northern Kuriles area to bombard Matsuwa Island. There was concern that the task force would be in great danger.

The next day, the first scheduled daylight bombing mission over the Kuriles since September 1943 took to the air in support of the task force. Led by the squadron executive officer, Lieutenant M. A. "Butch" Mason, five volunteer crews attacked Miyoshino Airfield on Shimushu. The element of surprise was in their favor, bombing results were good, and no losses were suffered in the target area. Mason and Lieutenant Lewis "Pat" Patteson continued over Paramushiro and took the first photos of Kakumabetsu Airfield, on the western side of the island. The entire mission results encouraged the squadron to continue the practice of daylight attacks even though one Ventura, piloted by Lieutenant (j.g.) Jackson W. Clark, ditched in Massacre Bay upon return when fog obscured the runway. All hands survived.

On June 14, two 3-plane bomber formations plus a single reconnaissance Ventura departed from Casco Field on another daylight mission.

Ensign Morgan was the lead navigator in his group. The three aircraft took off with minimum spacing, then joined in a loose triangle. The weather was clear across the Bering Sea and North Pacific. As the Kuriles were neared, Morgan became concerned about the lack of cloud cover needed to help protect the Venturas

Plane crew #6 before being forced to divert to Kamchatka during a mission to the northern Kuriles. Top row, left to right: Lieutenant (j.g.) J.E. Brassil, Lieutenant H.P. Schuette, Ensign B.A. Morgan. Bottom row, left to right: AMM2c A. Michelotti, RM3c E.J. Jage, AMM1c W.A. Dunaway, AOM2c W.H. Morris.

from fighter attack. He suggested to his pilot, Lieutenant Schuette, that instead of turning south before reaching the Kamchatka coast, they might continue over the coast, then use the mountains to shield their approach to the Kuriles. Schuette agreed even though it violated Soviet neutrality, then made a radio call to the other crews regarding the deviation.

At the radio listening post on Shimushu, linguists along with Warrant Officer Fukuno were monitoring radio transmissions in the communications building. The radar at Kagenoma on the southeastern side of Shimushu was operating, its antenna searching for contacts inbound from the north and the northeast. The Venturas were detected, and scramble orders went out. Pilots raced for their aircraft. Japanese Air Group 203 had sixty aircraft available to intercept the American strike force.

The Ventura formation crossed the Kamchatka coastline at seven thousand feet, turned south, and skimmed alongside the volcanoes on their way toward the Kuriles. As they bore down on Cape Lopatka, Schuette pushed the power up. Morgan, his job done for the moment, began clearing his navigation table, stowing his dividers, E6B navigation computer, and ruler. AOM Petty Officer Second Class Walter H. "Wally" Morris, in the gun turret, charged his twin .50s and squeezed off a test burst. Adrenaline began to pump through every member of the crew as the smell of cordite wafted through the compartments.

Morgan took a look out the astro bubble and saw Shimushu dead ahead in the clear, ten miles distant. He stepped forward past the radioman, Eddie Jage, then braced himself between Schuette and Brassil on the flight deck. Morgan pointed out Miyoshino Airfield, its single fifty-four-hundred-foot runway, aircraft revetments, and gun pits. Clouds of flak blossomed in the sky above it. Then Schuette asked Morgan to go back to the astro bubble and call out heavy flak concentrations so they could avoid them. Morgan scurried aft while Brassil, the copilot, activated the bomb bay door switch. The Ventura began to vibrate as the doors swung open and the roar of the slipstream filled the plane. By the time Morgan got in position, Schuette had already lowered the nose, diving into the thick of things to begin his bomb run at the airfield.

Morgan now had a bird's-eye view of the action and saw aircraft on the runway taking off. He called it out over the intercom. Headsets crackled with excited chatter as AMM First Class Willie A. Dunaway, the plane captain, and mechanic AMM Second Class John F. Beggin watched from the tunnel hatch. Up above, Morris swivelled his gun turret, looking for fighters.

At fifteen hundred feet in the dive, Schuette pressed the pickle button, releasing three 500-pound bombs. He swung hard left away from clouds of exploding flak. Brassil reached down and cycled the switch to close the bomb bay doors. The Ventura picked up speed and the noisy ride smoothed out as the doors slid shut. From the rear, Beggin shouted out his report: "Hits on the runway!"

As the plane cleared the island, Schuette pushed the power to 2600 rpm and set the manifold pressure up to 48 inches. He lowered the nose, and the Ventura surged ahead at maximum speed as it descended toward the water. Half a mile off to the right was Lieutenant (j.g.) Mabus's aircraft. A Japanese fighter was closing in behind it. Moments later, Morris in the gun turret called out another fighter, this one coming their way.

Morgan looked aft and spotted it. "It looked like a toy back there. I couldn't imagine anything so small could do us damage."

The Ventura was now a hundred feet above the water, indicating 280 knots flat out. As Morgan looked rearward, the fighter was no longer looking like a toy. The nose of the fighter rose slightly, and red winks appeared on the wings as its 20-millimeter cannon opened up. The maneuver caused the fighter to lose ground in the chase. Morgan saw splashes appear in the water behind them as the Ventura rushed away at wavetop height.

In the top turret, Morris couldn't lower his .50-calibers enough to take a shot because the tail rose too high at that speed. Slowing down was not an option. Neither was climbing, since that would expose the now defenseless underbelly of the aircraft. Morgan told Morris not to fire without a clear shot, since wayward tracers zooming well above the fighter would convince the Japanese pilot that he was not vulnerable.

The fighter soon closed the distance again. Once in range, he raised his nose to get the bomber in his sight, then opened fire, only to drift out of range once more. The fighter repeated the maneuver several more times during the next twenty minutes. Then the pilot climbed away, back toward Shimushu.

With time now to assess the situation, Schuette looked over the gauges. The starboard main fuel tank showed it was down to fifty gallons. He called back to Dunaway to look outside and check the right side for a fuel leak.

Dunaway peered out at the wing. A fine mist was trailing like smoke. "Mr. Schuette," Dunaway reported, "I can see gasoline comin' off that wing! We got us a real gas leak."

Brassil added up the remaining fuel. There was not enough left to make it to Attu. The choice was to continue on and make an ocean landing short of home field or head for Kamchatka. The crew was unanimous in their opinion: "Russia!"

Schuette swung in a long, sweeping arc to the left, seeking the new course that Morgan had given him for Petropavlovsk.

Recalling the implications, Morgan wrote:

> We were turning away from Attu, from the war and all that it meant. We would not return to the rough, steel-matted runway, to the mountains of Attu, to the wet, cold tundra and the wood-slatted walkways over the tundra to our Quonset huts, rounded like low mounds of earth, to military trucks and jeeps wearing the mud down deeper into more and more mud and water, to the faces in the squadron, vital and alive, seeking something in that next mission, some incident, some action which would give a point of reference to that flight into the gray sky over north water, dead and molten gray, like lava that slowly moved in rhythm to some great beast beneath.

Schuette radioed his predicament and intentions to Lieutenant Sparks in one of the other two planes.

"Okay," Sparks answered, "I'll notify them back on Attu what happened. I'll get word to [your wife] Edna. Good luck."

The radio then erupted with last-minute messages.

"Hey," Morgan broke in, "this is Morgan. Tell Lester to take care of my dog."

The radio stayed busy with chatter until the voices from the other planes faded out as Schuette and crew continued toward the Soviet Union.

Aboard the aircraft were two classified electronic boxes. The identification, friend or foe (IFF) transmitter was used to send a coded signal that could be read by friendly radar sites. It had an internal detonating device which the copilot activated. The other item was the new Loran gear. Beggin and Dunaway used a fire ax to chop it loose from its mount on the navigation table, then threw it overboard. Morgan's navigation charts were torn up and also tossed into the slipstream. Satisfied that no secrets would be revealed to the Soviets, the crew peered either out the windscreen, gun bubble, or side ports in an attempt to spot a runway.

Just then a plane flew over the top of them. It circled behind and pulled up on a wing as Morris held the squat fighter, a Mosca, in his twin-.50 sights.

Schuette put down the landing gear, the international signal of peaceful intentions. Then Brassil switched his radio to the frequency he had been briefed to use with the Soviets. He rattled off the appropriate Russian phrases telling whoever might be listening that the crew wanted to land. He got no response, but the Mosca stayed glued to the wing.

Ahead, a large, grassy area came into view. In the center was a single concrete runway. Schuette reduced power, dropped flaps, and brought the plane in for a smooth landing.

Once on the ground, for Schuette and his men there would be difficult times ahead, but their war with the Japanese was over.

Chapter 9
Internment in Kamchatka

What fate might have awaited the crew of Bomber 31 had they intended to make safe passage along the peninsula and landed their crippled plane at Petropavlovsk?

—Kamchatka crash site

The crews diverting to Kamchatka by and large expected to be treated with hospitality befitting an ally, but when Ensign Byron Morgan and the rest of Lieutenant Schuette's crew landed at Petropavlovsk, the tone of their reception was quite unexpected.

Lieutenant Schuette parked his Ventura clear of the runway and shut down the engines. Minutes later, a Soviet soldier approached the entry door, bayonetted rifle in hand, and motioned for the crew to get out of the plane. Morgan, who was by the hatch, slipped back inside and told Schuette and Brassil that they were being met with guns. The soldier followed right behind Morgan onto the flight deck and continued to motion for the crew to leave.

Morgan recalled that Brassil turned to the Soviet and said, "Okay Boris, okay. Take it easy. We are leaving." Brassil then laughed "in his square-jawed, Boston Irish way" as he motioned for the soldier to move back so they could squeeze through the narrow passageway.

As Morgan started out, he remembered a notebook he kept in the drawer of the navigation table. He retrieved it, but the soldier tried to snatch it from his hand. A momentary tug-of-war developed until the soldier got angry and started yelling. Morgan let go. The notebook was not worth getting shot over.

The crew was herded in a tight group and made to sit in tall grass near the aircraft. Along the edge of the field Morgan spotted several B-24 bombers with engine nacelles vacant, the paint on the fuselages fading. The planes had been sitting there since the September 1943 raid, and to Morgan looked like "an elephant graveyard of U.S. aircraft from the Aleutians." Another PV-1 was parked at a distance, the crew of which was also seated in the grass. Dunaway got to his feet and said, "Hey, that's Bone's crew!" The rest of the men rose and started walking toward the other Ventura, but the soldier blocked their path. At that moment, laughter erupted behind them. Near Schuette's plane, a group of Soviets was having a raucous chuckle over the tail art painted on the side of the fuselage aft of the door. It was a cartoon of a fat Japanese general in elegant attire. Reporting to him was a battered Japanese pilot whose bullet-riddled plane was resting beside a palm tree. The caricature broke the ice with the Soviets. Soon Soviet navy and air force officers came over and began animated exchanges, bridging the language barrier with laughter and pantomimes.

With tensions easing, Morgan noticed another officer approaching along a road beyond a row of birch trees. "Every step seemed to be a new adventure for him; he walked as though someone was pushing him along against his will. He didn't bend his knees, and when he put his foot down, it didn't seem to want to stay where he put it. From his broad-toed, black boots to the black-visored, green-topped garrison cap, he seemed to be constantly in motion." He came to a stop in front of the crew, and clicked his heels together in a jittery movement. Then his hand fluttered to his cap brim in salute.

"My friends," he said, "listen me now. I am interpreter. Please sit down." While bracing himself with one hand and grasping the grip of his holstered revolver with the other, the man eased himself to the ground. He then introduced himself: "I am Suborta Lieutenant Dondekin."

Dondekin had suffered a head injury from a land mine explosion on the Manchurian border while fighting against Japanese army regiments. The palsied veteran had a score to settle with the Japanese. "I am sick man," he said. "Monkeys do this to me. You bomb monkeys. . . . good." In addition to speaking Russian and English, Dondekin also was fluent in Chinese and German. He became the Americans' basic communication link to the outside world and a valued friend to many of the internees.

As others before them had, Schuette's crew entered internment, wondering whether the Soviets would indeed enforce international law concerning their breach of neutrality in the Asian war and keep them in custody for the duration. Premier Josef Stalin was still locked in a fight to the death with Hitler's army. To irritate the Japanese and have them attack along the tense Manchurian-Siberian frontier, where troops of both nations stood gun barrel to gun barrel, was something Stalin desperately wanted to avoid. So Soviet protests were lodged for each aircraft incursion, and the planes and crews were not allowed to return to American control. Stalin had a secondary reason for quarantining the aircraft: exploitation. He knew American aircraft had the latest technology. Venturas, along with their airborne radar, Loran navigation gear, IFF identification electronics, and reconnaissance cameras were all items the Soviets lacked.

These airmen, much like those who had diverted to Kamchatka before them, hoped to be returned to U.S. control quickly. After all, they reasoned, the Soviets were allies in the war. Following their pre-mission instructions, the American crewmen told the interrogators that they had been on training missions. The Soviets were buying none of that, since these and other planes had landed with as many as a hundred bullet holes puncturing the wings and fuselage. The Americans tried another line, explaining that the aircraft strayed and came under attack while on the training missions. The Soviets looked inside some of the bomb bays. The were rightfully skeptical that planes landing with high-explosive ordnance on board were on training missions.

The typical internment procedure began. The Soviets took down the names of all crew members, then transliterated the names into Russian-language characters. The roster was forwarded to Moscow, where it was re-transliterated into English and sent to the U.S. embassy. In the process many surnames became badly transcribed, so notification of next of kin became a difficult chore. Doubly translated names often had no match among the missing-in-action list provided by the units on Attu.

After the Doolittle raid on April 18, 1942, during which an American B-25 bomber diverted to Vladivostok, officials in Washington had begun negotiations with Moscow on the release of interned crews. Delicate sensitivities were involved. The United States was sending massive support to Stalin's forces using American-built but reflagged cargo vessels under the Lend-Lease program. These Soviet-operated vessels, full of food and supplies, crossed the North Pacific to the port at Vladivostok or Magaden, where nearly half of all the wartime Lend-Lease goods arrived in the Soviet Union. According to the classified portion of the 1941 Tokyo-Moscow protocol, the ships plying the Pacific were supposed to contain noncombat items. Over in the Atlantic Theater, tons of food and war matériel came by American-operated Liberty ships across the ocean to Murmansk. Planes were ferried over the Atlantic, too, but many transited Alaska and passed through Siberia to the Eastern Front. Since vital supplies from America were crucial, Stalin did not want to alienate his ally, while at the same time he remained fearful of opening a second front with Japan. As a result, a highly classified program was developed whereby the crews were allowed to "escape" internment.

The first of these "escapes" involved Captain York's five-man crew from the B-25 Doolittle raid. After landing at Vladivostok on April 18, 1942, the crew was interned near Khabarovsk. Eventually they were moved overland in aircraft and by ground transportation until reaching Meshed, Iran, thirteen months later. In Iran they sought refuge with British vice consul R. M. Hadow at the British consulate on May 11, 1943. Iran was selected by the Soviets since it had been overrun by British and Soviet forces in 1941 when the shah refused an Allied demand to expel German advisers and technicians. The shah was replaced by his more accommodating son, Muhammad Reza Pahlavi, and the country was divided into two occupation zones. The northern zone was controlled by the Soviets; thus "escapes" through Iran were more easily arranged there than through other "neutrals." After the York crew was spirited into Iran, they were taken farther into South Asia and eventually wound up in Washington, D.C., where they were advised that "secrecy of their former internment and escape is of vital importance."

Since "secrecy" was paramount in preventing the expansion of the war from Manchuria into the Soviet Union, getting to safety in Iran would never be easy for the American aviators who would follow.

Upon arrival in Petropavlovsk, the first wave of Aleutian airmen from the August and September 1943 raids were billeted in a log barracks, where their movements were restricted. Each crew member was interrogated by a Soviet team. Suborta Lieutenant Dondekin had done most of the interpreting.

The interrogations were straightforward, with the Soviet officials asking questions and the crews giving name, rank, and service number while continuing to claim they were on training missions. Once the Soviets became convinced that they were only going to be lied to about "training missions," the quiz sessions ended.

The crews learned little about their surroundings, since they were not allowed to roam outside their barracks area. On one occasion the internees from the August and September raids were escorted to the harbor and taken aboard a ship so they could shower, a greatly appreciated luxury.

Meals were spartan since the Soviets had little to spare for uninvited foreigners. Typical fare was smoked salmon, black bread, fish soup, and coffee. Extra clothing also was in short supply, and many crewmen had only the flight gear they arrived in to wear during their initial internment. Medical treatment was surprisingly good in spite of the minimal equipment and medicine available. As noted, a Soviet doctor had successfully removed the spleen from Staff Sergeant Donald L. Dimel, the waist gunner aboard the B-24 that crash landed near Kamchatka's shore on August 12, 1943. Transfusions from other crew members were accomplished using a crude apparatus to transfer blood directly from the donor to the patient. Waist gunner Technical Sergeant Thomas E. Ring suffered a broken hip and pelvis. He also was successfully operated on and was recovering nicely, but suffered a blood clot and died from a stroke. He would be the only American to succumb during internment in the Soviet Union.

For the surviving crewmen, a routine set in. Meals, served three times a day, consisted mostly of seafood cooked in fish oil and in soups. They also were given two ounces of spirits, usually vodka, at least weekly. Card games, chess, and cribbage dominated the activity and went on endlessly. Outside, the men played volleyball using a ball provided by the Soviets. Then they fashioned hoops, attached them to trees, and used the volleyball to play basketball.

For Schuette, Morgan, and the other Americans interned in the summer of 1944, they began the monotonous ordeal their predecessors had endured. Days turned into weeks, and weeks into months, with no word about their repatriation status. Boredom set in. Tempers became short while the men simply waited.

Chapter 10
North Pacific Bombers

As the snow pack melted in May, Bomber 31's engines began to slide down the side of the mountain, inching ever closer to each other, and fifty yards above, the bodies of her crew were surrounded by wild flowers.

—Kamchatka crash site

By May 1944, the war had turned in favor of the Allies on all fronts. Headlines around the world touted one major victory after another. The Soviet attack against the Germans holding Crimea had liberated the region. In Italy, the town of Monte Cassino fell to the Allies on May 18, crumbling the Nazis' Gustav Line and opening the road to Rome. On the nineteenth, the Wakde Islands, 115 miles west of Hollandia along the New Guinea coast, were seized by U.S. Army units under General MacArthur. The first thousand-bomber raid in Europe hit Cologne on May 30.

With things going well in every theater, the army's Eleventh Air Force commander, Major General Davenport Johnson, decided to resume Kurile bombing operations, which had been halted after the heavy losses in September 1943. Nearly six tedious months of patrols, reconnaissance, and training and equipping of new crews were about to end. On Shemya, the Seebees and the Army Corps of

Engineers had finished the ten-thousand-foot matted runway for use by the heavy bombers and put in a four-thousand-foot cross-runway usable by fighters. The time seemed right for the army air force to get into the fray again.

The 77th Bomb Squadron and their B-25 Mitchells at Alexai Point on Attu and the 404th Bomb Squadron B-24 Liberators on Shemya geared up for renewed runs on the Empire Express.

At Alexai Point, the B-25 twin-engine bombers were modified much like the Venturas of navy Patrol Wing 4. Half the bomb bay was taken up by a 225-gallon fuel tank. Two jettisonable 110-gallon wing tanks were added. The payload suffered, however. Planes were able to carry only four 300-pound bombs or ten 100-pound bombs in the remaining bomb bay space.

On May 13, 1944, the first 11th Air Force antishipping sweep since the previous September disaster was led by Lieutenant Andrew Witmer, flying a B-25 from the 77th Bombardment Squadron out of Attu.

Lieutenant General Buckner left Alaska in June 1944 to take command of the 10th Army for its final push from the South Pacific to the home islands of Japan. Lieutenant General Delos C. Emmons replaced Buckner and continued to support Major General Johnson's renewed bombing campaign over the Kurile Islands. These 11th Air Force missions complemented sorties flown by the two navy Ventura squadrons at Casco Field, which continued flying their heavy schedule, both day and night, against the Kurile Islands.

No pilot lost sight of the fact that when flying across frigid Arctic seas, fuel awareness was critical. For the Ventura missions, Lockheed recommended cruising at 145 knots, but had not tested the plane with all the added weight. The "how-goes-it curve" determined months ago at Attu was still considered bible. Fuel on board remained above the curve minimum, or the pilot turned back. Failure to do so risked putting the plane in the drink.

Two of VB-135's planes quickly came to be known as "gas burners" in that they were unable to remain above the "how-goes-it curve." On one occasion when there were not enough other planes available, a gas guzzler was assigned to Lieutenant J. F. Rumford's crew. Since he assumed he would be turned back anyway, he decided to "shoot the coal to it," cruising at 155 to 165 knots to more quickly bust the curve and head home. Amazingly, he stayed above the curve all the way to target and returned with more fuel than anyone else. By experimenting, the navy discovered that there were two airspeeds for each power setting, one on either side of the best glide angle-of-attack. Fly slower than that angle, and induced drag from lift would increase faster than aerodynamic drag from friction decreased, thus requiring more and more power to hold a given speed as the plane slowed. Fly above that speed, and drag from angle of attack decreased while aerodynamic resistance initially increased more slowly. A pilot could get about twenty extra knots flying on the high-speed side using the same power setting.

On June 17, VB-139 was relieved on Attu by VB-136. Under the command of Lieutenant Commander Charles Wayne, their planes came factory-direct with both the Loran and the second instrument panel for the copilot. Improvements had been made on the Bendix automatic direction-finder (ADF) receiver for homing on radio signals, the very-high-frequency (VHF) radio for communications, and the oxygen system. Added was a much-needed automatic fuel transfer system, and the chin armament was increased to three .50-caliber machine guns.

The PV-1 daylight missions took off carrying one 500-pound general-purpose bomb, one fragmentation cluster, and either one incendiary cluster or one napalm bomb, all with delayed-action fuses except for the napalm. The mission change to applying 24-hour pressure on the Japanese in the Kuriles necessitated these adjustments. Low-level attacks were the preferred daytime method of delivery, hence the need to delay activation of the bomb fuses to allow the pilot enough time to clear the fragmentation envelope of the explosion. Any thought of attacking after sunrise from medium or higher altitudes was considered suicidal, since the Ventura would be vulnerable to the heavy fighter protection now available to the Japanese. Approaching on the deck or at wavetop height allowed the Venturas to slip under radar coverage, and with their high speed, denied the Oscars, Hamps, Tojos, Rufes, and Zeros the opportunity to attack from below and behind.

Ventura crews, however, had more to contend with than just flak, fighters, and weather. On June 19, Lieutenant George A. Mahrt and crew from VB-135 approached Paramushiro at night as part of a four-plane strike. In checking his fuel status, Mahrt discovered that about five hundred gallons of fuel had been accidentally siphoned from one of his main tanks. Unable to return to Attu, Mahrt radioed his dilemma and took up a heading for Petropavlovsk.

Still in the dark as he crossed into Soviet territory, Mahrt found the area fogbound. He orbited above the clouds until dawn, when he spotted a hole in the weather. Mahrt slid the bomber through the gap in the clouds, then saw rising terrain ahead. Too late to react, the Ventura plowed through a stand of trees. One wing slammed into solid lumber. The nose was ripped off forward of the cockpit as the plane plowed trough the forest. Fortunately, the crew escaped serious injury and there was no fire. The Soviets interned the crew.

On June 21, the Bats of VP-139, having flown their last combat sortie, rotated back to Washington State. They had logged approximately a hundred sorties and completed 78 photo/bombing missions while losing six aircraft out of fifteen. During their deployment, five men were killed and seven remained missing.

To keep the pressure on the Japanese, U.S. Navy Task Force 94 slipped in under heavy fog on June 26 to shell Karabu Zaki Airfield on Paramushiro for thirteen minutes. More than a thousand rounds of five-inch shells were fired at them. Japanese Air Group 203 recorded eight Zeros destroyed, seven more heavily damaged, and sixteen others lightly damaged. Only nineteen out of sixty Zeros remained operational. On the other side of the island, PV-1 reconnaissance photos taken on the same day revealed that the concrete runway at Kakumabetsu had been increased in length by six hundred feet in the previous ten days.

For VB-135 and VB-136, the squadrons remaining on Attu, losses continued as both units ramped up air operations. On July 22, Lieutenant (j.g.) Jackson W. Clark, whose VB-135 crew had barely escaped death in their water landing off of Attu six weeks before, found himself and his crew once more over the Kuriles. Dawn was breaking as Clark began his bomb run on Shimushu, but four Japanese fighters latched onto the Ventura as Clark turned for home. For a hundred miles the fighters poured fire into the PV-1 before turning away. Though no one was hit aboard the plane, Clark assessed the damage. The right engine was steadily losing oil, and remaining fuel was too low to recover in the Aleutians. He

Plane crew #2 were forced to divert to Kamchatka after suffering engine damage while attacking a Japanese picket boat. Top row, left to right: Ensign D.R. Wilson, Lieutenant J.P. Vivian, Ensign T.H. Edwards. Bottom row, left to right: ARM2c F.A. Virant, AMM3c E.A. Nommenison, Jr., AMM2c K.G. Anderson, AMM2c P.J. Shasney.

reported his situation to Attu by radio, then turned northwest toward Petropavlovsk, landing there without difficulty.

The next day Lieutenant John P. Vivian and his crew were inbound toward Paramushiro when they came upon a Japanese picket boat about a hundred miles east of the Kuriles. Knowing that the vessel's radio operator would try to relay the sighting back to Paramushiro, Vivian decided to attack the vessel before continuing. He set up a low-angle dive run and dropped his bombs as 40-millimeter tracers sought him out. Vivian then rolled and banked, observing the bombs impact the 60-foot boat. It started to sink. In the process, Vivian noticed his right engine oil pressure dropping. The engine had been hit. "I nursed the engine along as we set course for home," he recalled, "but it just wasn't going to run." As he headed east, a fog layer slid beneath the nose. Not knowing how long the engine might run and not wanting to descend into the fog if he had to ditch, Vivian looked rearward, to the west. On the horizon, he could see several volcanic peaks. "Kamchatka stood out in clear weather with not a cloud around it." Vivian's navigator, Ensign Thomas H. Edwards, came up with a new course to Petropavlovsk, and Vivian swung west.

As Vivian's PV-1 crossed the beach near Petropavlovsk, coastal batteries opened up. By now the Soviet antiaircraft gunners on Kamchatka had been ordered to fire behind American aircraft to ward off any Japanese fighters that might be following. Vivian looked aft: "The bursts were behind us but correct on altitude."

Vivian's landing went badly. He overshot the concrete runway and came to a stop in the sod overrun. He glanced across the field and spotted three disabled Venturas lined up and weathering in the open.

The Venturas that made it back to Attu on the 23rd, came back heavily damaged with wounded aboard. By the last week in July, VB-135 had lost twelve of their original eighteen assigned aircraft, and three entire crews had been killed. Five other crews had diverted to Kamchatka and were assumed to be interned.

Ensign R. Rice, wounded by Japanese gunfire during an armed reconnaissance daylight mission over Paramushiro, is being assisted from his plane.

The PV-1 encountered Japanese fighters on its armed reconnaissance daylight mission over Paramushiro. Note the topside of fuselage showing entry of 20-mm explosive shells.

C.W. Scott, AMM2c, plane captain, was wounded in the encounter with Japanese fighters. With him are Lieutenant J.R. Close and, to the left, Comdr. P.L. Stahl, commander of VB-135 operating from Attu.

Meanwhile, in and around Kurile waters, U.S. Navy submarines accomplished one of the most destructive missions of World War II, with the USS *Sunfish* alone sinking sixteen Japanese vessels. The USS *Skate* sank the destroyer *Usugumo*. Though the Japanese were taking serious losses, the buildup in the Kuriles continued apace.

Chapter 11
Cowles

How much punishment could a Ventura take? Was it possible for Bomber 31 to become riddled with bullet holes in both engines, lose electrical and who knows what systems, then still be able to fly fifty miles from the Kuriles to that mountain impact?

—Kamchatka crash site

President Roosevelt had always been enthusiastic about the idea of using the Alaskan Theater as a springboard for bombing Japan, for supplying Lend-Lease equipment to the Soviet Union, and possibly for drawing Stalin and his Far Eastern forces into the contest against Japan. The ten-thousand-foot runway on Shemya was designed to eventually be used by B-29s to reach deep into the home islands of Japan. Roosevelt was well aware of the progress being made with the atomic bomb, and that bases where secrecy could be maximized were in need. Isolated Shemya fit that description.

Roosevelt had backed the offensives that drove the Japanese from the Aleutians and flew up from Hawaii to visit the fogbound servicemen there on August 2, 1944. He stopped at Kodiak, and his appearance was well received by the army and navy men present. While there, the president had his picture taken fishing in a small lake; the photo shows him, buttoned up against cold rain, holding a small trout, a metaphor for what many in his military headquarters and administration thought of the effort in the Aleutians.

On the seventh, Roosevelt shifted to the destroyer USS *Cummings*, and in company with two other escort ships departed for Bremerton, Washington. With the distraction surrounding the visit over, the Aleutian admirals and generals returned to the prosecution of the war.

On August 12, 1944, Lieutenant Carl W. Lindell and his VB-136 crew took to the air on their thirteenth mission as part of a six-plane daylight raid on Paramushiro's canneries and an airfield. Unexpected winds blew the formation a hundred miles south of the island. Once they confirmed their position, they turned north, but because of low fuel, jettisoned their bombs and took up a course for home. Lindell's plane then encountered antiaircraft fire and came under attack by two fighters. According to Lindell's gunner, AOM Petty Officer Third Class Russell L. Manthie, "The bomber received several hits, and the starboard engine was running rough." Lindell feathered the propeller and took up a heading for Kamchatka, where he landed and ran off the end of the runway, coming to rest in a grove of trees. No one was hurt, but VB-136 Squadron had lost its first aircraft on the tour.

On August 19, 1944, Lieutenant (j.g.) Jack R. Cowles and crew from VB-136 took to the air in Ventura no. 49507. Aboard was copilot Ensign Leonardo Panella, navigator Ensign Millard B. Parker, radioman ARM Petty Officer First Class Harold R. Toney, and gunner AOM Petty Officer Third Class John R. McDonald.

The mission was a daylight strike against Paramushiro. Six planes took part in two-plane sections. Lieutenant Larson led Cowles in the last section.

Upon reaching the target area, a two-thousand-foot thick layer of fog obscured the eastern side of Paramushiro, covering Kurabu Zaki and extending well out into the Pacific. Beyond the central mountains, the western side of the island and the Sea of Okhotsk, farther west, were clear. Cowles listened as the first section used their radars to locate and attack Kurabu Zaki while the second skirted alongside the bay at Kakumabetsu on the western side, strafing ships seen at anchor as they passed. They then proceeded to do a radar bombing attack on Kurabu Zaki.

Finally, Larson began his attack on the airfield, and Cowles lined up for his radar bomb run. Due to a switch setting error, none of Cowles's bombs released over the target. Cowles followed Larson toward Attu for about fifteen minutes, during which time Cowles discovered his mistake and rearranged his bomb panel. He determined that his fuel was sufficient to allow a return to the target area for another run, alone. He radioed Larson his intention and swung west. Instead of flying directly at Kurabu Zaki, he headed toward the spine of mountains running down the center of the island. Cowles's plan was to look for a target in the open on the other side, make a quick attack, then head for home.

As the Ventura topped a peak, Cowles called for a camera forward and lowered his nose. Toney came up on the flight deck, camera in hand. He looked ahead. "There was the prettiest line of ships lined right up in the harbor that you ever saw in your life. And it looked like easy pickings." Sixteen to eighteen Japanese vessels were at close anchor in Kakumabetsu Harbor. Cowles knew the defenses had been alerted—smoke was rising from fires he thought were from the strafing attacks done by the second section. Nevertheless, he opted to attack the ships, described as, "picket boat type about 80 to 100 feet long with a couple of small cargo vessels about 150 feet included."

Toney began taking pictures with his camera as shore batteries opened up. Turbulence from a near miss jolted the camera out of Toney's hands. Then the surface ships opened fire with cannons and machine guns. A shell plowed through Cowles's port wing, ripped it open, but failed to explode.

Because copilot Panella's "seaman's eye" during training had been more accurate than Cowles's, the job of releasing the bombs became his. Tracers converged in a wicked crossfire, yet Panella made what Cowles considered "a perfect drop." An instant after bomb release, a cannon round exploded in the right engine. The plane went into a skidding turn. More rounds struck as Cowles and Panella struggled with the feathering control, trying to streamline the propeller. The nose dipped toward the water, and Toney, who was still standing between Cowles and Panella, saw the water rushing up. He shoved the pilots apart, reached forward, and pulled back on the yoke. Cowles shouted, "I got it!" He took back the controls and rolled the Ventura's wings level while Panella finished securing the damaged engine.

The radio was hit, the navigator's sextant disintegrated, a 25-millimeter exploded in the empty ventral gunner's position, and the cockpit gunsight had been knocked out. Gasoline began spurting onto the fuselage floor. Cowles pointed the nose at a twenty-five-hundred-foot pass, hoping to slip through it, then drop into the fog on the other side before any fighters could attack. He climbed on one engine to two thousand feet but could get no higher, so he turned away from the pass. Within seconds, three Japanese Oscar fighters appeared above the ridge to the east.

Cowles dove to pick up speed and headed west, out beyond Japanese-controlled Araito Island, a small, rocky mountain that protruded from the sea northwest of Paramushiro. His only hope was to shake his pursuers upon reaching Soviet airspace north of the island.

The fighters began making runs, and as the first Oscar peeled off to begin his pass, McDonald called out the attacker's position. Cowles rolled in the direction of the fighter. When the Oscar opened fire, Cowles tried to spoil the pilot's aim. He kicked top rudder, causing the Ventura to appear nose-up in a skid while losing altitude in the process. One after another the Oscars came in, firing. Cowles even made several of these skidding turns into the failed engine, a delicate and dangerous undertaking that could easily have caused a spin.

During these maneuvers, Japanese bullets began to find their marks. One creased Panella's jacket and another passed between Cowles's legs. Navigator Parker saw bullets penetrate the empty tail gun area. Rounds shattered Parker's observation window, and slugs passed under each arm. Another clipped a radio antenna. It wrapped around the top turret, making it impossible for gunner McDonald to turn the mechanism to its full extent. One barrel jammed. McDonald tried to clear the blockage, but the cable on the charging handle snapped.

Cowles kept losing altitude during these maneuvers and was concerned that the Oscars might discover that his underbelly was defenseless. He dove to wavetop level. Because of the slow speed on one engine, McDonald had no trouble bringing his sights to bear on the fighters. Seeing holes appear all around him was terrifying. He lost control of his bodily functions, but the gritty gunner kept on firing. After some twenty attacks, McDonald was nearly out of ammunition when yet another Oscar came in from the side, guns blazing. McDonald swung the turret and opened up with his single .50-caliber barrel. The Oscar burst into flames, rolled over, and crashed into the sea. The other fighters then broke off the engagement. At that point, the battered Ventura was approaching Russia's Kamchatka Peninsula. Cowles began a climb while Toney spliced several cable wires in an attempt to repair the radio. He could only get half an ampere of current to the antenna, but started sending out a distress message anyway.

The fuel transfer pump had been damaged by machine-gun fire, causing the main tank to be nearly empty after the long, hectic minutes at maximum power. Cowles had Toney switch to the emergency bypass system, which would bring fuel from the cabin tanks directly to the engine, but the lines had been shot away. Toney switched back to the main tank. As the plane neared land, the source of fuel was exhausted and the engine quit. A few seconds later, it coughed back to life after the faulty pump brought a little more fuel to the tank. The engine surged back to power for a few seconds, then quit again. Cowles nursed the plane over the coast of Kamchatka, losing altitude all the way. At three hundred feet above ground he set up for a crash landing. Flaps would not come down because the power to lower them was knocked out. At a hundred feet he concentrated on making a full-stall landing and shut off the fuel to the operating engine. Everyone was now braced for landing. The tail made contact first and was partly ripped off as it dragged through scrub pines. The windmilling engine's propeller slammed into the ground. One blade from the feathered engine snapped off and the right wingtip was ripped from the fuselage as the plane plowed along on a metal-shrieking, bone-jangling journey through muskeg.

When what remained of the Ventura finally came to a stop, a spark ignited fumes inside the plane. A flash fire swept through the crew compartment. Parker and McDonald, their exposed skin and faces burned, scrambled forward toward the cabin door, but it had jammed. They crawled through flames aft to where the fuselage had split open and leaped outside. Up front, Panella opened his side hatch and began squeezing out onto the wing. Toney unstrapped and moved behind Cowles, whose headset cable got hung up while he tried to exit on his side. Instead of taking off his headset, Cowles attempted to pull the cable plug out. Toney shoved his shoulder between Cowles's legs and pushed with all his might, snapping the cable. Cowles spilled out onto the wing, with Toney following right behind. All five men scurried through flaming fuel to safety just as the plane exploded. They stood huddled together, clothes smoldering, faces blistered, and watched the plane burn. Then Cowles moved closer and counted more than a hundred holes in what was left of the aircraft.

After the fire waned, the crew followed Cowles toward the beach. Three Soviet soldiers with rifles appeared. The Americans had sidearms but did not draw them. One of the Soviets put a hand up, signaling the crew to halt. Then the soldier raised his index finger and motioned for one man to come forward. Cowles went ahead. He knew only one useful Russian word, and when he got within earshot, he yelled "Americanski." Toney recalled years later how "the Russian grabbed him and bear-hugged him like he was a long-lost brother."

The crew was taken to Cape Lopatka, where according to Cowles, they were treated well considering the Soviets' "extreme poverty." The soldiers were annoyed that some American bombs had fallen on the cape in the past and wanted to know why. Cowles tried to explain that difficulties in navigating could cause the radar operator to easily confuse the cape with the southern part of Paramushiro, but the Soviets were skeptical and just shook their heads. After six days, two Soviet PT-type boats came and took them to Petropavlovsk and internment.

Eight days later, Lieutenant (j.g.) John A. Dingle and his crew were on a six-plane mission to attack shipping and shore installations on Onekotan, an island south of Paramushiro. Dingle selected a picket boat as his target but was bounced by three Japanese fighters. Heavily damaged by the fighters, Dingle headed north, still under fire. He radioed his distress and intention to land on Kamchatka. Once over Soviet territory, the Japanese withdrew, and thirty minutes later, Dingle set up for landing at Petropavlovsk. On touchdown his brakes locked, and the Ventura went careening off the pavement. The crew exited the plane with cuts and bruises and were immediately interned. This was the third but not the last of VB-136's crews to be killed or interned during their tour.

Chapter 12
Empire Express Combat Intensifies

Could any of the crew from Bomber 31 have been able to walk off the mountain in the dead of winter? How deep was the snow? What obstacles were in the way? How far would anyone have had to travel before reaching civilization?

—Kamchatka crash site

By now, both sides in the conflict had settled on tactics and a routine that would repeat themselves time and again. The American bomber forces attacked in waves, each plane or group of planes separated by not more than ten to twenty minutes. The Japanese reacted to these incursions by alerting their antiaircraft batteries and scrambling fighters while the rest of their forces hunkered down in bunkers. The gunners put up a barrage of flak to shoot the American bombers down or at least disrupt the ability of the planes to make precision attacks on their targets. Meanwhile, the fighters engaged the strike force from head on, with guns blazing. This tactic was particularly important for the pilots flying the Oscar or Tojo, since they had only .50-caliber machine guns as armament. The Zero had both machine guns and two 20-millimeter wing cannons, so it could approach from the stern and fire from just outside the range of the Ventura's machine guns, but even these pilots preferred the frontal attacks because they could not overtake the PV-1 at high closure speed.

For the bombers, having a fully functioning aircraft and crew were crucial to survival, since they had no friendly fighters available to fend off pursuers. If the bomber suffered damage or a critical system malfunctioned, the ability to recover to Attu was doubtful. Reduction in performance of even part of any engine meant that the aircraft could no longer outrun Japanese fighters. The inability to properly control the propeller setting on either engine, for example, would be enough to make the difference between a successful egress from the target area and a decision to divert to Kamchatka. More importantly, once an Oscar or Zero pilot realized he could rapidly close the distance behind a damaged bomber, his attack options expanded dramatically. He could accelerate ahead of the fleeing bomber and peal off to employ the preferred procedure: slashing attacks from the bomber's front quadrants. The recourse a stricken bomber had at that point was to bank and dive in an attempt to destroy the attacker's ability to aim. Each maneuver cost precious airspeed and altitude until the bomber was forced to try eluding the fighters at wavetop height. Under those circumstances, the Japanese pilot could maintain altitude while pushing ahead of the stricken bomber, then reverse course to begin a diving pass. When strafing from the target's twelve-o'clock position, there would be no "tracking" involved. The fighter pilot would simply maneuver to place his gunsight beneath or ahead of the target's nose as the two planes converged. Then he would squeeze the trigger. A curtain of fire would rain in front of the already wounded bomber, which had to fly through the maelstrom. Trading bullets at point-blank range also brought into consideration such things as midair collisions and unintended flight into the water, which often extracted as heavy a toll as did the gunfire.

With September 1944 came cooler temperatures and an increase in fog. Both 11th Air Force and Patrol Wing 4 bombers continued the

VB-135 copilot Ensign Robert J. Hanlon is helped from the aircraft after being wounded in action over Paramushiro on September 9, 1944. The Japanese continued to put up stiff resistance to these bombing attacks.

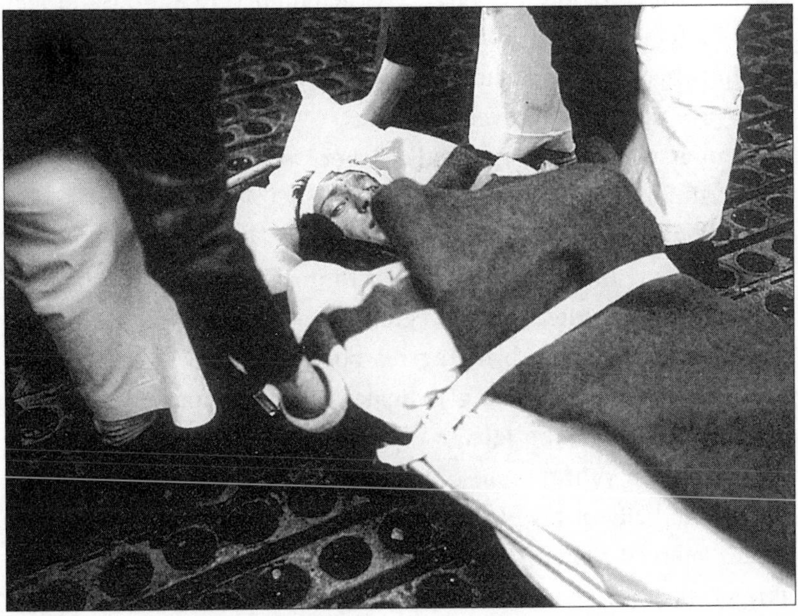

grueling missions to the Kuriles. The army was the first to have an aircraft divert that month, when on the tenth, First Lieutenant William W. Head, Jr., and his crew landed their crippled B-25 in Petropavlovsk. On the eleventh, Lieutenant (j.g.) D. F. McDonald and crew from VB-136 was part of a bomber force that attacked a beached cargo ship that apparently had run aground off Shimushu's northern shore. Following the attack, McDonald climbed above a thin cloud layer and was immediately bounced by five Japanese fighters. The Japanese scored hits on the Ventura's right engine. Though pursued until he reached Soviet airspace, McDonald was able to hold the plane together while he radioed ahead to the tower at Petropavlovsk regarding his intent to land. Upon touchdown on the runway, the right landing gear collapsed. The plane spun around as it careened down the asphalt, sparks flying and metal shrieking. The six-man crew was shaken but received only minor injuries.

On September 14, PV-1 Ventura pilots Lieutenants Morrison and Littleton attacked targets on the eastern coast of Paramushiro. Morrison struck a cannery at Hayake Gawa, then flew along the coast in search of another target. As he climbed to a thousand feet for a better look, two Japanese fighters jumped him. He dove to wavetop height and pushed his speed to 280 knots. The fighters soon gave up trying to overtake him.

Lieutenant Littleton attacked a fishery at Kasuga Zaki. After his bomb run, he spotted four Nakajima Ki-44 Tojo fighters well to his right, blocking his escape. The Tojo's big Ha-109 Type 2 radial engine gave it an appearance similar to the U.S. P-47 Thunderbolt, but no P-47s operated in this region.

Littleton pulled up, bringing his bow guns to bear on the lead Tojo which was positioning to make a head-on pass. When Littleton opened fire, the Japanese pilot must have seen the muzzle flashes off the Ventura's nose, because he pulled up, exposing the vulnerable belly of his plane. Littleton continued firing as the two planes merged. The Tojo swept overhead, and Littleton's turret gunner engaged the now smoking fighter as it passed. Moments later a crewman took a photograph of the damaged Tojo before it crashed into the sea.

Two days later, on the sixteenth, Lieutenant Commander Wayne, skipper of VB-136, found himself under attack by fighters while over Paramushiro. To escape, he poured the coals to the Ventura, and dove for the deck with the Japanese in full pursuit. One engine was hit, and the plane suffered additional damage. Wayne spent nearly an hour with the engines in full supercharger, and the damaged engine failed just moments after the Japanese turned for home. Wayne kept to his heading toward Attu, but Lieutenant John W. Murphy, his copliot, persuaded Wayne that recovery at Attu was impossible, especially when the sole remaining engine began to act up. Wayne reversed course for Kamchatka, but the aircraft started losing altitude and airspeed. Wayne spotted a flat, swampy area short of Petropavlovsk. He crash-landed in the estuary without injury to the crew.

Upon arrival at the internee camp, Wayne found himself the senior man. With three of his own crews interned, five crews from VB-135, and several from the army, Wayne was not lacking for subordinates.

With the loss of their commander, further daylight raids by VB-136 were put on hold.

The 11th Air Force, however, pressed on with daylight strikes from both Alexai Point and Shemya. Diverts continued. On September 25, a B-24 from the 404th Bomb Squadron had to recover on Kamchatka, and a week later a B-25 crew from the 77th Bomb Squadron also made their way to Petropavlovsk.

Then, on October 19, 1944, VPB-131* arrived on Attu to replace VPB-135. The squadron brought with their aircraft a new weapon: five-inch rockets. Daylight missions for the navy over the Kuriles were put back on schedule.

Antiaircraft fire struck an 11th Air Force B-25 over Paramushiro

* On October 1, 1944, the designation of all PV-1 Ventura squadrons was changed from bombing (VB) to patrol bombing (VPB).

on November 1. The plane diverted to Petropavlovsk with two wounded crewmen aboard.

By now the Japanese feared an invasion of the home islands coming from both the north and the south, so the increasing daylight attacks over the Kuriles put them further on edge. In fact, in the fall of 1944 plans *were* being made in Washington, D.C., to invade Paramushiro and Shimushu. The code designation for the invasion was Keelblocks. Orders arrived to photograph all the beaches on the western sides of both northern islands, the area deemed most suitable for amphibious landings. Fleet Air Wing 4 was given the task.

Since flying level at the altitudes necessary for daylight photo missions would be suicidal given the fighter protection available to the Japanese, a special plan was devised. A maximum effort was assembled, including ten PV-1s that would create a diversion by striking the airfields at Karabu Zaki, on the southern part of Paramushiro, and Miyoshino, on Shimushu. Five more Venturas equipped with large F-56 cameras, would streak down the western coasts and take both high and low oblique photographs. Two PBY-5A seaplanes were to orbit off the coast of Kamchatka to assist with pickups of any downed aircraft. The mission was tried on November 2, but due to clouds covering the photo targets, the planes aborted and returned to Attu.

On the fourth, VPB-131 flew its first Kuriles mission of this deployment, targeting Torishima Retto. Lieutenant Robert Ellingboe and crew were jumped by an estimated eleven Japanese fighters and were shot down, with the loss of all hands.

Two days later, another photo-reconnaissance attempt was made along the Paramushiro coast, using nine PV-1s. The mission was pulled off successfully in spite of heavy fighter and antiaircraft fire.

On the sixth, a B-25 flown by Lieutenant Alfred Muldoon took a hit that destroyed the outboard portion of his right wing. The plane struck the water, flipped over, and sank with the loss of the crew. The destruction of the B-25 was captured on film.

A Japanese Oscar approaches in a head-on attack against two B-25 Mitchell bombers near Torishima Retto in the northern Kuriles. The bomber on the right, piloted by Lieutenant Alfred Muldoon has been hit; the right engine is smoking and losing power.

Lieutenant Muldoon's B-25 slowly rolls to starboard and crashed moments later when the right wing failed.

Starting on the 13th, PV-1s no longer carried bombs for normal combat operations. Only machine-gun and rocket ammunition was authorized, due to concerns about the excess weight, which had risen to more than three thousand pounds above the recommended maximum.

On November 18, five B-24D Liberators from the 404th Bomb Squadron arrived over the Paramushiro target area. One was a B-24 with distinctive nose art and its accompanying inscription, *Bugs Bunny, What's Up, Doc?* The bomber, flown by Second Lieutenant

Later in the war, rockets were mounted on the wings for daylight strikes against Japanese shipping in the Kuriles.

Donald H. Taylor from Des Moines, Iowa, and his crew, began lining up for the bomb run. Suddenly the plane came under attack by fighters that made repeated passes with machine-gun and cannon fire. The bomb bay doors jammed, so Taylor was unable to close them for increased speed. Two of the four engines were hit and losing power. A cannon round penetrated the cockpit, then exploded, sending shrapnel through Taylor's foot. His navigator, Flight Officer Edward H. Wheeler, from North Wales, Pennsylvania, was hit in the hand and left leg. Taylor, with blood pouring from his injured foot, muscled the bomber into a right turn away from the target in an attempt to reach cloud cover. With the roar of the slipstream in his ears, he dove for clouds to the north. Once inside the gray protective curtain, he turned the controls over to his copilot, Second Lieutenant Lester R. Yelland. Hydraulic pressure was falling, and several electrical busses were damaged. The radar had been hit and was useless in revealing the Kamchatka Peninsula. Fuel was leaking inside the aircraft. As they continued to egress, crew members gave medical aid to Taylor, who then insisted on taking back the controls. The plan was to head for Petropavlovsk, but the plane was being buffeted by strong winds. Snow obscured forward visibility, and Taylor soon realized that finding the runway would likely be impossible. Then he spotted a hole in the weather and slipped the bomber underneath the cloud mass. Taylor picked up a coastline to his left, gray and ominous behind a veil of driven snow, and followed it north. With two engines out, the bomb bay doors open to the howling wind, and no way to release the heavy bombs, the plane began steadily losing altitude. Taylor spotted a flat beach area and decided to try a crash landing.

The crew braced themselves as Taylor brought the smoking bomber lower and lower toward the icy sea. As he crossed the coast, he banked to get lined up, then rotated the nose. Touchdown was soft. The plane skidded and bounced its way along as sand and snow were flung into the air while the men held on and hoped for the best. Finally, the B-24 came to rest headed northwest, with its right wing touching the ground. Fuel fumes filled the cabin area, and Taylor ordered his radioman not to transmit a distress signal for fear that an electrical spark might set off an explosion. After the fumes dissipated, the men moved back inside the fuselage and stayed the rest of the day and all night as a blizzard raged outside.

In the morning, they dug their way out and tried to remove the blanket of snow that covered the plane so it could be seen from the air. The radio operator, Corporal Bernard P. Bendorovich, tried to make contact with Shemya, but the signal output was too weak. Bendorovich discovered that a cockpit switch left on overnight had drained much of the battery power. Starting an engine to recharge the battery was out of the question, but Bendorovich surmised that with the switch turned off, the battery would recover some of its power after a while.

Taylor realized that neither he nor his navigator were in any condition to walk. With no certain idea where they were on the peninsula, Taylor asked for volunteers to go out on foot to find help.

Bombardier Flight Officer Leo C. Lodahl, nose gunner Corporal Billy J. Burnett, and radar operator Sergeant John Smith stepped forward.

At age twenty-four, Smith was the oldest member of the crew and took the lead the following morning. His team, equipped with two hatchets from the survival kit, headed south. Later in the day, they encountered an impassable stream and decided to return to the aircraft. On their way back, freezing rain drove them to seek shelter under a pile of utility poles. They built a fire and huddled together through the night.

Meanwhile, Bendorovich's faith in the battery was vindicated, and his signal was received at Shemya. The squadron notified the 11th Air Force, and the downed aircraft location was passed to the Soviets via the weather reporting circuit and through the U.S. embassy in Moscow. The commander of the North Pacific Force, Vice Admiral Frank Jack Fletcher, also was advised. He ordered a special mission flown to drop supplies to the downed crew.

The three crewmen who had trekked south finally made it back to the plane, learned of the radio contact, and discussed alternatives. Making contact with the Soviets was still considered the required action, so plans were made to take the aircraft's inflatable raft with them the following morning. By the twenty-second, the crew began their third day on the ground. At sunrise, four men headed south again, this time rafting across the stream.

At Shemya, Captain William Beale's B-24 was loaded with survival gear and took off at midmorning in search of the plane and crew. The radio station at Shemya had taken a bearing off the signal received from the downed bomber. When Beale estimated he was about a hundred miles from the peninsula, he dropped beneath the weather, continued in at three hundred feet above the waves, and aimed for a point slightly north of the place where the bomber was expected to be found. After landfall was made, he turned south. Shortly after rounding Cape Zelty, the nose gunner spotted the aircraft. Six men were seen near the plane, and on the beach the message "4 men south" had been spelled out, using red fabric from their survival gear and by trampling the snow.

Food, clothing, medical supplies, and a 24-volt battery were dropped by parachute from the B-24. Before heading back to Shemya, Beale swung south in search of the four missing men. He found them headed in the direction of the aircraft. They had come upon a steep cliff and once again had turned back.

"The food, medical and survival equipment probably saved our lives," Smith later wrote. "Needless to say, we ate that night and we slept in sleeping bags."

The men sat it out inside the aircraft until eight days later, when a Soviet ship came bobbing into view off the coast. The ship's crew unsuccessfully tried to launch a small boat in roiling water, then disappeared to the north. That same night a Red Army lieutenant and six soldiers arrived with two horses. The wounded men were placed on the horses, and the group began walking north. After hiking all night, the men reached a military outpost. Though it would be months before the men were repatriated, the critical juncture in their fight to survive was over.

The incessant bombing, the "regular delivery from President Roosevelt" continued to wear down the Japanese defending the northern Kuriles. Compounded by early snowfall and icy wind blasting in from Siberia, the men flying and maintaining the aircraft were having the worst of it. Icing on canopies, wings, and control surfaces resulted in numerous accidents. Salt-laden moisture got blown inside the tiniest of openings, the resulting corrosion wreaking havoc with engines, instruments, and aircraft structural components.

On September 10, a Kate was lost with a crew of three. A Tojo went down on the seventeenth, another on the twenty-fourth. In October, a fighter was downed on the fourth, two more on the eighteenth, and at least two other pilots died after crashing into the mountains in fog and snow in November. The Japanese had installed radio beacons for

Japanese gunners on the lookout for U. S. bombers during the winter of 1944–45. Shimushu, northern Kuriles.

navigation at their major airfields, but these improved safety only slightly, considering the prevailing low ceilings and visibility.

Warrant Officer Trueman Fukuno's naval telecommunications station was on a hill just below the Kataoka airstrip. From his post, he could see down to the bay and across the narrow passage to Paramushiro. Fukuno's barracks complex was built into a slope and consisted of interconnected A-frames, with only the roofs visible. These were built of heavy lumber, the ceilings covered with layers of tundra weighted down with rocks. Drainage was not a problem, but "during the frigid temperature of winter, the blizzards often resulted in snowdrifts as deep as 5 to 10 meters, requiring all hands to shovel the stuff off roofs and literally dig ourselves out."

Everything was in short supply. The army troops manning the antiaircraft guns and protecting the islands from assault came by the navy area from time to time with socks and sweaters they had hand-knitted themselves to trade for food and sake.

Antiaircraft gunners slept in six-to-eight-man bunkers located near their heavy-weapons positions. Warning of attacks was received by phone line, based on contacts made by the radar site at Imazuki or via radio relay from picket ships. Voice tubes were used by the battery commander to communicate with the gun teams once the firing positions were occupied.

The Japanese navy men had virtually no free time (not that there was much to do), with the exception of their twice-a-week bath and the extra sleep they got when the weather was so bad that no American bombers were inbound. Some of the officers did a little cross-country skiing, but other outside sports activity was virtually nonexistent. Martial-arts-type activities such as kendo and karate were permitted on Kataoka Naval Base and among the army troops deployed on the islands. The Japanese had already become enthusiastic about baseball, but the leadership considered it "an enemy game," according to Fukuno. Thus, even when the weather eventually improved, baseball was "out." Discouraging baseball was hardly necessary, though, because as the skies cleared, the bombers came, and no one had time for games.

Mail delivery was unreliable and heavily censored in both directions, to keep both the military and the civilian population in the dark about the tide of the conflict. By late 1944 it was generally known that Italy was out of the war and that Germany and Japan were retreating on all fronts. Fukuno was aware of much more, since his job in Section A (English-language intercepts) was to listen to U.S. radio transmissions and news broadcasts. He also exchanged information with Lieutenant Hattorri of Section S (Soviet intercepts), who was fluent in Russian and recorded those communications. The two men kept Commander Haruki Itoh, the base commander, informed. Itoh once warned Fukuno after being briefed that "he would have me shot if I divulged [the information] to my peers or the rank and file."

In addition, as conditions deteriorated, the commander of the Fifth Area Army dispatched sixteen aircraft of the 38th Air Regiment south to the Philippine Islands on October 21, 1944, to take part in the "decisive battle" (Operation Sho-1). Japanese sailors and soldiers in the Kuriles certainly knew that bombing attacks were becoming more frequent, that naval shelling by surface ships was increasing as well, and that the number of their planes rising to meet these attacks was dwindling. To many, it was only a matter of time before the "decisive battle" for the northern sector would take place.

Chapter 13
Repatriation

A diplomat's words must have no relation to actions—otherwise what kind of diplomacy is it? Words are one thing, actions another. Good words are a concealment of bad deeds. Sincere diplomacy is no more possible than dry water on iron wood.

—Josef V. Stalin

Following the repatriation of the Doolittle raid crew on May 11, 1943, interned airmen were moved from Kamchatka by flying boat, C-47, or by train to destinations deep inside Manchuria and Siberia. The second group to be repatriated included the first crews from the Aleutians. Sixty-one Americans who had diverted to Petropavlovsk in eight aircraft were released on February 18, 1944. All of them were army air force fliers from the Paramushiro attacks in August and September of the previous year. Within weeks of arriving in Kamchatka, the men were taken on a circuitous route by air, most stopping first at Kharbarovsk, near Manchuria, then hopping across Siberia to Tashkent. Eventually they crossed the Iranian border south of Ashkabad in a truck convoy. From there, they were taken to Tehran and turned over to U.S. authorities.

The navy crews, led by Lieutenants Bone and Schuette from VB-135, who landed on June 15, 1944, experienced similar treatment.

They went from the airfield at Petropavlovsk to a two-story building that had served as a Soviet officers' club. From there they were soon transferred to a remote naval air station on the shores of a lake. The men set up housekeeping in a three-room building that also served as dispensary.

During their roughly six-month confinement, the crews made attempts to learn to speak Russian. Women linguists were brought in, and the men welcomed language lessons as a means to fill idle time. Several of the internees had Slavic family backgrounds and spoke Polish or Serbo-Croatian. Language similarities between those tongues and Russian provided a basis for developing a semblance of fluency in Russian. Yiddish was spoken by several Jewish internees, who discovered Soviet Jews working at various jobs inside the camp. Later, displaced Jews from Eastern Europe and the Soviet Union were encountered at "escape" stop-off points in Siberia. Though conversation was often awkward and slow, eventually many of the men were able to express basic needs and utter simple responses in Russian.

When Lieutenant John P. Vivian arrived in Petropavlovsk on July 24, 1944, he found himself the senior man in confinement and took charge. With the addition of his and Clark's crew, which had arrived the previous day, the internees now numbered thirty-four, too many to house in the dispensary building. Tents were put up outside, and three to four men were moved into each.

The new internees played basketball using the hoops attached to trees by the previous internee population who had already moved deeper into Siberia. The volleyball was long gone by then, so they fashioned a no-dribble ball from old socks and rags. "Ours was strictly a run-pass-shoot basketball game," recalled army second lieutenant Ralph W. Hammond, who diverted his B-25 to Kamchatka on September 10, 1944. "One afternoon we played some of the visiting Red Army artillerymen from an antiaircraft battery that had fired on us over the bay. Needless to say, our game with them got a little rough."

After numerous false starts, a twin-engine C-47 transport arrived in Petropavlovsk on October 9, 1944, to take the next (third) batch of internees, including the first navy men, to freedom. After more than a week of unexplained delays, the Americans were divided into two groups. Fifteen in the first party eagerly boarded the U.S.-provided Lend-Lease aircraft and departed for Magadan, a port city on the Sea of Okhotsk, on the seventeenth. There they were billeted in comfortable quarters while awaiting the rest of the men, who subsequently became delayed by bad weather.

On October 24, this first group was then flown south to Khaborovsk and housed in a Red Army camp along the Amur River north of the city.

Back at Petropavlovsk, the departure of the remaining thirteen detainees continued to be delayed day by day because of weather. On November 7 they boarded a C-47 transport along with seven more army air force crewmen from Second Lieutenant William D. McQuillin's B-25, which had diverted to Kamchatka six days earlier.

The C-47 took off, but because of weather was redirected from its intended landing at Okha, on Sakhalin Island, to Magadan. Soviet officials at the port were unprepared for their arrival, the date being the start of celebrations for the anniversary of the Russian Revolution. The Americans were billeted in the city and were allowed to freely roam the streets.

Magadan had been a small fishing village until the 1930s. During that decade Josef Stalin accelerated his great purge. Soviet citizens, often whole families, were sentenced to labor colonies all over the Soviet Union for the most trifling of offenses. Stalin needed cheap labor to pull the country out of the depression and was arbitrarily condemning thousands of innocent people to the mines; railroad line construction; logging camps; and, for many, almost certain death. Stalin's approach was described by German playwright Bertolt Brecht as "the more innocent they are the more they deserve to die." Many of the prisoners transited through

Magadan on their way to inland Siberia. They came in slave ships that arrived at times swollen with five thousand to six thousand souls. Prisoners built the docks, breakwaters, and the city itself, as well as the region's most important project, the Kolyma Highway. The road led due north from Magadan to the gulags or work camps, *lagpunkts*, often named according to their distance from the city. Camp 47 was forty-seven kilometers north of Magadan, for example.

While walking the city, the American internees came across a procession of prisoners dressed in rags, thin from lack of food, many of them dragging frightened children by the hand. The internees stood silently by as an endless line of despairing faces were being led through the streets under heavy guard. Second Lieutenant Gilbert S. Arnold was the navigator on First Lieutenant John E. Ott's B-25. Ott and crew had diverted to Kamchatka on September 25, 1944. Arnold retained vivid recollections of these gulag-bound Soviets more than forty-four years later. "Those miserable wretches, as well as Japanese flak and fighter planes, are etched on my memory today as if I saw them yesterday."

On November 11, after a frigid cross-country flight, the last of the American fliers rejoined the main group at the Kharbarovsk camp.

On the fifteenth, thirty-nine of the internees boarded a Trans-Siberian Railroad train. Kept in third-class coaches, the men endured 40-degree-below-zero cold in compartments heated by a single coal-burning stove whose fuel supply was not replenished along the way. The windows became covered with ice. Second Lieutenant Ralph W. Hammond remembered one night when the train stopped. "I saw the woman car attendant carry a white-hot metal grate in a bucket into the car. The grate had been heated in the locomotive firebox. She deposited the grate in the middle of the car. The radiated warmth from this grate was the only heat I can recall." They shared a few bedbug-infested blankets while attempting to sleep on wooden benches during the eleven-day journey through deep snow across the continent to Tashkent, in Uzbekistan.

Arriving at Tashkent, they were met by Soviet officials, driven in trucks through the city, then motored thirty-five more miles southwest, to Vrevskaya. There, a school compound had been transformed into a permanent internment camp. The main building was large enough to handle the flood of internees awaiting their "escapes" from the Soviet Union. Sixty-two internees were already there when the new group arrived. The earlier internees had endured barracks life with no electricity. Kerosene lamps had been provided until the Soviets finally wired the facility. No on-off switches were available, so the lights were operated by manually hooking together the bare ends of two wires.

The new arrivals had with them Lieutenant Commander Charles

Nona Solodovinova, chief interpreter at the internment camp near Tashket between September 1943 and February 1945.

Wayne, who was senior to Vivian, so Wayne assumed command. The men were introduced to their cook, Reuben, and various camp personnel, including Nona Fedorovna Solodovinova from Leningrad, who was the chief interpreter. Nona had large, alluring blue eyes, a flawless complexion, and light brown hair. Apparently widowed, the still strikingly attractive woman in her early forties became a mother figure to many of the internees, a number of whom were not yet twenty years old. The young men referred to her as "Mama," a name she seemed to relish. Some internees suspected she had connections with the People's Commissariat for Internal Affairs or NKVD, the Soviet internal security apparatus, because her authority seemed to exceed her position as interpreter. Regardless, she proved herself a caring person time and again, and on one occasion, in November 1943, she brought copies of Shakespeare's plays to two internees in confinement. They had been caught trying to flee from the camp to China. By local standards, Nona was very well atired, appearing wearing silk hose, fancy dresses, and was known to possess a formal gown. She even owned an expensive fur coat. A number of the housekeeping staff were replaced during the period internees stayed in the camp, but Nona was an affectionately remembered fixture up to the end.

Mealtime fare at the camp lacked variety and the portions were small, consisting of black bread, butter, soup, and at times fried grain, which one of the internees speculated was buckwheat. Life for those already there had settled into a dull routine. As the days passed, more internees arrived, and no word of their release came. The internees were, however, regularly escorted to the Vrevskaya community bathhouse and to the village bazaar, where they mixed with Uzbeks, displaced persons, and local villagers, who soon became accustomed to the sight of Americans in their midst.

After several false starts, at dusk on December 5, 1944, a hundred army and navy internees assembled with their gear and five days' rations. They loaded onto trucks for the drive to Tashkent. There the men were dropped off in the railroad yard, where they boarded three coaches for their "escape." Most of the men tried to sleep, but were awakened when a locomotive shunted them out of the yard and coupled them to a train that departed at midnight.

Two brutally cold days later, the train approached Ashkabad, and as planned, the three cars carrying the Americans were uncoupled and switched to a side track. Though the cars were supposed to continue to Tbilisi, an event in America changed everything.

A week earlier, Drew Pearson had broken a story in his nationally syndicated column, "Washington Merry-Go-Round," about the first escape, that of Lieutenant York and crew from the Doolittle raid. Someone in contact with one of the crew, perhaps a family member or friend, had gone to the media with a fabricated tale about the release of the fliers. Though Pearson's column was in error in almost every detail, Henry C. Cassidy of the Associated Press filed a more accurate story on December 2, detailing the internment and "escape" of the York crew.

While the internees marked time in the cold near Ashkabad, the Soviets, who had by now learned of the newspaper reports, waited for the Japanese reaction. On December 10, the U.S. attaché from Moscow, Lieutenant Colonel Robert McCabe, brought the bad news to the internees that because of the news leak, the men would be returned to the Vrevskaya camp. The announcement was greeted with stunned silence. Within two hours, however, thirty-four of the hundred internees took to the countryside in a spontaneous escape attempt. They split up into groups, destined for the border of Iran, some eighteen miles to the south. Eventually most of the men returned, many of them exhausted. The rest were captured by alert Soviet guards.

The next day, ninety-three of the internees—seven were not captured until December 12—were taken by train back to Tashkent. At Vrevskaya, the men reentered the icy building that had been their barracks. The health and morale of the men began to deteriorate, and discipline problems surfaced. Men were placed in solitary confinement by their American commander for infractions and misconduct. "The spirit of the men was at a low ebb," B-24 pilot Major Richard M. McGlinn observed. "Sickness of one type or another was prevalent, and the men brooded, wondering whether they would ever get a chance to leave the Soviet Union alive."

On the sixteenth, the camp population was increased by twenty-nine more men from two B-29s and from one B-25 crew. The next day, the seven men who had eluded escape for twenty-four hours at Ashkabad were returned to the camp. Radioman ARM Petty Officer First Class Harold R. Toney, who had crash-landed on Kamchatka with Lieutenant (j.g.) Cowles and crew, was one of them. Toney and the others "looked hard," Second Lieutenant Arnold recalled years later. The seven had been confined in an unheated room in Ashkabad for three days, interrogated repeatedly, then loaded aboard a boxcar and shipped to Tashkent.

Christmas came and went, though the Soviets permitted a Christmas Eve party, complete with a rare treat of sliced beef with fried egg, green onions, and cake for dessert. Wine and vodka also were provided. The internees amused themselves with skits and carol singing, but the boost to morale was short-lived as the year ended with no word of their release.

Diplomatic efforts in Washington and Moscow continued. Since there appeared to have been no adverse reaction to the articles from the Japanese—they were reeling on all fronts and hardly in a position to enlarge the war—the Soviets reversed their position on "escapes." On January 8, 1945, the U.S. embassy was informed by General Ivanov of the NKVD that an attaché should go to Tashkent and complete the internee "escape" according to plan. Major Paul Hall, who had replaced McCabe at the end of his tour, made the six-day train trip to Tashkent. He carried a letter from Major General John R. Deane, chief of the U.S. military mission in Moscow, to Lieutenant Commander Wayne, the senior internee. Regarding secrecy, the letter stated, "I can think of no better way to emphasize the necessity for secrecy on the part of your group than to point out how publicity concerning internees has affected each of you, personally. For the sake of those internees who come after you, it is imperative that no one, including your parents and closest friends, be given any of the circumstances concerning your release until after the conclusion of the war."

Because the escape route for the previous attempt was now blocked by heavy snow in the mountain passes, the route was modified—no easy task, given the need for security.

Weeks passed with no word of movement, and the men became increasingly restless, at one point pelting a Soviet officer with mud-caked snowballs, an infraction that was overlooked by the Soviets since the commander, NKVD lieutenant colonel Ivan Siminov, seemed sympathetic to the men's frustration and certain the men would soon be out of his hair.

On January 25, the announcement was made by Major Hall that the men would be leaving that night. Each was required to sign a letter of confidentiality, pledging not to divulge the means of escape from the Soviet Union. Again the men were issued food for five days. After nightfall all 130 internees were taken to the Tashkent rail yard. This trip, however, did not involve a stop outside Ashkabad, but instead continued 150 miles westward beyond the city to Kizil Arvat, where the three coaches were uncoupled and shunted to a siding. After daybreak on the twenty-eighth, ten Lend-Lease trucks pulled abreast of the railroad cars. Two of the tarpaulin-covered vehicles carried extra fuel cans. Sixteen internees each were loaded aboard the other eight trucks and began a 48-hour trek, mostly in silence, toward Iran. The rough, dusty roadway ran along the southeastern rim of the Caspian Sea to Bandar-e-Shah, then curved across the Elburz Mountains. The men shivered during the cold second night, but reached Tehran safely the following morning. Numb from the chilly, sleepless nights and dusty, bumpy ride, the internees were dropped off at Camp Amirabad. The exhausted men poured out of the trucks and into the rear entrance of an empty hospital wing. Seven weeks after their first attempted "escape," they finally found themselves safe among U.S. medical and security personnel, all dressed in civilian clothes. The men enjoyed American-style food in unlimited quantity, clean bedsheets, and were issued fresh uniforms. The taste of freedom was sweet, but it would be five more weeks before their odyssey fully ended and the men once again set foot on American soil.

Chapter 14
The Rising Sun Begins to Set

All gave some and some gave all
And some stood through for the red, white and blue
And some had to fall
And if you ever think of me
Think of all your liberties and recall
Some gave all.

—From singer/songwriter Billy Ray Cyrus's debut album

In November 1944, discussions about the northern Kuriles invasion—Operation Keelblocks—continued at the staff level. Vice Admiral Frank Jack Fletcher wrote to CINCPAC admiral Chester W. Nimitz suggesting that, although seizure of the northernmost islands would allow secure lines of communication across the sea-lanes in maritime Siberia, workable bases for an advance on Hokkaido and Honshu would not exist. Fletcher felt that the Soviet Union's entry into the war with Japan was still a question mark, and establishing bases on Soviet soil was necessary and required their full involvement. If the Soviets came on board in the Far East, bases in Kamchatka could be utilized instead, bypassing the Japanese facilities on Shimushu and Paramushiro. The Soviet peninsula would be the launch point for invasions of the more southerly islands of Matsuwa and Etorofu.

In December 1944, Admiral Nimitz requested clarification from

Admiral Fletcher regarding the plans for seizing Japanese islands. A meeting was held in Hawaii on December 5, and from that session came Keelblocks II, which relied on the entry of the Soviet Union into the Pacific war. The northern Kuriles were not to be bypassed, however. In the revised plan, Paramushiro would still be invaded and its southern airbase facilities converted to Allied use.

The New Year began with a ramp up of pressure on the Japanese. Day and night attacks were conducted by B-25s, B-24s, and PV-1s on targets throughout the northern Kuriles. On January 3, 1945, navy cruisers and destroyers comprising Task Force 92 sailed out of Attu's Massacre Bay, and two days later conducted a twenty-minute bombardment of Suribachi Airfield on Paramushiro. The next day, B-24s from Shemya bombarded the same target, with the aim of preventing aircraft from taking off to engage the fleet. Unknown to the U.S. Navy, however, all Japanese planes had departed from Suribachi and had been deployed south, to defend the Philippines and Okinawa. Even so, snowblowers were still operating to keep the runway clear.

The Japanese were being pressured on all fronts, and the redeployment of their aircraft amid an increase in attacks meant only two things to the soldier or sailor left behind on Paramushiro: a favorable outcome of the war was hopeless, and invasion of their island was imminent.

On January 19, the chiefs of the Japanese army and navy General Staffs reported to the emperor that an advance on the Kurile Islands was expected. The headquarters then submitted the Outline of Army and Navy Operations, which established policies to deal with this eventuality. Following it came Navy Order No. 37 to fully prepare for the invasion. Later followed Imperial Japanese Directive No. 2433, stating that the troops were expected to fight to the last man to "annihilate the attacking barbarians."

And fight they did. Sergeant Iwayama, an army Oscar pilot flying out of Kitanodai on Paramushiro, had both arms wounded while attacking American B-25 and B-24 bombers on January 25.

He tied his handkerchief around the control stick, and as his arms became useless, he manipulated the controls by placing the end of the handkerchief in his mouth and bumping the stick with his knees to keep the plane level. He safely landed the plane before passing out from loss of blood. In addition to this and other combat losses, half a dozen of his squadron mates would crash into the mountains in the abysmal weather before the month was over.

On March 12, VPB-139 returned to Attu to relieve VPB-136, which was winding up the longest of the Ventura deployments, having been on station for nine months without a break. The squadron lost eight aircraft during that period, more than half the squadron allotment. The Bats of 139 brought with them a new aircraft, the PV-2 Harpoon. Led by Lieutenant Commander Glenn A. David, the unit began a training/patrol workup after arriving on Attu. With a redesigned wing and tail section, the Harpoon could carry an additional two thousand pounds of weapons. The plane sported nine .50-caliber machine guns (five in the nose and two each in the top and belly turrets). Eight 5-inch high velocity air rockets (HVAR) could be mounted four to a wing, and four thousand pounds in bombs or depth charges fit inside the bomb bay. Two additional thousand-pound bombs could be carried on the wings in place of drop tanks. The extra payload came at the cost of speed, however, since the Harpoon utilized the same power plant used in the lighter Ventura. To the men arriving at Attu, it was clear the war was coming to an end. No one wanted to become the last casualty. One question in the minds of the crews was whether the Japanese would notice the Harpoon's reduction in speed and take advantage.

The first loss of a Harpoon occurred on March 26, when Lieutenant L. J. Dulin diverted to Shemya due to bad weather at Attu, then overshot Shemya's runway in a severe snowstorm and crashed. Two of the crew were injured with lacerations but recovered.

PV-1 Ventura losses continued right along with those of the newer planes. On April 7, 1945, a VPB-131 Ventura flown by

Last full measure. Death in the Aleutians came often and was always grim in nature. Here the body of a crewman is recovered by navy Seabees after the April 7, 1945, crash of a PV-1 Ventura that stalled on final approach.

Lieutenant J.E. Patton crashed into Casco Bay, Attu. The plane appeared to stall on final approach, a quarter mile from the runway. All aboard were killed.

The second and final Harpoon lost in the Aleutians during the war went down on April 22, 1945. Flown by Lieutenant William D. See of VPB-139 and a crew of six, it disappeared from radar contact 90 miles out from Attu. These losses were especially painful since the knowledge that the war was coming to an end was clearly evident to all the men on Attu. It was becoming evident to their opponents to the west as well.

The Allied Yalta Agreement had been reached in February 1945, and bit by bit, word of it had filtered down to the Japanese army and navy men in the Kuriles. By April, with the fall of Germany certain, the troops understood that the pact required an unconditional surrender. Though little of the details regarding Japan were passed down, there was no longer any sugarcoating by the Imperial General Staff regarding the future direction of the war. The mood of the military on Shimushu and Paramushiro was subdued at best.

On May 8, 1945, Germany surrendered unconditionally. The war in Europe was over. The Allies were now free to concentrate their efforts on subjugating Japan. Celebrations were short-lived in the Aleutians, however, because two days later began one of the saddest periods in Eleventh Air Force history.

Second Lieutenant Milt Zack. As navigator/bombardier, he rode in the vulnerable nose compartment of the B-25 bomber.

Lieutenant Lewis's crew.

On May 10, a concentrated effort of B-24, B-25, PV-1, and PV-2 bombers was scheduled to strike ships in the harbor and narrow channel between Shimushu and Paramushiro.

The plan had the slower B-24 heavies from the 36th Bomb Squadron taking off first, from Shemya. Two hours later, on Attu, the 77th Bomb Squadron B-25 medium bombers launched from Alexai Point, followed by the navy planes out of Casco Field. The B-24 element was to use radar if necessary to determine if there were ships in the waterway, then radio back to the following flights.

Leading eight B-25s was Lieutenant John Daughtrey from Dadeville, Missouri. The Mitchells were spread out in two flights of

The lead B-25 roars over Shimushu to attack shipping in Paramushiro Strait at sunset. Kataoka Naval Base is to the left and above the bomber's wingtip. Kashiwabara Harbor on Paramushiro is directly across the narrow ocean passage. Drifting smoke from a damaged freighter is apparent in the left foreground. Six vessels were attacked and either damaged or sunk.

four aircraft each. Flying on the far right side of the formation was Second Lieutenant Raymond Lewis. Inside his bomber was Second Lieutenant Milt Zack, from Boston. Zack was the navigator/bombardier and sat on a flak vest atop two ammunition cans in the nose of the bomber. From his station, he watched as the planes jockeyed into position, then settled into formation. Hour after hour, the planes lumbered along under an overcast. The pounding noise of the propellers penetrated right through the Plexiglas that thinly shielded Zack from sound and cold. Zack was alone up front, and his boredom was interrupted by brief scraps of interphone chatter that quickly came to sound far off and hollow. Below loomed the uninviting gray mass of white-capped ocean. Above, the sun made a shiny spot on the cloud deck and seemed bent on racing the planes to the far horizon.

About two hours from the target area, the radio cackled with the coded message that indeed ships were in the harbor. A cloud layer slid underneath, and the B-25 formation maneuvered between layers, suspended in space. Finally, after another hour and a half, out of the gloom appeared the ragged coast of Kamchatka, its snowcapped volcanoes poking through broken clouds. Zack confirmed his position, then passed word to the rest of the crew to get set for battle. Zack cycled the breech twice to load a round into the chamber, then squeezed off a preparatory burst from his single .50-caliber in the nose. The smell of cordite drifted through his compartment. Adrenaline began pulsing through veins, and the men started rubbernecking the sky, looking for bandits. This was it.

Lieutenant Daughtrey swung the B-25 force south, skimming above a white blanket that hid the earth and water below. Minutes later, the formation swept over Shimushu. A hole in the clouds revealed the entire harbor area, where numerous ships were at anchor. Daughtrey pealed off to begin his bomb run.

Lieutenant Lewis followed his leader in from the right side. In his position up front in Lewis's plane, Zack had an unobstructed view of the battle scene as sea and ships rushed toward him. In the center of the bay, a freighter was burning, set afire by the previous B-24 flight. Flames, whipped by the wind, blazed across the darkening water. The islands on either side looked a lot like Attu, with muddy roads and barren hills interrupted by clusters of huts and tents. Docks stretched out from shore, and above the beach were the same kind of warehouses as seen in the Aleutians. The only difference was the flash of antiaircraft fire rising in ever-increasing amounts from ship and shore batteries.

Zack shifted forward as Lewis lined up on a picket boat. With the bomb pickle button in his left hand, Zack aimed his machine gun with his right. When the ship came within range, he opened fire. Tracers raced ahead, and the ship's deck came alive with sparkles. For a moment Zack thought the ship's crew was shooting back, then realized the flashes were from the exploding ammunition he had fired, armor-piercing incendiary rounds. When the picket boat grew huge in the windscreen, Zack pressed his bomb release button.

B-25 Mitchell flown by Second Lieutenant Leonard G. Larson on May 10, 1945, just prior to crashing with its five-man crew still aboard.

As they passed beyond the ship, Zack's attention was diverted to the right as another B-25 swept perilously close. The plane's left engine was on fire, the flames trailing red and distinct. The tail gunner in Zack's plane, Corporal Walter Bailey, snapped a photo just before the plane nosed over and smashed into the sea.

The downed bomber had been piloted by Second Lieutenant Leonard G. Larson, who Zack remembered always wore a distinctive red scarf when he flew. Larson had flown with the Finnish air force and the RAF earlier in the war. His crew had lived in the hut next to Zack's. "My immediate first reaction," Zack recalled, "was to think 'I'm glad it's not us.' Then I got hit by a terrible guilty feeling, like I had actually thought I was glad it was them, not us."

There was nothing anyone could do for the Larson crew, so Lewis simply inched closer to the forbidding water, keeping his bomber barely above the swells as he streaked for home. Behind him, flames from the downed aircraft rose in the sky as a crimson sun finally set in the west.

Ahead, the clouds turned blue and the night sky began to emerge, starry and coal black. Once clear of the Japanese islands and with no fighters in pursuit, Lewis began a climb. Zack settled in for the long ride home, then happened to glance at his bomb-rack panel. "I almost had a heart attack," he remembered. Four lights were on, meaning the bombs had not released and were still in the bomb bay. He advised Lewis, then opened the bomb bay to salvo the weapons. As the munitions dropped toward the cold Pacific, Zack wondered how he would explain things back at Alexai Point.

After enduring four more hours of chill and ear-pounding engine noise, Zack peered into the blackness, eyes straining to find the runway as the plane descended toward Attu. Finally the cloudbank fell away, and flares that were lit along the matted surface appeared, glittering in the night.

Lewis brought the bomber in and after they shut down, the crew found only one hole, in an engine nacelle.

At the debriefing, Zack learned that a B-24 and another B-25 were so badly damaged, they were forced to divert to Kamchatka and that several other bombardiers had bomb release systems that had malfunctioned. His concern about what he might have done wrong lessened.

Zack and the rest of the crew hefted their flight gear and trudged back up the wooden steps to their hut. On the way, they passed the empty hut that had belonged to the downed crew. Inside were the personal possessions of Leonard G. Larsen, pilot; Joseph F. Jellinghausen, copilot; Reno D. Zambonini, navigator/bombardier; and gunners Israel S. Port, William A. Biggs, and Thomas E. Barnes. These were somber moments as each member of Zack's crew dealt with mortality. Soon someone would arrive to gather the missing crew's belongings for shipment to next of kin and a new crew would move in, and memories of the fate of the lost crew would diminish until the next plane went down.

A little over a week later, on May 19, Lieutenant Daughtrey led another force of eight B-25s against radar facilities and fisheries.

Again, Zack had a bird's-eye view from the nose of Lieutenant Lewis's bomber, but this time in the second plane, second flight of four. As the formation approached Shimushu, Japanese fighters appeared.

First over the target, Lieutenant Daughtrey's plane was shot down in flames, with the loss of the entire crew. Another B-25, flown by Lieutenant Harold Beever, was badly hit. The crew headed for safety in Kamchatka.

The best defense was low altitude and high speed, so Lieutenant Lewis pushed the power up and dove. The plane leveled off, barely skimming the wavetops. Seated in the nose, Zack was in a position to see the water much better than the pilot. They were too low. Each passing swell seemed to be reaching up to grab the plane. "I was about to call to tell him to pull up a few feet when it felt like the plane hit a brick wall." The engines seemed to hiccup, then recover to a roar. "I looked out to the right and did a double take. There was no propeller on the right engine." The left engine still had its prop, but the plane was veering to the right.

Certain the plane was mortally damaged, Zack knew "that I had to get out of the nose of the ship in a hell of a hurry." He wore a parachute harness and inflatable Mae West under his flak suit, but had to shed the suit to fit through the tiny crawl space back to the flight deck, where his parachute was located. He pulled the red tab on the suit, hoping it would work as advertised and cause the suit to split in two at the top. It did. It was a tight fit through the narrow opening, as he still had on his harness and flotation device. He started sliding through, feet first, on his stomach. "My throat mike was still attached and it pulled out of its fitting, but I kept going. I made it into the pilot's compartment and remember the copilot [Second Lieutenant Edward Burrows] turning and giving me a sick grin."

Only the pilot and copilot were strapped in, so Zack grabbed part of the aircraft structure and held on. "The next thing I knew we were on the ground, skidding in a crash landing."

Attacks like the one above (B-25 just beyond the piers) were conducted at low altitude where antiaircraft fire was intense and collision with the water a real danger, as well. These photos illustrate effective attacks on Japanese vessels near Paramushiro and Shimushu.

The plane impacted on Shimushu's shore at high speed. "There was two or three feet of snow on the beach and no rocks, so we seemed to go on skidding on our belly forever. When the plane finally came to an abrupt stop, one of us, I don't remember which, immediately released the escape hatch on top of the plane and my pilot, copilot and I scrambled out . . . . The radioman [Corporal William Bradley] and tail gunner [Corporal Walter Bailey], who were in the rear, were already out. They had broken the machine gun window and exited that way. The engineer [Corporal Robert Trant] was the last to get out, since he was in the top turret and had to come down from there, then up into the pilot's compartment and out the same escape hatch we had used. Other than some bumps and bruises, no one was seriously injured in the crash. But the whole bottom of the plane was ripped out, and when I looked in my compartment in the nose, I saw it was full of snow."

While the crew debated what to do—stealing a boat somewhere and rowing to Kamchatka being one suggestion—a Japanese fighter circled overhead and was obviously radioing the position of the downed aircraft. Soon Zack spotted a company of Japanese soldiers approaching in the distance. "When they were about 100 yards away or so, they started shooting in our direction and there was nothing left to do but raise our hands and surrender. It was the most hopeless, desolate feeling in the world, and I'll never forget that moment."

As they closed in, the soldiers stopped shooting and surrounded the Americans. They took all of the crew's personal items, watches, wallets, everything except their clothing. Then the men were led away through the snow.

The sun had set, and as they stumbled and slid along the slippery beach path, Zack motioned to one of the men that he had to relieve himself. The soldier indicated that Zack should move to the side and take care of it. Zack headed off the trail in deepening darkness. "I took two or three steps and broke through some ice and fell into water over my waist. The soldier pulled me out, and I don't remember if I took care of my business or not. But I was so cold and wet after that it didn't matter much."

The Americans were marched to a group of buildings where one Japanese soldier came out and began slugging each of the crew with his fists. When he swung at Zack, "I moved a bit so his blow didn't do much damage, but I dropped to the ground anyway to make him think he had hurt me." By now it was dark, and the men were tossed into a barracks-like building where they spent the night freezing in damp or wet clothing, with no heat or food.

The next day the men were taken out together and were blindfolded, with their hands tied behind them. With a Japanese soldier on each side to hold and guide each prisoner, the men were marched for some time until they stopped and were placed with their backs against a wall.

Zack was able to lift his head enough to peek out under the blindfold and "saw what I expected to see, five or six soldiers facing us with rifles in their hands. Obviously that could mean only one thing, we were about to be shot."

Zack waited for what he thought was the end of his life. "Strangely, when I was resigned to the fact that I would never get out alive, I just wanted to get it over with and be done with it all." After a few minutes of pure terror, the men were led down to the port and taken by boat across the strait to Paramushiro and placed in individual cells. Thus began Milt Zack's life as a prisoner of war.

During his confinement, Zack saw Lieutenants Lewis and Burrows and radioman Corporal William Bradley being led away. Presumably they were to travel by ship to one of the main islands of Japan, a hazardous undertaking given the number of U.S. submarines operating in the northern Kuriles as the war drew closer and closer to Tokyo. A week later, Zack was placed aboard a ship and was taken to Sapporo, Japan, where he was confined in the stockade at an army camp.

In one month, two 11th Air Force B-24s and five B-25s had either been shot down or interned. Morale at the 77th Bomb

Squadron, having lost the five Mitchells, was at an all-time low. Pinned to the officers' bulletin board was a magazine ad offering "Free Engravings on Purple Hearts."

Bombing missions over the northern islands continued unabated. The Japanese by now had most of their command and control operations well dug in. Warrant Officer Fukuno recalled, "At my duty station deep underground I could hear and sometimes feel thumps and rumbles of bombs hitting the airstrip installations. Sometimes dust entered our rooms through the air shafts that ventilated the tunnels. Once, when I happened to be outside during a raid, I saw our provisions warehouse sustain a direct hit."

The Japanese government began seeking the means to achieve an armistice to be followed by a "conditional" surrender. Diplomatic efforts were being made in Moscow to attempt to broker the deal. That the war might end was one of the few things that sustained a semblance of esprit. Then, according to Fukuno, "When Admiral Kubo and his entire staff flew home after declaring he was 'advancing' to defend the homeland just weeks before the end of the war, morale plummeted."

By mid-June, no one in the Kuriles or the Aleutians doubted that the defeat of Japan was certain. The only question was how long it would take and how many would die in the desperate last throes of Imperial Japan. Casualties were mounting on both sides as kamikaze attacks took a heavy toll of American ships and men during the Okinawa and Iwo Jima invasions. So severe were American losses that they were kept secret until well after the war had ended.

On June 16, the 404th Bombardment Squadron at Shemya launched four B-24s on an antishipping sweep of the eastern and western coasts of the northern Kuriles. In the number-two position was a Liberator flown by Second Lieutenant Richard S. Brevik. In the bomb bay were fifteen 300-pound bombs. The crossing of the Bering Sea and North Pacific was uneventful, and landfall was

A Japanese soldier relaxes inside his semi-submerged barracks on Shimushu. The roofs were reinforced with thick beams and covered with tundra to camouflage them and protect them from bomb damage.

sighted seventy-five miles east of Paramushiro. The formation split into two elements. Lieutenant Brevik and Lieutenant Kolva's bombers proceeded to the western side of Paramushiro, where Kolva spotted three picket boats headed "southeast at five-to-seven knots."

Kolva began his bomb run, south to north, dropping five bombs and scoring near misses against the leading vessel. He made two more runs, then pulled away to watch his squadron-mate make a run against the second ship. Brevik's bomber flew low over the target as a string of bombs exploded, one a direct hit on the vessel. Shrapnel flew high in the air and peppered the water around the ship.

The nose of Brevik's bomber came up, then appeared to mush as the plane gradually lost altitude.

Inside the bomber, twenty-three-year-old gunner Corporal William V. Cavanaugh from Staten Island, New York, was standing just in front of the forward bomb bay as the plane pulled off target. Seconds later, Cavanaugh felt the concussion from an explosion:

"There was a jolt from underneath the plane." Cavanaugh was hit in the face, arm, and below the right ankle by shrapnel. He staggered toward the flight deck and was near a bulkhead when, "Lieutenant Martin [the copilot Second Lieutenant Harold E. Martin] cut power to the four engines and we struck the water almost immediately. I remember going forward with tremendous force."

With explosions going off while the U. S. bombers were so close to their Japanese shipping targets, the planes were often well inside the fragmentation envelopes of the bombs.

Lieutenant Kolva watched from overhead as Brevik's bomber slammed into the sea, creating a huge splash. The resultant spray obscured the bomber momentarily. When the water settled, the plane was floating upside down, broken in half, and partly underwater. One man was seen swimming near the sinking plane.

Cavanaugh was knocked unconscious by the impact. "Next thing I knew I came to, and it was pitch black. I knew I was in the water. All of a sudden it started getting lighter, and I popped to the surface."

Cavanaugh saw Lieutenant Brevik alive in the turbulent sea, and who he thought was Martin floating facedown nearby. They were the only ones he saw outside the plane.

Cavanaugh spotted a fully inflated raft that had been thrown clear of the plane. He swam to the raft and heaved himself inside. Then he helped Brevik get aboard. Lieutenant Martin was nowhere in sight. Meanwhile, the last of the Japanese picket boats that was still afloat scurried away at high speed.

Adrift at sea in the raft, Cavanaugh noticed that Brevik had a deep cut on his forehead just above the left eyebrow and a swelling above his right ear. Brevik also suffered from what he described as unbearable pains in his stomach. He had been strapped in at impact and probably sustained internal injuries from the seat belt or from contact with the control yoke. While they waited for possible rescue, Brevik told Cavanaugh that they had scored a direct hit on the ship and the concussion from their own bombs had thrown the plane out of control.

Cavanaugh found the raft's medical kit and dressed Brevik's head wound. In sight was Araido island, a Japanese-occupied "rock" that protruded out of the Sea of Okhotsk. Cavanaugh assumed the Japanese would soon be out to pick them up, but no one came. Darkness closed in, and Cavanaugh helped his pilot as best he could until Brevik appeared to fall asleep. Since it was summer, darkness lasted only about two hours. Even so, Cavanaugh became thoroughly chilled from his wet clothing. While tending to his own cuts, Cavanaugh realized that his right calf had been badly bruised in the crash. He tried to rest, dozing on and off until daybreak.

As the sun rose above the horizon, Cavanaugh tried to rouse Lieutenant Brevik but got no response. The lieutenant had died during the night, and the loss hit Cavanaugh hard. Of the nine men in the crew, all of whom had trained together in the States, he alone was still alive. For Cavanaugh, this was the low point in his ordeal. He got out the two paddles that were in the raft and tried to row toward Araido but could make no headway, so he gave up. All day, Cavanaugh floated over the cold sea, unwilling to toss the body of the dead officer over the side. He survived on the small amount of rations cached in the raft and the hope that an American submarine or a PBY might appear to rescue him. Since no U.S. planes flew overhead, the chances of being spotted by friendly forces diminished with each passing hour.

On the third day, he was startled by an explosion "that almost lifted the raft right out of the water." He later learned from the Japanese that one of their transports had been hit and blew up. That night, a Japanese destroyer that had been dispatched to pick up survivors came alongside the raft. The Japanese were surprised to discover the Americans drifting in the vicinity of their sunken vessel, but took both aboard. Cavanaugh was blindfolded, and he and the corpse of Lieutenant Brevik were taken to Kataoka Naval Base on Shimushu. Brevik was soon buried, but not before his watch and that of Corporal Cavanaugh were removed by two Japanese officers.

Cavanaugh had trouble walking, and was placed in a room where he spent the night. The next morning a Japanese naval officer and an interpreter, Warrant Officer Trueman Fukuno, entered the room. The naval officer began an interrogation, but Cavanaugh gave out no military information. One of the questions asked was whether Cavanaugh thought the Japanese would try to attack Attu again. He replied, "No, your supply lines are much too long." That seemed to satisfy the interrogator.

The next evening, Fukuno returned to the room alone, carrying a bowl of rice. He put his index finger to his lips to ensure that their conversation was private, then said, "Don't let those SOBs get you down." He introduced himself by his nickname, "Turpy," a name the Japanese had bestowed upon him and of which he was not particularly fond. "Turpy" explained that he had grown up in San Diego and described his personal situation, that of having been trapped in Japan when Pearl Harbor was attacked. He gave the food to Cavanaugh and spoke nothing else of the war. Cavanaugh suspected that this might be a ploy to get him to lower his guard and provide intelligence information. Fukuno, however, did not try to learn anything of military value, focusing his conversation on life in the U.S., hoping someday to get to Times Square in New York. Cavanaugh mentioned the loss of the two watches, and though he didn't mind surrendering his own watch, asked Fukuno to try to get the watch belonging to Lieutenant Brevik returned so Cavanaugh could give it to his widow for a keepsake. Fukuno promised he would look into the matter. When Fukuno approached the two officers, they explained that they were having the watches examined for "bugs."

Cavanaugh was never given Brevik's watch, and several days after the session with Fukuno was taken aboard a ship. There he was confined to a small room near the captain's quarters where food was brought to him. A day out at sea, the engine quit and the boat floated dead in the water. Twenty-four hours and after a lot of haranguing by the captain later, the crew got the engine restarted. As the boat continued south, an old Japanese seaman came into Cavanaugh's room and with his weathered hand passed him a cigarette. The seaman then lit it. It was a small act of kindness between two adversaries who did not speak each other's language, but the effort meant a lot to Cavanaugh and was never forgotten.

Several days later, the ship pulled into port on Hokkaido. Cavanaugh was brought to a local prison, where his injured leg was examined by a doctor who indicated there were no broken bones.

From there he was escorted into town, where he was given a shave and bath and had his clothes steam-cleaned. He then boarded a train in his spruced-up khakis and caught a lot of stares from the population. He wound up at Ofuna prison camp, southwest of the center of Yokohama. Conditions for the last American POW from the Kurile Islands campaign were about to change.

Confined in Ofuna were captured British servicemen and U.S. army air force, navy, and marine fliers, including World War II ace, Major Gregory "Pappy" Boyington. Established in the spring of 1943, the prison was run by Japanese Naval Intelligence for the primary purpose of gaining military information.

Ofuna's barracks were located around a large, open area and were surrounded by a tall fence topped with barbed wire. The prisoners' barracks were divided into cells, each of which was entered from an aisle in the middle. The cells had a sloping ceiling, and were six feet wide by eight feet deep, with a small window at the back. The sleeping area was covered by a thin bamboo mat. In the corner were three cotton blankets, which were kept folded at all times during the day. Cracks between the floorboards were so wide in places that the ground underneath could be seen. The locked door leading into the cell had a peephole.

Cavanaugh was allowed out in the morning to clean up and use the toilet, but during these times the guards would take every opportunity to mistreat prisoners. The Japanese maintained a belief that a prisoner had "lost face" and deserved whatever they got in the way of punishment. As bombing raids intensified on Tokyo and Yokohama, guards named Nishi, Mori, and Nakakichi in particular would come into prisoners' cells at night to administer beatings with clubs. "The treatment," Cavanaugh recalled with obvious restraint after his release, "wasn't the best." Speaking was strictly forbidden, and if they were caught doing so, the punishment was severe and often in front of the others. Food was handed out two, sometimes three times a day and consisted of a bowl of rice, soup, and a cup of Japanese tea. Once in a while the soup would be replaced by a fried herring. Prisoners got their drinking water out of the faucet near the squat toilet or in the area where they washed up in the mornings. When in their cells and needing to answer a call of nature, they notified a guard, who followed them to the toilet and back, but at night the guards often pretended not to hear them, so they sometimes had to urinate in their cells. This rule violation was another excuse for corporal punishment, but eventually these beatings lessened because prisoners urinated through the cracks in the floor or worked a plank loose underneath their bamboo mats. Clothing was not issued, so prisoners wore what they had on at arrival.

Conditions such as beriberi, scurvy, and dysentery were rampant, but only added to the prisoners' worry about what might happen to them once the main islands were invaded by Allied forces.

Chapter 15
The End of the Beginning

Kolyma . . . the remoteness and isolation, the severity of the climate, and the harsh living conditions made this frozen hell stand apart from the rest of Siberia. . . . The people of the Soviet Union feared Kolyma more than any other region of the Gulag Empire. "Kolyma znaczit smert" was the common phrase whispered at the time, and translates to "Kolyma means death."

—*Stanislaw J. Kowalski,* The Land of Gold and Death

The first atomic bomb struck Hiroshima on August 6; the second hit Nagasaki three days later. The effects of those two weapons instantly overshadowed the years of combat that preceded their dropping.

By war's end, some fifteen hundred sorties had been flown over the Kurile Islands during the conflict. Yet, when compared to the European war, where a single air raid often involved a thousand or more bombers with at times dubious results, the effect of the Kuriles campaign against Japan was clearly huge in proportion to its size. Hundreds of Japanese vessels, as many as five hundred fighters and bombers (in 1945, that amounted to a sixth of the combined Imperial Air Forces), along with forty-one thousand ground troops were tied up defending the northern isles. These men, machines, and all their supporting needs, including food, parts, medicine, fuel, and ammunition, were things that General

MacArthur and Admiral Halsey did not have to contend with in the South Pacific. For the men who suffered and died above the ring of fire and ice, their efforts impacted the outcome of the war far greater than any of them would ever have imagined.

Emperor Hirohito recorded a statement to the Japanese nation on August 14, and at noon the following day it was broadcast to his subjects on the radio in the formal language of the Imperial Court. Though many Japanese had trouble understanding his court dialect, the meaning was clear, as for the first time in history, the voice of the Japanese emperor was heard by the masses:

> To our good and loyal subjects: After pondering deeply the general trends of the world and the actual conditions pertaining to our empire today, we have decided to effect a settlement of the present situation by resorting to an extraordinary measure.
>
> We have ordered our government to communicate to the governments of the United States, Great Britain, China, and the Soviet Union that our empire accepts the provisions of their Joint Declaration.
>
> To strive for the common prosperity and happiness of all nations as well as the security and well-being of our subjects is the solemn obligation which has been handed down by our imperial ancestors, and which we lay close to heart. Indeed, we declared war on America and Britain out of our sincere desire to ensure Japan's self-preservation and the stabilization of East Asia, it being far from our thought either to infringe upon the sovereignty of other nations or to embark upon territorial aggrandizement. But now the war has lasted for nearly four years. Despite the best that has been done by everyone—the gallant fighting of the military and naval forces, the diligence and assiduity of our servants of the state and the devoted service of our one hundred million people, the

war situation has developed not necessarily to Japan's advantage, while the general trends of the world have all turned against her interest. Moreover, the enemy has begun to employ a new and most cruel bomb, the power of which to damage is indeed incalculable, taking the toll of many innocent lives. Should we continue to fight, it would not only result in an ultimate collapse and obliteration of the Japanese nation, but also it would lead to the total extinction of human civilization. Such being the case, how are we to save the millions of our subjects; or to atone ourselves before the hallowed spirits of our imperial ancestors? This is the reason why we have ordered the acceptance of the provisions of the Joint Declaration of the Powers.

We cannot but express the deepest sense of regret to our allied nations of East Asia, who have consistently cooperated with the empire towards the emancipation of East Asia. The thought of those officers and men as well as others who have fallen in the fields of battle, those who died at their posts of duty, or those who met with untimely death and all their bereaved families, pains our heart day and night. The welfare of the wounded and the war sufferers, and of those who have lost their homes and livelihood, are the objects of our profound solicitude. The hardships and sufferings to which our nation is to be subjected hereafter will certainly be great. We are keenly aware of the inmost feelings of all ye, our subjects. However, it is according to the dictate of time and fate that we have resolved to pave the way for a grand peace for all the generations to come by enduring the unendurable and suffering what is insufferable.

Having been able to safeguard and maintain the structure of the Imperial State, we are always with ye, our good and loyal subjects, relying upon your sincerity and

> integrity. Beware most strictly of any outbursts of emotion which may engender needless complications, or any fraternal contention and strife which may create confusion, lead ye astray and cause ye to lose the confidence of the world. Let the entire nation continue as one family from generation to generation, ever firm in its faith of the imperishableness of its divine land, and mindful of its heavy responsibilities, and the long road before it. Unite your total strength to be devoted to the construction for the future. Cultivate the ways of rectitude; foster nobility of spirit; and work with resolution so as ye may enhance the innate glory of the Imperial State and keep pace with the progress of the world.
>
> 14th day of the 8th month of the 20th year of Showa.

After being taught all their lives that Japan was invincible, the land of the god-emperor, and that every man, woman, and child was to fight to the last breath, the surrender came as a shock. How could "god" possibly lose? A military faction tried to revolt against the government officials whom they felt had forced the emperor into making his surrender speech, but the majority of Japanese citizens were tired of the war. They well knew how badly things had gone for Japan in spite of the propaganda streaming from newspapers and radio, and thus accepted defeat.

Many in the Japanese military were aghast at surrender. It violated Bushido, the "death before dishonor" code of the Samurai. To surrender was dishonorable, and many senior officers were quite ready to die for the emperor, but there were many more soldiers, airmen, and sailors for whom the end meant going home alive. Orders were received to turn in all weapons, and the units began to disarm.

When that word reached the guards at the Japanese POW camp at Ofuna, they ran off, leaving the prisoners to fend for themselves. Corporal Cavanaugh and the rest of the POWs took over the installation and learned of the surrender when newly arrived reporters from the U.S. news media approached. The prisoners climbed on the roof of the barracks and marked out the letters P O W, using debris from the camp. Soon a U.S. Navy torpedo bomber circled overhead, and a few hours later several planes returned to drop food, clothing, shoes, and medical equipment. The former prisoners ventured out of the camp, and the local population gave them wide berth.

In the northern Kuriles, the feeling of sadness over the surrender was mixed with nervous relief among Japanese, since the Soviets had declared war against Japan a week earlier, on August 8. After the surrender announcement, division commander Lieutenant General Fusaki Tsutsumi held a conference on Paramushiro with his military and civilian leaders. He made sure everyone was committed to surrendering in good order, yet was worried about the occupation. Tsutsumi received word that in spite of the surrender announcement, the Soviets were bombarding the northern coast of Shimushu, using their long-range 130-millimeter shore batteries at Cape Lopatka. The four guns on the peninsula were only eight miles from Shimushu. Tsutsumi set in motion plans for the evacuation of the women and children living in the northern fishing villages to Hokkaido.

On Shimushu, Warrant Officer Fukuno's commander ordered him to draft a message in English to the commander in chief of U.S. forces in the northern Pacific, urging the United States to occupy the island and take the Japanese surrender. The message was sent, but no reply was received.

The last U.S. combat sortie from the Aleutians was airborne even as the surrender announcement was made. Launched out of Attu by VPB-139, the mission was flown by pilot Lieutenant Joseph Marlin, copilot Ensign Sydney Weij, navigator Ensign Robert Hart, radioman William Collins, and turret gunner Robert Medlock. The bomber was targeted against Shimushu and had almost reached the island when a coded message from Attu ordered the plane to return to base; the war had ended. The crew discussed turning back.

Pearl Harbor and the Bataan Death March were mentioned. They took a vote according to gunner Medlock, and the outcome was unanimous. "We voted to complete our mission." They agreed to later claim during debriefing that they had jettisoned their bombs over the ocean. Instead, they continued to Shimushu and dumped their bombs in the relatively uninhabited center of the island and sped homeward. Though a serious transgression that the crew regretted on the return trip, it would pale in comparison to what Stalin was about to unleash.

In the weeks prior to the surrender, the Soviets had moved large numbers of troops, ships, and planes to the Far East, and while the Japanese on Shimushu still had their focus on repelling U.S. air attacks, a Soviet landing force left Petropavlosk on the sixteenth. The convoy passage took place in dense fog on the night of the seventeenth across the narrow strait separating Kamchatka from Shimushu.

The Japanese on Shimushu were awakened to the sound of heavy-weapons fire in the early morning hours of August 18. Initial thoughts were that American forces were invading.

Warrant Officer Trueman Fukuno rushed to the underground listening post and, after some moments of confusion, the situation was clarified. The Soviets were the attackers in the north. He was ordered to draft another message, asking the U.S. forces to intercede. Fukuno was then issued a weapon for the first time, a shotgun, but was given no ammunition.

A Japanese negotiating team was ordered to proceed toward the Soviet line, carrying a white flag of surrender. Soon they reported back that the Soviets were ignoring the white flag and were continuing to shoot and move forward.

Though the fog allowed the assault to take the Japanese defenders by surprise, it also prevented Soviet air units from flying from Kamchatka's airfields. The weather lifted at midmorning, and several groups of eight to sixteen Soviet aircraft, including American P-63 Kingcobras, which they had received just weeks earlier, took to the air. The planes made raids on the Kashiwabara staging area at noon to prevent movement of Japanese troops from Paramushiro to Shimushu.

Repeated refusal of requests to the Soviets to cease firing roiled General Tsutsumi, who then ordered Colonel Sueo Ikeda, commander of the 11th Tank Regiment on Shimushu, to counterattack. The Soviet advance was halted temporarily as the Japanese engaged them in heated combat.

While the ground battle raged, the Japanese launched aircraft to strike the Cape Lopatka shore battery that was giving long-range fire support to the landings. The planes also engaged Soviet landing craft and their escorts.

On August 21, after inflicting more than three thousand casualties on the Soviets while losing every tank sent into the battle, the Japanese garrison on Shimushu ceased hostilities. Surrender was unconditional, following orders from its Fifth Army headquarters in Sapporo. The surrender document was signed on the twenty-second by Lieutenant General Tsutsumi and Major General Aleksei Gnechko, commander of the Kamchatka Defense Group. Once again, Japanese soldiers began turning in their weapons. On the twenty-fifth, the Soviets occupied Paramushiro without a fight.

As things remained in turmoil in the Kuriles, the final 52 internees of the 290 airmen held by the Soviets were repatriated on August 24 in Tehran, Iran. The Japanese POW camp at Ofuna was officially liberated on August 29, 1945. B-24 gunner Corporal William Cavanaugh, the last Aleutian warrior captured during the war, became a free man. The Allies began rounding up the Japanese camp guards and their commander.

B-25 navigator/bombardier Lieutenant Milt Zack, engineer Corporal Robert Trant, and tail gunner Walter Bailey were released from confinement. Lieutenants Lewis and Burrows and Corporal William Bradley from the same crew had not survived. Zack was told by the Japanese that the three men were aboard a freighter that was sent to the bottom by a U.S. submarine.

Etta Jones, whose husband, Charles Jones, was killed on Attu during the Japanese invasion in 1942, was released from confinement in Yokohama along with a group of Australian nurses. Twenty-four of the original forty-two native Attuans survived the war and were released at Otaru City, Hokkaido. The U.S. government did not allow them to return to Attu. The island had become a major military installation. The Attuans were resettled on Atka.

In the Kuriles, Japanese servicemen were being detained in garrison awaiting movement off the islands. Warrant Officer Fukuno, who had wanted to fight for the United States, but wound up in "the wrong navy," thought he would eventually be transported from Shimushu to his uncle's home in Yokohama. The Soviets were clearly intending to take the northern archipelago as their own territory, so Fukuno assumed they would all be evacuated. When word finally came in early October that they were to move out, some of his navy friends gathered their Japanese script, money that was now worthless, and stuffed it in their duffel bags. Others packed the heavy blankets they were issued. Certain he would soon be home to a warmer climate, Trueman Fukuno marched to the dock carrying only two of "the lightest blankets I could find." His personal belongings beyond that consisted of his navy blue military-issue underwear, the uniform and cap he wore, his watch, and a pair of glasses. Along with the first group of four thousand Japanese, Fukuno was loaded aboard an American-built Liberty ship. The boat slipped out of Kataoka Harbor, but instead of heading south, the overcrowded vessel swung north. Fukuno and every Japanese serviceman on board soon realized they were not headed home. After two days, the ship pulled into Magadan. The Japanese disembarked at the same Soviet port that several groups of American pilots had transited through on their way from internment to eventual release in Iran. The reception accorded the Japanese at Magadan, however, was much different.

Premier Josef Stalin had been perfecting the gulag system since the early 1920s, and for more than two decades he oversaw the methods being tried to extract the maximum amount of labor out of incarcerated human beings. In the course of the experimentation, Stalin and his bureaucrats discovered that slave labor was most profitable when "norms" or daily work goals were set and met. Food was forthcoming for those who performed up to expectations. The weak ate less and died quickly without much expense. The strong lasted a little longer.

Well before the start of World War II, Stalin's gulag program was spread far and wide within the Soviet Union. With more than 1.8 million in confinement plus another million sent into exile, the labor camp system was the largest single employer of manpower in the world by 1938. Under NKVD chief Lavrenti Beria, the camps had rapidly become what Stalin envisioned: a place to rid himself of his perceived internal enemies while forming a productive element in the development of the Soviet economy. Mines such as the main one for gold at Kolyma, nickel at Norilsk, salt at Chong Tuz, and coal at Vorkuta were but the most notorious of the many subterranean operations established. Forestry camps were spread far and wide (e.g., Kargopollag, Vyatlag, Kraslag) in the far-flung regions of Stalin's empire, with prisoners supplying all the labor. Even high-ranking scientists, engineers, and administrators of the gulags were often current or former slave laborers. If a certain skill was needed deep in Siberia, the NKVD simply grabbed someone with anything that remotely resembled that ability and had the person sent there. Electrical engineers wound up heading bridge construction projects. If they did well, they got "promoted" within the system.

Following the surprise German attack in 1941, Stalin's grand scheme was disrupted. His 1938 purges within the Red Army decimated the senior officer corps, and manpower intended for the labor camps needed to be siphoned off to the military to stem the German invasion. Prisoners of war made up for the losses, so the growth in gulag population never decreased. Once the war began winding down, however, Stalin's focus returned to gulag economics. Inmates had never been thought of as human beings but rather as "units of labor." What better way to begin reconstruction than to use captured German and Japanese soldiers? The lives of "fascists" and "imperialists" mattered even less than those of common Soviets.

By the time the Japanese surrender was accepted by Stalin, the total number of POWs held by the Soviets surpassed four million, including six hundred thousand Japanese, a stunning number considering the brief time the Soviet Union was at war with Japan.

On arrival in Magadan, Fukuno and many of his four thousand companions were immediately put to work on the docks that night, unloading wheat from another Lend-Lease Liberty ship. For the next week, Fukuno hefted sacks of wheat, backbreaking labor, in temperatures that dropped rapidly after sunset. Then the prisoners were abruptly marched into the city. Fukuno and about three hundred Japanese were separated, loaded aboard trucks, and taken out of town along the single road built by the slave laborers who had preceded them. The convoy traveled thirty-two kilometers north to *lagpunkt* 32, a satellite camp in the complex collection of Kolyma gulags.

By Soviet law, the camps were laid out in either a square or a rectangle; no irregular shapes were permitted. The enclosures were surrounded by barbed wire and a five-meter "death zone," where those who trespassed were assumed to be attempting escape and would be shot. Each *lagpunkt* had a cluster of makeshift wooden buildings set around a large open space in the center, where prisoners stood at attention twice a day to be counted.

Fukuno's group occupied four huts plus a large canvas tent. He was given space inside the tent and was issued heavy "duck" boots, cotton pants, cotton gloves, and a jacket. Here is where Fukuno and his companions were introduced to the "norm," the daily work goal. Here is where Fukuno would begin to understand why life expectancy in Kolyma was but one winter.

For the most part, the Japanese in Fukuno's camp worked outdoors, cutting wood. The Siberian winter was beginning to set its teeth, but the ground had not yet frozen. Mud covered everything. Men worked and slept in wet clothing. The prisoners rarely took anything off except their boots when they were near one of the two steel drums used as stoves to heat the tent. The drums had no pipes to carry the smoke outside. Fukuno wore his two thin blankets day and night. As days passed, the mud froze solid, darkness pervaded, and frigid air whistled inside his "soot-covered igloo," which soon was full of holes. If the temperature was above –40 degrees Celsius, the laborers would march out under guard and begin sawing, chopping, and gathering wood. At night, as the wind penetrated their thin canvas protection, the exhausted men slept huddled around the stoves. Prisoners refused to go outside to relieve themselves. Going outside to the bathroom was a dangerous undertaking in nighttime temperatures that hit 50 to 60 degrees Celsius below zero. "Those who left their place close to the stoves for any reason automatically forfeited their space." Dysentery soon began claiming lives as often as the cold. The stench from excretion and body odor was by this time the least of anyone's concerns. Fukuno's socks disintegrated. He carefully cut strips from one of his blankets and wrapped his feet, then shoved the result back inside his boots. The winter of 1945–46 was bitter cold. Men lost fingers and toes to frostbite, and many froze to death. But the wake-up call at each dawn meant another "norm" to meet.

The men were fed a meager breakfast of bean porridge and frozen carrots or beets. Then roll was taken as men stood stamping their feet to keep up circulation in the freezing cold while the guards counted, then sometimes recounted the assembly. Whatever implements were necessary for the work were pulled from the tool shed, then either carried or loaded on sleds, which were manhandled, often through waist-deep snow, to the forest work site to cut timber. The weak would fall along the way, and would be either placed on the sleds or left in the snow, if the guards were certain they could not get far away. The temperature often dropped so low "the tree trunks would become hard as concrete, maybe harder," according to Fukuno, and the axes "wouldn't bite." The steel head would ping off the trunk and hit the prisoner's leg. Fukuno had that happen so many times, "My boots were all cut up." They were allowed one break during the day, when they were issued several hundred grams of black bread.

After a tree was finally brought down, the men had to saw it into six-foot sections for loading onto more sturdy wooden sleighs attached to diesel tractors. The sleigh had to be filled above the top, the "norm," so the men tried to leave as much of the bulky branches and foliage on the cuttings as possible. The guards would come and order the men to knock the limbs off. When the norm was finally met, the tractor pulled the sleigh to the road, where the logs were loaded on trucks for transport to Magadan. On the way back to camp, they loaded the bodies of those who had died from exhaustion or frozen to death that day onto the tool sleighs. Clothing from the dead was still of use to the living.

According to Fukuno, "The dead were not buried at No. 32. There was no cemetery in the area, and, in any case, the ground was frozen to concrete hardness, making burial impossible. The bodies were taken away for disposal elsewhere. Later we learned they were taken to Magadan's only morgue, where they were kept until they could be buried in a cemetery in the city's outskirts when graves could be dug in the spring."

The Japanese suffered in particular from what to them was strange and virtually inedible food. The bread was made in the shape of a brick. Because of the bran used in its manufacture, the loaf was black in color and of coarse texture. Baked with a great deal of water, it was heavy and gave the impression it was more nourishing than was the case. Men argued over the drier ends, and as one gulag survivor recalled regarding a prisoner's approaching death, "He no longer watched for the heel of the loaf or cried when he didn't get it. He didn't stuff the bread into his mouth with trembling fingers." Other prisoners killed and ate anything that moved or appeared to be nourishing. Rats would invade the tent area, only to become a meal. The Japanese even dug up frozen frogs near bogs.

One morning, when Fukuno entered the tool shed to gather his ax, he was stunned to find one of the prisoners hanging from the rafters. The man had killed himself during the night. "That set off a series of suicides," according to Fukuno. After a number of similar deaths, no one wanted to open the shed door for fear of finding another corpse.

Spring comes late in Siberia, and as the ground thawed, berries, herbs, beetles, and snakes appeared. These were consumed along with wild mushrooms, some of which were poisonous, even deadly.

With the arrival of warm weather, the Japanese were allowed their first bath. At the Russian *banya*, or bathhouse, Fukuno was given a pail of lukewarm water to clean himself. He took off the navy-blue underwear he had been wearing since capture. The prisoner's clothing was deloused at just the right temperature to hatch thousands of lice eggs. His shirt was handed to him "shimmering, silver and black. I will never forget the horror of seeing mine crawling with hungry, newborn lice." Fukuno rinsed off, shook his things out as best he could, and put his clothing back on.

After the ground thawed, Fukuno was placed on a trench-digging detail. The trenches were for mass graves, but not for the already dead. These graves were for those expected to die during the next winter at No. 32. Instead of being sent to Magadan, they would be carried to the holes and their frozen bodies covered with loose dirt piled nearby.

Some sixty thousand Japanese died the first winter of 1945–46 according to Soviet records. The trend was not expected to decline.

In summer, the surface of the tundra was muddy, so walking became difficult and the mosquitoes rose in hordes. They got in the prisoners' eyes, their noses, their mouths. The taste was sweet, like blood. The insects went after the warmth of the porridge bowls, and the prisoners ate mosquitoes as they in turn were eaten by the bugs.

Warm weather lasted only a few months before Fukuno was transferred to another camp near Magadan. With him up to that time were the two officers who had taken the wristwatches from Corporal Cavanaugh and Lieutenant Brevik back in June 1945. The warrant officer who had taken the lieutenant's watch was sent to a camp in the Urals in 1946, and the few returnees from that area testified to the high mortality rate there. The officer with Cavanaugh's watch had been Fukuno's company commander in captivity in Siberia. He kept the watch on his person at all times, even when he slept. He was eventually charged with "sabotaging" the work effort, and a Red MVD tribunal court sentenced him to twenty-five years hard labor at a gold mine. Full body searches are conducted after sentencing. Since personal property is confiscated by the MVD in such cases, Cavanaugh's watch likely wound up in the possession of the Soviet secret police.

According to Fukuno, the only mitigating thing about Japanese camp life was that the Germans had it much worse. Work at the nearby German camps was often designed principally as a means of torture and abuse.

When back in the camps, the Japanese were constantly barraged with propaganda, which often issued from loudspeakers or from political hacks at mandatory meetings. Socialism was the theme, and Stalin's hope was that the prisoners would be won over to communism and eventually be returned as fifth-column insurgents in their home countries. The prisoners listened to the incessant retoric, but the lectures had little effect. Required responses were recited back, but few true conversions took place. At one point, Fukuno was told he was to be included in the next group release only to be pulled out of the line by an NKVD officer and sent to another camp. Fukano did not know the cause, but suspected that his ability to speak English or his American background may have been part of the reason. These facts may have been revealed to the Soviets by another prisoner in an attempt to obtain an early release.

Fukuno was moved from camp to camp until in the summer of 1947 he wound up back near Magadan. His compound at Nahodtka was a few miles from a prison that housed women. "Judging from the size and number of barracks in the compound it is possible at least a thousand women were incarcerated there." In the fields, work details from both camps would often come in contact. Through another male prisoner, Fukuno's knowledge of the English language came to the attention of one of the prisoners in the women's camp. She sent a note to Fukuno introducing herself as "Mary" and wanting to know who he was. She asked Fukuno to read her message, make a verbal reply, and then destroy the note in the presence of the sender. He complied. Over the next two years as he moved back and forth between camps, Fukuno managed to communicate regularly with the woman, even getting a glimpse of her several times. Mary claimed that she had come to the Soviet Union with her engineer husband in the thirties, all imbued with communism. After the war, she and her husband were arrested, as were all foreigners or those who had contact with foreigners. Her husband's fate was unknown to her. She was desperate that the U.S.

Japanese artist's rendition of prisoners being marched to work in Kolyma during the winter. Approximately 80,000 Japanese prisoners died in the camps.

government become aware of her situation since she was sentenced to twenty-five years in Siberia, a virtual death sentence. A detached affection blossomed over the months as more short notes and verbal messages were passed.

Then in December 1949, Trueman Fukuno was once again told he was about to be released. He gathered his belongings and was ordered aboard a flatcar as darkness descended on the camp. He had no illusions. Fukuno had been selected for repatriation before, only to find himself pulled from the group by the NKVD and taken to yet another camp. A few yards ahead of the train stood Mary swinging a lantern beside the crossing just beyond the station. She had sent a message asking him to notify the U.S. embassy of her status if he actually won his release and to look for her near the train. She wanted him to acknowledge receipt of the message. He spotted her at the crossing and decided to tell her as the flatcar passed. The train finally lurched forward, but an NKVD officer suddenly appeared at the end of the platform. As Fukuno approached Mary's position, he saw her, "all wrapped in rags, looking like an old woman, her face barely visible as she swung the lantern. I couldn't say anything with the NKVD so close, so I just nodded as we passed within yards of each other." He thought she saw his signal, but couldn't be sure.

This time, however, Fukuno was set free. He had survived four winters in Siberia at camps 32 and 47, at Magadan, back to 47, Magadan, at 47, 63, and 47, at Magadan, Nahodtka, to an unknown camp close to Havarosk, and finally at Nahodtka. He had lost sixty pounds and weighed just seventy-nine pounds on landing at Maizuru Naval Base, Japan, where repatriates from Siberia were examined by medical personnel and released. He soon contacted the U.S. embassy. A UPI reporter picked up on the tale of the American woman incarcerated in Siberia, and the story made the U.S. newspapers.

Back home in the U.S., former POW William Cavanaugh read the article in his local paper and noticed that the nickname of the

Japanese serviceman was listed as "Turpy." He wondered if he was the same Japanese interpreter who had befriended him on Shimushu. Cavanaugh contacted Fukuno to discover that he was indeed the same man. Though Fukuno and Cavanaugh have been exchanging letters ever since, the fate of Mary has never been clarified.

As each year came and went after the end of the war, the Siberian snow fell across the Soviet Union, covering the remains of tens of thousands of Japanese prisoners who died there, while farther east it settled on the wreckage of lost bombers and crews scattered among the volcanoes of Kamchatka and the northern Kuriles.

Chapter 16
The Last Flight of Bomber 31

There came a point when all the training and skills the men of Bomber 31 possessed would be called upon, one final act of courage and daring.

—Kamchatka crash site

After my return from that first visit to Kamchatka in the summer of 2000, I obtained from the U.S. Defense Prisoner of War/Missing Personnel Office (DPMO) a full copy of the report on their interview with Mikhail Khotin, the Geology Technical School graduate who had been part of the 1962 survey team that first encountered the wreckage of Bomber 31.

The report noted that the four bodies found at the site were clad in leather flying jackets, flight suits, and boots. The condition of the first two skeletons and clothing indicated that over the years the remains had been disturbed by wild animals. Because machine-gun ammunition and small bombs were strewn about the area, the team members had to tread their way carefully among the debris to the side of the aircraft. Near the tail, the third victim was discovered. They then made their way to the nose of the aircraft. The barrels of two machine guns were found protruding from the fuselage.

Both were stuck in the ground. Beside the guns, they found the fourth body.

Inside the fuselage, ammunition belts for the nose and top turret guns were strewn about, the tips of the bullets painted in alternating colors of red, black, and blue. Several boxes of ammunition also were discovered.

After examining the site, the survey team returned to the bodies and removed two gold watches. Three rings were taken, and one, which looked like a wedding ring, was examined by Khotin. It had an inscription on the inside, a first name, he thought, but the writing was not Cyrillic. Among the remains were scattered a number of silver coins. Khotin could read the dates, and all were minted prior to 1942. The personal items were collected by the survey team leader, Yuri Slepov, who turned them over to the local KGB representative, a Captain Likhachev. Khotin described Likhachev as a "drunkard."

About a year after the discovery, Khotin encountered Captain Likhachev again and asked him whether the Americans had been contacted about this aircraft. Likhachev told Khotin that some things were better off not questioning. At about the same time, Khotin was once again surveying in the area of the wreck. He noticed this time that the plane had been chopped up. The engines were at that time facing uphill and were fairly close to the fuselage.* Some distance south of the crash site, Khotin came across an abandoned shelter, which he speculated had been used by hunters. He found a small cloth ammunition case, which he recognized was from the wreckage of the plane.

After comparing the Khotin report with physical evidence and doing additional research on the Aleutians-to-Kuriles bombing

* In 2000, the engines faced downhill and were about 75 yards from the main wreck. A metal hoist rig was nearby, indicating that at some point an attempt to move the engines might have been made via the hoist. This probably was the same method by which the bombs were lifted from the aircraft bomb bay for disposal.

campaign, I submitted the article manuscript about the missing PV-1 Ventura and crew to my editor at the Retired Officer Association's magazine. The feature was published in January, 2001, under the title, "One Down in Kamchatka." Concurrently, the subject came to the attention of folks at NBC News and at Parallax Film Productions, a documentary company headquartered in British Columbia, Canada. Both subsequently obtained copies of my article. In addition to a Parallax decision to undertake a documentary effort, NBC planned to do a news item plus a *Nightline* feature on the subject.

In July 2001, producers Michael Barnes and Julie Crawford contacted me about the Parallax documentary. They asked if I would be interested in participating as an on-scene expert, a "tech adviser." The opportunity to spend time doing a more complete visual inspection of the wreckage was impossible to turn down. After being informed of the timetable CILHI and JTF-FA had established for the return trip to Kamchatka, Barnes agreed that I should arrive about midpoint during the thirty-day expedition period. This decision was reached after I described my prior five years' experience observing similar MIA recovery missions and on anthropologist Dr. Ann Bunch's comment the previous August that this was a "big site." Progress would be slow. Several days would be required at the front end just to get settled into the site and set up the "dig."

To get there this time I had to catch a Boeing 767, operated by Aeroflot, out of Los Angeles for Moscow, Reeve-Aleutian Airlines having gone bankrupt the previous winter. From Moscow, the next leg was via a thirty-year-old Ilyushin IL-62 jetliner across Siberia to Petropavlovsk, arriving on Wednesday, August 15.

In Petropavlovsk, the recovery operation was by that date expected to be in full swing, but sadly was not. Though the U.S. team had been in-country for nearly two weeks, they had just that day gotten to the site. Problems stemming from the abbreviated initial evaluation (IE) the previous summer and incomplete follow-up by the headquarters in Hawaii had materialized.

The Russians were not prepared for the amount of equipment brought in on a U.S. Air Force C-17 cargo aircraft. Included was a pallet of bottled water, made necessary because CILHI had not qualified the bottled water available in Kamchatka, a locale where clean water is plentiful. In addition, there was an incomplete equipment manifest, so the Russian customs agent was unable to compute the required charges. In fact, the team was unaware that *any* fees would be levied. Apparently no one had looked into the duty requirement during the IE, and as a result no cash was available to pay the charges. When trying to arrange helicopter transportation to the site, a similar glitch arose. The tour companies would accept only cash payment. When told that the U.S. government would reimburse them later for the use of the aircraft, the representatives shook their heads. In their experience, government guarantees to pay debts have generally turned out to be empty promises. In high season (July to September), the companies had waiting lists of passengers for the many tourist attractions on the peninsula. None of the tour companies was willing to pull a helicopter out of service to work with the recovery team unless cash was placed on the barrelhead. Nearly two weeks later, the team resolved the cash situation with the help of CILHI headquarters in Hawaii and a tour company consultant in Petropavlovsk. The recovery equipment was cleared through customs, and the team flew by helicopter to their camp site the day before my arrival in Petropavlovsk.

Parallax had arranged an overnight stay at a local bed-and-breakfast for me after I reached Petropavlovsk. The next morning I was driven to a heliport nearby. There were several tour helicopters at the field, but the one I was led to was an eye-opener. The right front windscreen was cracked and had been patched with cellophane tape. Inside, there were no seat belts, not even the pilot position had one. The pilot, a burly Russian in need of a shave, did his preflight, then took the left front seat. Our tour company liaison hopped in to sit behind the cracked windscreen. Two Russian civilians involved in the recovery operation found spots to sit near me. The pilot set up his switches, and hit the starter button to fire up the right engine. When the fuel control was moved forward, the exhaust gas temperature needle swung without a pause right into the red zone. The pilot shut off the fuel supply and, looking a bit perplexed, stared at the temperature gauge. Next he decided to try the left engine. Same result. Confusion reigned. A moment later, a maintenance man appeared out of a nearby shack. He took one look, then pointed to a spot above the fuselage. The pilot let out a howl, opened the door, and got out. He had forgotten to remove the intake covers from the engines.

With that show of skill and cunning completed, everyone on board was having second thoughts about the whole operation. Minutes later, however, we were airborne and on our way, though "wayward" might be more descriptive. Soon the pilot began an angry exchange with the guide. She had a map spread out on her lap and was doing her best to aid him in his quest for the correct routing. After searching for landmarks for ten minutes or so, we finally established where we were and took up the proper heading.

On sighting the camp, my eyes were greeted by the familiar blue tents used by the U.S. recovery teams in their operations. One of the tents appeared to have blown down, but otherwise all seemed well as we slowed to a hover beside a pristine lake in a canyon.

Around us, snowdrifts intermingled with lush, green foliage that hung down the sides of the mountain like tapestry. The location was chosen because it was beside a small mountain lake where water for showering and cleaning was plentiful. Unfortunately, it was a mile north of the crash site, and a steep five-hundred-foot ridge separated the camp from the wreckage of Bomber 31.

Once outside the still-running helicopter, I was introduced to producers Michael Barnes and Julie Crawford, soundman John Garrett, cameraman Jonathan Gilbert, and Tom and Kathy Rains.

Tom Rains is the son of Samuel Crowne, the radio operator aboard Bomber 31. Tom had come in the previous day, hoping to visit the wreckage and find some sign of his departed father. Both Tom and his wife's physical conditions precluded a climb over the ridge, so they were patiently awaiting our helicopter's arrival. In addition, I met the NBC crew led by correspondent Dana Lewis (currently with Fox TV).

I was told that a windstorm the night before had shaken things, hence the flattened tent. While we sorted out our next task, an Mi-8 helicopter landed. At that point the recovery team assembled with their personal belongings and started boarding. Dr. Bunch's last words to me were, "We don't have the right clothing, and it's too dangerous here." Minutes later the helicopter lifted off, leaving the Rains couple, the Parallax and NBC personnel, the Russian contingent, and me behind. The recovery team had not set up anything at the crash site and had obtained only enough money from headquarters for one round trip on the helicopter.

Tom and Kathy Rains had endured a tough 24 hours, having first gotten lost on their helicopter ride in. The pilot had to set down after becoming disoriented and with fog blocking his route. They spent several hours in the wilderness trying to determine their location. Tom later mentioned that things became tense, and at one point he began to wonder if his fate might mirror that of his father. Eventually the fog lifted, and they made their way to the camp site, too late to consider visiting the wreckage. The storm later that night also unnerved the couple. They were anxious to visit the crash site, then return to Petropavlovsk on our helicopter.

Michael Barnes and Julie Crawford decided to immediately take the film crew, the Rains couple, and me to the crash site. None of us spoke Russian and the pilot spoke no English, so instructions were passed to him to bring the aircraft down in the vicinity of the plane wreckage. However, instead of landing near the crash site, as was done when I visited the previous year, he chose a landing site atop the ridge. There, turbulence was at its greatest. He eventually set the helicopter down on the muskeg but was having a brutal time keeping it stable. When no one made a move, he shouted what we immediately translated to mean, "Get the hell out!" We mustered aft toward the rear door, and I was the last to exit. Before I could clear the rotors, our dauntless pilot poured the coals to it and started to lift off. I dropped flat to the ground. Gusting winds caused the rotor blades to tilt toward my head. A moment later the helicopter swung clear on its way back to the camp, and I've no doubt my epithets were heard above the sound and fury of the rotor wash.

We brushed ourselves off and began to hike the two-hundred-foot or so drop down to the crash site while the film and sound duo recorded the Rains's reactions. Tom seemed to retreat within himself as they approached the place where his father, Sam Crowne, had died. Film was taken of the couple pacing the crash scene and responding softly to questions from Michael Barnes. Nothing of note seemed to have been disturbed since my visit the year before. When the shoot was completed, the group began the climb back up the ridge so Tom and Kathy Rains could return to Petropavlovsk before dark.

Crawford had offered to carry in her backpack one of the sound tech's microphones, a furry item the size of a loaf of bread. We two arrived on top in short order, but Tom and Kathy Rains plus the loaded-down film crew were making a slow go of it. I looked over the other side of the ridge at the blue tents some five hundred feet below and saw that our helicopter had not yet started up. Crawford wondered if we could walk down. I moved east along the ridge and could see a clearing about halfway down the side of the incline where snow had collected. If we could reach that open spot, it seemed to me an easy descent from there. Since the helicopter had not yet departed, we figured we could be down before it left. The two of us began working our way through thick brush. Branches tugged at our clothing and progress was slow. When we finally made it into the clear, Crawford checked her backpack only to discover it had opened and the microphone was missing. I suggested she wait a few minutes while I retraced our route through the underbrush in search of the microphone. Climbing back up through the dense growth was a real chore, and soon I was soaked in sweat. No microphone appeared. Meanwhile, the helicopter had taken off and picked up the rest of the crew atop the ridge. I returned empty-handed to the clearing ten futile minutes later, and by now the helicopter was orbiting in search of the pair of us. I headed down the slope with Crawford, working our way alongside a pack of snow. When I was sure she could manage the rest of the descent alone, I turned back for one more attempt at finding the lost item. After groping through tangles for another half hour without any luck spotting the microphone, I descended to camp. Meanwhile, the helicopter had departed with the Rains couple. Over dinner, Barrett informed us that the microphone was valued at more than $3,000. We ate in relative silence, feeling very penitent over the loss.

After breakfast the next morning, Irina, our Russian cook, headed up the mountain and after less than ten minutes of searching found the missing item, to our great relief and joy.

Meanwhile, the NBC crew was getting antsy. They had a deadline to meet and no recovery operation to film. Dana Lewis and Michael Barnes decided to take their crews to the crash site for some preliminary filming without the presence of the Hawaii group, since their eventual return was in doubt. I accompanied both media crews. We trudged up through snow pack and undergrowth for forty-five minutes, then over the ridge to the site.

Standing over the cockpit area, I began to explain what we were looking at when I noticed a Jefferson nickle lying head-down on a narrow metal aircraft stringer. A few inches away I spotted with almost certainty a phalanx, a human finger bone. Both were in easy view and attested to the haste with which the initial examination had been conducted the previous summer. I advised the film crews not to take images of the remains, since that was a CILHI rule, and even though the Hawaii team had abandoned the camp, the site was still considered under their jurisdiction. CILHI is adamant about not having images of remains publicized, in deference to family sensitivities.* The media folks agreed with my direction not to film the bone. Dana Lewis then reached in and picked up the coin. He flipped it over and read the date: 1943. We then moved down the slope to the engines.

All the possible crash scenarios had been playing out in my mind since August 2000, after I had first examined the powerplants from Bomber 31. Several things were apparent to the naked eye, which was all that was available to us on-site.

If Bomber 31 had flown into the mountain in fog such that Whitman (or Hanlon, if he was at the controls) had no idea what was coming, the nose of the aircraft would have in all probability been the first thing to make contact with the slope. The engine propeller hubs (or spinners) would have impacted next. Damage to all points of initial contact would have been severe from compression. Explosion would have been likely, survival unlikely. If whoever was at the controls saw the mountain in time, he would have either pulled up or tried to turn away. If his pull-up was unsuccessful, a stall and nose-down impact would result with less severe, though usually fatal results. The debris field would generally be compact, with parts strewn in a tight pattern. With an unsuccessful turn, the low wing would impact terrain first, then the plane would cartwheel. The first wing to make contact often separates on impact. The engines would either remain together on the wings or be found far apart. The debris field would generally be spread over quite a distance. Survival might be possible depending on many other obvious factors. In both cases, however, explosion would be likely.

If Whitman had tried what is called a crash-landing, it means he

*Months later, when the Parallax documentary was aired, a scene was shown with Dr. Bunch handling what appears to be bones from the site. The "bones" were actually plastic replicas, and the segment was shot in Hawaii sometime after the expedition.

Lowe's Crash. Note the prop damage. The engine props on Bomber 32, which crashed May 18, 1944, show effects of ground impact. Vertical blade tip is bent forward indicating engine was powered. It likely only struck the ground once since no backward bending is evident. The lower blade is bent forward as well but sheared at the midpoint. The engine either stopped or the drive shaft failed.

had some level of control over impact with terra firma. In that case, usually the underside of the aircraft makes contact first. If the landing gear was extended, it would have been ripped from its mounts. Propellers spinning below the wings, mounted mid-fuselage on the Ventura, would hit next. The condition of the propeller blades in any mishap reveal a wealth of information.

When a propeller makes contact with a solid or liquid object, several rather straightforward things occur. For example, if the engine was providing power to the propellers when the aircraft struck a hard object such as a boulder or an asphalt runway, the first propeller blade to strike the surface will bend severely and often separate (fracture) at the hub, the break axis almost perpendicular to the rotating prop axis. Because the hard surface has no

This PV-1 flown by Lieutenant A.G. Neal ran off the runway on landing. Note that the engines were shut down and there was no damage to the propellers.

"give" to it, the tip will show high impact damage. Subsequent blades will normally show progressively less damage unless the engine was operating at a high power setting. Striking solid objects at low-power settings, such as during landing when the throttle is usually at idle, often will result in severely bent blades, though tension fractures also can occur.

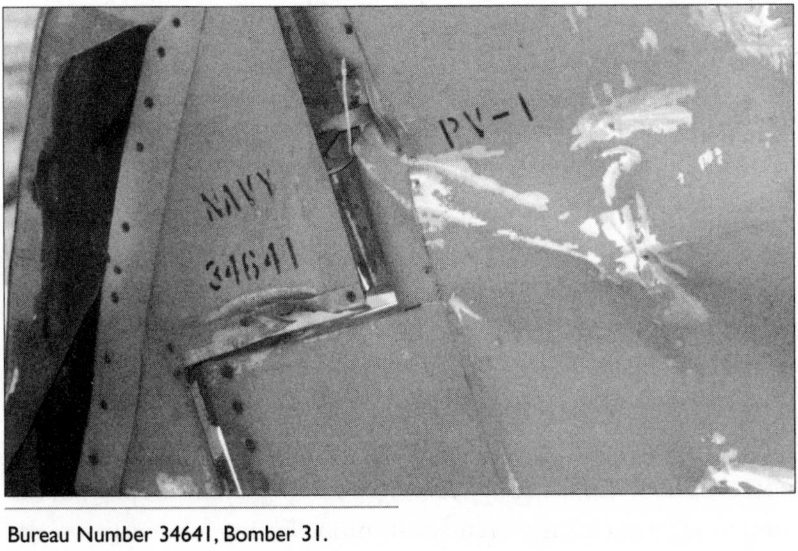

Bureau Number 34641, Bomber 31.

The engines with propellers showing little impact damage.

Propellers impacting soft soil, snow, or water (snow being the medium at the Kamchatka site) will show different effects. Under power, the tips will contact the surface, with the angle-of-attack established to provide the pulling motion or horizontal lift that otherwise propels the aircraft forward through air. Sticking one's curved hand out a moving car window and rotating the hand will demonstrate this effect. The lifting force increases or decreases depending on how you rotate the wrist. Because the propeller tip is "biting" into the air mass, it will initially try to do just that through snow, soil, or water as it cuts into the more dense material. Thus the blade tip actually twists and bends forward and up due to the shear force (twisting). While this is occurring, the aircraft continues to move ahead, and the rest of the propeller begins to bend backward, since the propellers make little headway through the more solid material. The blades may fail through a combination of tension and shear. Lab analysis is required to determine the finer points of how fast the propellers were rotating and the speed of the aircraft at impact. Measurement of propeller impact marks on the ground can aid in this determination as well, but the estimated nine feet of snow on the ground in March 1944, effectively rules that out. The end result from this kind of power-on impact is an s-shaped propeller shaft with the tip twisted and bent slightly up and forward while the rest of the prop is bent rearward.

In summary, had the engines on Bomber 31 been operating at even an idle power setting, the propeller tips would have bent forward on contact with anything solid, like packed snow or dirt, even though the main shaft of the propeller would then bend backward. But the tips were basically undamaged. Neither engine showed any evidence of being powered at the time of impact, nor was either prop in feathered (streamlined) position. None of the props had separated from the hub.

How a metal object fails also can tell a lot about what was going on at impact. Tension failures are caused by pulling motion, as happens when one yanks on a licorice stick. The material elongates before failure. Compression failures result from a push until the material collapses. There is no elongation. Shear failures are caused by twisting at both ends. Bending and twisting at the same time results in a combination of effects.

As the unpowered (possibly windmilling) props on Bomber 31 made contact with deep snow, the downward pull—tension—peeled the engines from their mounts, and they rolled under the wings. Examination of the engine mounts still attached to the wing confirmed this. The attach fittings were bent downward at the fracture points, and elongation or narrowing (the licorice stick stretch) was visually evident on most fittings.

Both R-2800s wound up downslope, while the rest of the plane continued up the incline. Had the pilot inadvertently flown into the mountain, the engines would have been driven back through the wing fire walls, but that area was relatively unscathed.

Except for obvious battle damage from a projectile that exploded inside one of them, the propeller hubs showed no impact damage, indicating that the plane made relatively flat contact with the terrain. Impact probably injured some or all of those on board, especially since from the 1962 account by the Soviet geologist, at least four crew members apparently stayed with the aircraft and perished there.

I explained all of the above to my producers, but without the U.S.

Props are bent slightly, but tips show no damage. Spinners showed no impact damage either.

government recovery team on site, they and the NBC crew felt they had an incomplete story. Dana Lewis used his satellite phone to call the home office for suggestions on how to get the CILHI unit to return. Calls and messages flew, and the following day, the U.S. team returned on a helicopter leased by NBC. The personnel from CILHI and JTF-FA immediately reoccupied their tents and made preparations to excavate the crash site the next day. Included in their gear was a heavy power saw, the kind used by rescue teams to cut open wrecked cars. Two team members were qualified to operate the saw, yet the expedition commander elected to use each one on separate days. Cutting began at the wingtips, with two-to-three-foot sections sliced off at a time. A mystery to me was why they did not cut the wings near the fuselage to allow the wing sections to be lifted away. Then they could get under the main fuselage, where remains were more likely to be found. Dr. Bunch explained that they were following their normal way of dissecting an aircraft. The process required three days just to reach the fuselage area, where more remains were eventually found.

A week after arriving at the camp, Parallax rented an Mi-8 helicopter to help Major McDougall from DPMO fly down to Shimushu to search for the site of Lieutenant Brevik's grave. Brevik was the pilot of the B-24 that had crashed into the Sea of Okhotsk in 1945 with Corporal Cavanaugh aboard. Cavanaugh was taken prisoner and was the only survivor from the crew. When Warrant Officer "Turpy" Fukuno returned from the gulag in 1950, Cavanaugh learned from him that Brevik had received a military burial in the local cemetery near Kataoka Naval Base. This information was eventually relayed to DPMO investigators. Two cemeteries near Kataoka were subsequently identified by satellite photography as possible sites for Brevik's grave. Major McDougall wanted to check them out. Parallax wanted aerial shots of the islands for use in the documentary, so the company hired the helicopter, and McDougall got approval from the Russians to visit the islands.

As we flew south, a cloud base slid beneath the aircraft. Word was passed from the cockpit that we probably would not be able to complete the flight as planned. Our hearts sank. To the west, I saw Kambalny Volcano, its cinder cone poking above the undercast. I pointed out to Michael Barnes how these conditions were similar to what Whitman may have experienced: clouds beneath the aircraft, a mountain visible in the clear, except that he had both engines failing. "I'd have turned toward that mountain, too," I yelled above the reassuring noise of our Mi-8 powerplants.

Five minutes later, we crossed over Cape Lopatka. The islands magically appeared in the only clear spot, dead ahead. Elated, we dropped down and swept in low over Shimushu. The old airfield at Miyoshino in the center of the island was barren of buildings, but the outlines of the runway, taxiways, revetments, and gun pits were easily discernible. Like ancient ruins, they lie weathering in the pale sun, bearing testimony to hard times past.

We circled several locations, eventually sighting the two cemeteries near the bay on the western coast of Shimushu, at Kataoka. The rusting hulk of a fishing boat sat half submerged just offshore. We landed in a clearing beside one of the cemeteries. As I stepped to the ground, I suspected we were the first Americans to have the good fortune to set foot in the northern Kuriles since World War II.

Major McDougall went about inspecting the graves, searching for a marker with a Christian cross, possibly containing Lieutenant Brevik's remains. He found a few crosses configured in the Russian Orthodox fashion, dated post-1945. Of the many stone markers, all were of Japanese Shinto design. McDougall then headed off alone toward the other cemetery while we looked around the area. Bomb craters were still in evidence after almost six decades. Filled in with tall grass, the depressions "walked" across the landscape. A concrete pillbox, its gun barrels long gone, still sat as a sentinel overlooking the bay. Numerous homes and warehouses that made up the fishing village, all painted in the same blue-green tone, were abandoned. Not a soul was in sight. On the beach rested a Soviet landing craft, its front hatch dropped down onto the sand as though it had just disgorged its load of troops.

Suddenly our pilot started pointing and yelling in an agitated voice. We looked to the west to see a thick fogbank rolling in our direction. The group scurried back inside the helicopter and lifted off just as the dense mass crossed the beach.

Next we turned south toward Paramushiro. The Russians had converted the old Kashiwabara port facilities into a fishing operation. The town was small but populated. We circled above several aircraft wrecks in the hills, but none was readily identifiable as a military aircraft or was too difficult to reach on foot for further investigating. The weather seemed to be getting worse all over the area, so after a brief stop, the pilot climbed away and headed for Kamchatka.

Approaching Cape Lopatka, the cloud layer we had passed on the way down loomed ahead, seemingly higher than before. Helicopters are not known for doing well in instrument conditions, and up in the cockpit the crew began using a handheld GPS system to find their way. Five miles or so farther north, we dropped into clouds as thick as any I had ever encountered. A long two minutes passed before we popped into the clear, about two hundred feet above the Sea of Okhotsk. I looked around and saw the peninsula looking gray and ominous on our right, about a mile away. The pilot swung toward land, and soon we were sandwiched between the cloud deck and tundra. The crew seemed to know where they were going, since they made few heading corrections. Looking out the porthole on the left, I spotted a brown Kodiak bear the size of a Volkswagen. The animal was thundering away from us at incredible speed, with tundra flying high in the air behind it. Twenty seconds later the helicopter made a rapid swing to the left, came to a hover, and maneuvered to a landing. Everyone started piling out, and I wondered if we were going bear-watching. Once on the soft tundra, McDougall informed us that a plane wreck was on the other side of the helicopter.

We eased our way on top of thick brush to a point about twenty yards west of the helicopter. There lay an assortment of burned and battered remnants of a second PV-1 Ventura. When McDougall lifted the twin tail, bureau number 49507 was barely discernible. This was the plane that Cowles, Panella, Parker, Toney, and McDonald had been aboard on August 20, 1944. Lieutenant Cowles was the pilot who had returned over Paramushiro to make a second attempt to release his bombs. Japanese fighters had sieved his aircraft during multiple firing passes. Cowles had managed to crash-land here in the tundra. The "Americanskis" were interned by the Soviets and survived.

The feathered engine showed heavy impact damage. One propeller blade on it had sheared at the hub. The engine that Cowles had shut down just prior to impact had its propellers bent backwards. The blade tips were relatively undamaged, and looked much like those on Whitman's Ventura. Cowles's after-action report, written subsequent to his release in 1945, supported the visual evidence at the site. The right engine had been hit by enemy fire and had been shut down prior to impact. The condition of this wreck helped confirm my opinion that the last moments in the flight of Bomber 31 were flown without power to the engines.

Based on the visual evidence, interviews with combatants on both sides of the conflict, and the records of missions flown over the northern Kuriles, I have attempted to reconstruct the probable sequence of events during the final minutes of Bomber 31's flight.

We know that Lieutenant Commander Stevens was first in the air that foggy morning back on March 25, 1944. Due to a weather hold, he got airborne at 2:04 A.M., more than two hours later than the planned (midnight) takeoff time.

Lieutenant Moore crashed into Massacre Bay four minutes later. Lieutenant Neal was safely airborne after a further twenty-eight-minute delay. Norem was next, and Whitman took off at 3:06 A.M., three hours later than planned.

Wreckage of Cowles's Ventura. Engine on the left had been shut down and was probably still windmilling at touchdown, since it was not feathered. All blades were bent backward, but little tip damage resulted. The engine to the right of the standing photographer had been feathered. One prop had sheared at the hub, and was undoubtedly the first to contact solid ground. The wings showed multiple holes from battle damage.

Because of the weather, Neal relied on dead-reckoning navigation and at 6:40 A.M. made landfall on the Kamchatka Peninsula, early and well north of his planned route. He turned south. Thirty minutes or so later, radar indications showed he was over Cape Lopatka, so Neal continued toward Shimushu. The sun rose at approximately 7:23 A.M. at his location, and he released his bombs two minutes later, then turned outbound for home.

Below, the Japanese, who had become accustomed to night raids, were presumably surprised to find themselves under attack after sunrise. No daytime strikes had occurred since the September 1943 raid. Nevertheless, bombers always came in waves spaced several minutes apart, so the Japanese would have expected more were inbound.

Lieutenant Norem approached the target area next. He estimated reaching Cape Lopatka at 7:30 A.M. Unusual winds had blown him west of Kamchatka. With fuel running low, he used his radar to determine when he was over water, jettisoned his bombs, then headed for Attu.

Whitman's plane arrived last, and the crew found themselves over the Kuriles in broad daylight. The element of surprise was no longer available, and the Japanese surely had manned their antiaircraft artillery and launched planes to defend the islands.

In all probability, Whitman's plane was engaged by Oscars, Tojos or Zeros before he made his bomb run. Based on the way so many of the Aleutian bombers had sustained hits, it is likely that the Ventura was badly damaged by these attacks. As noted, Japanese pilots had been briefed to attack from the forward quadrant against bombers. The geometry of this head-on tactic would have been set up had Whitman also overflown Kamchatka due to winds (as had Norem earlier) and been required to turn back east to find the Kuriles. Both engines on Whitman's plane showed evidence of battle damage, the angle of impact indicating that the rounds came in from above. This would be the case had the plane been flying low over the water or been bounced in the clear above a cloud deck, and the Japanese were attacking from twelve o'clock high. With loss of power to either engine, Whitman would have turned toward Kamchatka, just as Cowles had done under the same circumstances. But was either engine damaged to the extent that Bomber 31 could no longer outrun its pursuers? The damage to the engine spinner has great significance in this regard.

Inside the spinner is an oil-driven mechanism for setting the pitch of the propellers. The pilot, copilot, or machinist's mate (engineer) makes the adjustments using the prop lever on the engine panel. The selected setting is passed by pulleys and cables to the propeller governor, mounted on the forward section of the engine. It in turn sends an electrical impulse that is picked up by a rotating contact inside the spinner housing. Within the spinner is a piston-like mechanism that moves in response to oil pressure that the governor's signal controls with a valve. As the piston moves, its aft end has a spline that engages teeth on the base of the propeller blades.

This prop spinner exhibited no impact damage from the crash landing, but a round had penetrated the housing and exploded inside. Damage would have made control of the propeller impossible.

Movement repositions the blades to full-power (maximum deflection or "bite" into the wind) or to minimum-power positions. In the event of engine failure, pulling full aft on the prop control lever will feather the propeller, streamlining it into the wind to reduce drag.

The damage to Bomber 31's spinner would likely have disrupted the works inside. Loss of oil pressure would have initially moved the setting to the lowest pitch (minimum "bite"). Even so, more power would be available than if the engine were feathered. In short, the propeller would still function, but would not have provided the necessary thrust to keep airspeed high. Just as Cowles had experienced with his engine problem and reduced speed, the attacks on Bomber 31 would have been relentless and punishing until reaching Soviet airspace. During this period is when the cryptic call "Down! Down!" was likely overheard by Norem. The extent of the engine damage to both of Whitman's engines indicates that multiple firing passes were made against his plane. He probably had wounded on board and may have suffered the loss of electrical power needed to open the

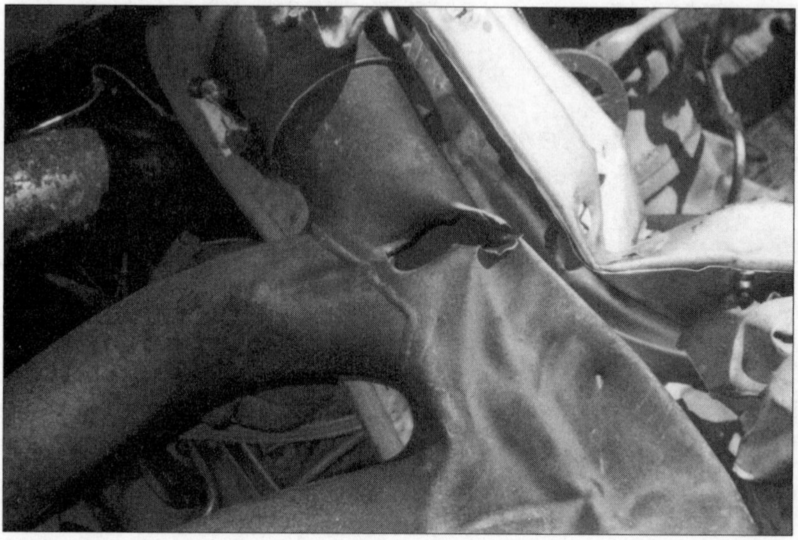

Heavy-caliber battle damage occurred to this exhaust stack on Bomber 31's right Pratt and Whitney R-2800 engine.

bomb bay and to jettison his bombs. One thing is certain: the damage to the prop spinner would have caused engine oil to begin gushing overboard. The oil would have spilled onto the hot cylinder heads of the engine, causing heavy smoke to trail the aircraft. This would have further encouraged coup-de-grace attacks from the Japanese.

In the cabin of the Ventura was an auxiliary oil tank that held approximately forty gallons. Petty Officer Clarence C. Fridley would have begun frantically pumping oil to the wounded engine in an attempt to keep it running.

Once clear of the Japanese fighters, some semblance of order would have been restored, and Whitman would have likely asked and received from his navigator, Donald Lewallen, a steer toward Petropavlovsk. A line drawn between the northern end of Shimushu and the runway at Petropavlovsk passes just left of the actual crash location.

As the plane proceeded north, eventually all the oil would have been expended, and the engine would freeze. When that happened, and assuming the prop could not be feathered, chances of holding altitude with the other damaged engine was unlikely.

From the debriefing reports we know there were low clouds over Kamchatka, so as Whitman continued toward Petropavlovsk, he was likely above a cloud deck. As power continued failing on both engines, he was faced with his next dilemma. Whitman's choices at that point were to head seaward and crash-land in the frigid Bering Sea; descend into the clouds, hoping to break out underneath before he struck a mountain; or try to land on the side of the volcano to his immediate right, where a relatively flat snow field offered a chance of survival.

If there were, in fact, wounded aboard, his or his copilot's options were reduced. In any event, someone aboard made the choice and turned the plane toward the mountain. A radio call during this period would likely not have been as short as the one heard by Norem, but instead would have provided the listener with the location "Kamchatka" and the fact that they were crash-landing on the side of a mountain. But time was running short, and whoever was

Both engines exhibited battle damage. This riddled exhaust stack from the left engine showed multiple holes from heavy weapons.

still at the controls was busy indeed. Assuming Whitman was still in command, he must have instructed his copilot or other surviving crewman to secure the engines, or at least the last one still operating, prior to touchdown. That was, with certainty, done to both engines before impact. Lack of damage to the propellers proves that the blades had windmilled to a stop. There was neither time nor need to feather either propeller, and it may not have even been possible to feather the engine with the damaged spinner. Touchdown was perfectly level, since both engines were simultaneously ripped downward from their mounts, rotated under the wings, and stopped side by side as the plane plowed its way uphill. There was no fire. Whitman or his copilot, Hanlon, had gotten them down. No other crewmen could have pulled off such a precise feat of airmanship.

The last flight of Bomber 31 was over.

In addition to remains, an empty boot with the name "Lewallen" sewn on it and a piece of a flight jacket with lieutenant, junior grade insignia was found at the crash site by the CILHI team. Copilot Lieutenant (j.g.) John W. Hanlon was the only j.g. aboard.

In July 2003, the Navy Casualty Office notified the appropriate next of kin regarding the identification of skeletal remains from Bomber 31. The delay was primarily due to the lengthy search locating relatives of pilot Whitman in order to get a DNA sample from the maternal side of the family, a requirement for mitochondria DNA matching.

Aviation Metalsmith/Navigator AM2c Donald G. Lewallen, Aviation Ordnanceman AOM3 James S. Palko, and Aviation Machinist's Mate AMM2c Clarence C. Fridley were confirmed as among the deceased found at the site. Identifications were made via mitochondria DNA analysis of bone fragments. It is reasonable to assume that Lieutenant Hanlon stayed at the site as well, since he would not have left without his jacket during the frigid temperature conditions on the mountain.

Khotin mentioned to interviewers that during a return to the area sometime after the initial discovery back in 1962, parts of the wreckage and personal items were discovered at a hunter's cabin some distance from the crash site. It is reasonable to think that several uninjured crew members had attempted to walk to safety, as Lieutenant Taylor's crewmen had tried to do after crash-landing in their B-24 on the eastern coast of Kamchatka in 1944. If someone in Whitman's crew had made the same attempt, he or they had undoubtedly run into either severe weather or impenetrable conditions much like those experienced by the Taylor crew. No trace of the cabin or other crewmen were found by the CILHI team, however.

One evening on my trip back from the crash site to the camp by the pristine lake, I chanced upon a pile of .50-caliber shell cases. They were in a neat pile at the very top of the ridge. Each casing had been burned, and none had a round still attached. All had exploded, but the primers were unmarked, indicating the ammunition had not been fired by a machine gun. Since the shells were on the ground and it was summertime, I initially presumed that the Soviets had burned the rounds there, but upon further consideration, think instead that someone from the bomber crew had gone through the belts of ammunition and removed the tracer rounds. That would explain why the ammunition was scattered about. Tracers were color-coded red for identification and were inserted in every fifth slot on the belt. Since the guns could not be fired without electrical power to the thumb trigger, it is likely the survivor or survivors decided to carry the rounds to the top of the ridge. There the tracers were set on fire, probably using aviation gasoline drawn from the fuel tanks. Though the tracers would not have traveled far without the use of a gun barrel, a few would have risen some distance above the ridge, and at dusk or night could have been seen or heard as an SOS for many miles. If that was indeed what they tried, it was a well-conceived attempt by desperate men to alert someone to their plight, but one that ultimately failed to save their lives.

Chapter 17
Attu Today

Attu's not the end of the Earth . . . but you can see it from there.

—U.S. Coast Guard saying

The Coast Guard C-130 still flies from Kodiak to Attu Island once every two weeks, weather permitting, and, much like the combat missions flown from the Aleutians, permit it did not on my first attempt to go there, in October 2002. A massive storm front with winds to eighty knots had blown in from the Bering Sea. At Kodiak I remained, on weather hold.

Waiting with me were navy veterans John W. Davis, who served on Kiska, Attu, and Adak (1943–45) and Albert F. King, who served on Attu (1946–47); they were hoping to revisit the haunts where they got their first real taste of navy life. In addition was Charles (Murphy) Pierce, the son of army officer Charles Murphy, who was wounded and awarded the Bronze Star during the 1943 Attu invasion but was later killed on Kwajalein in 1944. Along with Pierce was his history-buff neighbor Warren E. Schott, Jr. His father was an army veteran who survived the Pearl Harbor attack and served in the South Pacific. Both were looking forward to walking the ground where Pierce's late father had served with distinction.

By next morning, the storm had moved toward us at Kodiak, but the weather over Attu had improved. We loaded out, and two hours later, a crew headed by Lieutenant Commander Tim Tobiasz and Commander Harl Romine lifted the Hercules into the air and headed west. The four-engine turboprop was crammed with cargo, but ran out of space. One pallet containing the mail sacks was left behind, to the expected chagrin of the twenty men and one woman currently assigned to one-year tours on what these servicemen call "the lonesomest place on Earth."

An hour and a half later, the C-130 slipped gingerly into "yesterday's" storm. The plane bucked and swayed in response to a light chop, while twenty thousand feet below, an unseen mayhem ruled. As we came out the southwestern side an hour later, a look below revealed what force eleven winds (56 to 63 knots) can do. Huge waves swept across a churning surface, spawning rollers that appeared sixty or more feet high. They did not crest like surf, but instead avalanched down the lee sides, propagating dense streaks of white foam. Thoughts of the men who had to ditch in such weather during the Aleutians and Kurile Islands campaigns of World War II made me shudder.

Aboard our plane was engineer AM-1 David A. Weise, a twenty-three-year coast guard veteran. To my astonishment, I learned that Weise was aboard a C-130 that had crashed into the side of a mountain on Attu twenty years prior. The plane was destroyed, and two fatalities resulted. As we neared the island, I asked him how he felt coming back each time to the place where he had survived that ordeal. "It doesn't bother me anymore," he said, then stared in silence through the windscreen toward Attu, still out of sight in the distance.

Nearing Attu in clear weather, we first took a detour at my request to look for the PV-1 Ventura flown by Lieutenant V. C. Austin that nearly ran out of fuel on December 30, 1943. Over the radio, his squadron commander had gotten a weak bearing from the plane's radio signal and provided one last, desperate heading to a safe crash-landing on Agattu. We dropped to about a thousand feet over the island, where the plane reportedly went down. The C-130 swept across the barren speck of land for fifteen minutes without success when suddenly the coast guard spotter on the right side yelled, "There it is!" We circled as I took a few aerial shots of the plane, still beached beside a small lake. The PV-1's tail was detached, and the fuselage paint had weathered away. Still, the wreckage looked eminently restorable. Venturas are the rarest of war birds from World War II. Though there are several PV-2 Harpoons, both flyable and on static display in museums in the U.S., not a single Ventura has been located on display in America as of the date of this publication. Our side trip completed, Lieutenant Commander Tobiasz took up a heading for the short leg toward Attu.

We were now fifteen hundred miles from mainland Alaska, nearing the last bit of earth in America's Aleutians chain, a place where the international date line makes a left jog, rendering the island perpetually yesterday to the coast guard crew that operates

Lieutenant Austin's plane as it looked from the air in 2002. One of the rarest of warbirds, the PV-1 awaits recovery from Agattu Island and restoration.

the old Loran station. The Loran transmitter, known as Station X-Ray, has a 600-foot-tall antenna that emits a 470,000-watt radio navigation signal. The system has been improved over the years, but functions much the same as the one used by the Aleutian fliers during World War II. Kept in operation as a backup to the GPS system, Loran is still available for use by ships and planes transiting the Bering Sea and the North Pacific.

As Tobiasz made his approach, I caught sight of the wreckage of the C-130 that had provoked the wind and fog demons in 1982. The wings and separated tail section were still easily discernible. Weise had been the loadmaster, standing near the tail ramp that fateful day. He had just ensured that the wheels and flaps were down for landing and was about to take his seat. "I heard the engines scream and felt the nose of the airplane come up. I realized something was wrong. A couple of seconds after that we impacted the mountain." The plane broke apart behind the cockpit and near the aft paratroop doors. The right wing ripped off, and the fuselage spun around on the hill. "When the plane came to rest, I remember the copilot yelling at me to 'keep rolling.'" Weise's clothes were on fire. When he finally came to a smoldering stop, he noticed his anklebone sticking through his boot. His back was broken, and he had numerous lacerations. A crewman and a coast guard Station Attu passenger perished in the inferno. The story was a sobering one, but continuing to fly dangerous missions for two decades attests to the dedication of coast guard personnel such as Weise.

We flew over Casco's old abandoned runway, used by the navy fliers to launch toward the Kuriles. Then we circled to land on the longer runway, where concrete had replaced the Marston matting of World War II days. This time, C-130 contact with terra firma was uneventful. We taxied to the ramp area and exited the plane. A sign above a shack that served as a waiting room read, "Welcome to Attu International Airport."

The mountains surrounding the airfield looked foreboding, rust-colored and bare of trees. They loomed alien and primal. The

The Navy Brig, sole surviving Quonset from World War II.

island's sad history is echoed in the names of its locales: Massacre Bay, Murder Point, Mount Terrible. Beginning with the slaughter of native Aleuts by Russian fur traders, continuing with the second-bloodiest Pacific battle of World War II, and followed by the bombing campaign flown from her icy runways, it has borne and continues to bear witness to more than its share of tragedy.

Trees do exist at the lower levels, but number merely half a dozen scrub pines. The volcanic island's muskeg is covered in thick moss and lichen, giving the ground an elastic, trampoline quality, but wet and honeycombed with hidden sinkholes that can snap the leg of the unwary, as soldiers discovered during the war.

Along the southeastern coast toward Alexai Point, the World War II Quonsets have been flattened by the williwaws. The only hut left standing is the U.S. Navy brig, its tight confines and sturdy walls being the reasons for longevity.

At Engineer Hill, I stood by the monument to Colonel Yasuro Yamasaki, placed there by Japanese relatives, and imagined the appalling violence that shattered the early-morning darkness on

May 29, 1943. While walking the grounds, I nudged a small, flat stone near the monument and noticed a plastic-wrapped photo underneath. A young Asian woman gazed up at me from a faded color portrait. She was, no doubt, a descendant of one of the Japanese soldiers killed on the island. I carefully replaced the loose stone. Rain began to fall.

Weather determines all activity on the island, and we waited for a dry period two days later, when Warren Schott, Chuck Pierce, and I began the difficult climb toward Point Able. Pierce's father had scaled the heights in May 1943.

Along the steep way up, we encountered exploded mortar rounds. Spent shell casings from both American M-1 Garands and Japanese Arisaka type 99 rifles littered the damp landscape. Cresting the peak, I asked Pierce his thoughts. "We got here the easy way," he said, still drawing in great gulps of air after the exertion of the climb.

Pierce and I wandered along the ridge in a southerly direction, the one from which his father had made the ascent carrying a rifle

Japanese foxhole near the top of Point Able, from which the defenders rained bullets and grenades down upon the ascending U. S. troops.

Live Japanese bayonet clip from an Arisaka Type .99 rifle found atop Point Able.

and backpack under fire in the bitter cold. We made our way down about a hundred yards into an open area. I guessed Pierce was trying to imagine the gunfire and grenade explosions, the shouting and cursing, the cries of the wounded as battle-weary men, including his father, fought for every yard of mud and gorse in the icy, fogbound heights. Had we stepped upon the ground where the American soldier died as witnessed by aerographers Calderon and Carrigan through the theodolite scope? These were somber moments with little talk as we picked up and examined the debris of battle and contemplated the suffering of so many young men on both sides.

Later that night, at the coast guard station, I continued to read through the extensive library there, which covered the history of the island. I came across a high-altitude reconnaissance photo taken just before the 1943 U.S. invasion. The tiny shape of a Japanese floatplane was visible, beached at Holtz Bay. The notation beneath stated that the A6M2-N Rufe "appeared to have wing damage." Since the invasion came soon after the picture was taken, I doubted that the plane ever got off the island. I asked several members of the coast guard if any pieces of the floatplane were still at Holtz Bay, but no one had seen any remnants there. Intrigued, I borrowed a mountain bike and after a two-hour trek up and down Clevesy Pass and across raging streams, eventually made my way to the northern coast. There, just above the high-water mark, on the black-sand beach at Holtz Bay, sat a corroded 14-cylinder Sakae 12 engine. Undoubtedly it was from the Rufe fighter seen in the photo.

When I topped the berm to the south, the outline of the airstrip the Japanese had tried to complete stood out sharply. From the look of it, my guess is it will be discernible for a thousand years if left untouched. Closer in were mounds where ammunition bunkers and underground quarters had been dug in.

On the other side of the ridge at Chichagof Bay, not a building of any kind stood, nor could I find even a foundation to indicate that Attu Village had ever existed. The only item suggesting humans had once subsisted there was a badly weathered plaque naming the Attuans who had lived there in 1942 and commemorating those who had died under Japanese control.

Japanese 14-Cylinder Sakae 12 Engine at Holtz Bay.

I looked to see if I could discern the cave where Dr. Tatsuguchi had performed his final operations, where his patients had been killed, and where the doctor had emerged after the battle to unwittingly commit his "banzai to the emperor." Wherever the cave might have been, it was not in evidence, the entrance likely blown closed to prevent exposure to booby traps.

Working back south along the rutted trails, rusting American jeeps, tracked vehicles, and truck carcasses still littered the landscape, adding to the ghostly feeling.

Beside the road to Alexai Point, brown fire hydrants poked above bent grass, and out on the point lay scattered sections of the matted runways and taxiways. Now only ducks and geese take to the air from that windswept airdrome.

On the next-to-last day of my visit, I borrowed the mountain bike again and rode over to the abandoned runway at Casco. The asphalt rises a little at the end, where the Venturas topped off their fuel tanks. I stopped there, looking toward the bay where Lieutenant James Moore's plane had gone down and whose four crewmen still rest under the cold sea. The wind blew salt-laden drops against my raincoat. Shivering with chill, I could almost hear the sound of Whitman's R-2800s as they coughed back to life so long ago. Then I pedaled off the incline, the big-lugged tires of the mountain bike humming as speed increased, much like the wheels on Whitman's PV-1. Out of breath, I came to a stop at the end of the runway, looked across Massacre Bay and beyond Murder Point toward the Kuriles. There, the airmen of the Eleventh Air Force and the navy crews of Fleet Air Wing 4 had delivered their bombs on target or died trying, and in their modest, unheralded way wrote a glowing but little-recognized chapter in aviation history.

Epilogue
The Veterans

From August 25 to 29, 2002, I attended a reunion in Wichita, Kansas, as a guest of the former "Bats" of VB-139 and their relatives. Of the families who had lost a loved one on Bomber 31, the Lewallen and Hanlon clans were present in force, including Donna Lewallan, who was two-and-a-half-years old when her father was reported missing.

When I spoke with Donna, she said, "There was never a funeral. There was always doubt. I always prayed he'd come back." Upon learning the true fate of her father's final mission from the navy casualty office she recalled, "I was surprised I got so emotional. I was so choked up I could hardly speak. I thought he was lost at sea. My aunts and uncles always wondered if he had been captured by the Japanese."

The care and gracious treatment I received from everyone in Wichita, including attending to my swollen elbow—injured in a bicycle fall the previous week—were more than I would ever have expected. The veterans were eager to be interviewed and to share photographs, letters, and mementos of that tragic period in history. As it turned out, the documentary made by Parallax Films had been shown in the United Kingdom the night before the start of the Kansas affair. I had with me a copy of the video rushes that had been sent to me for review some months earlier by Michael Barnes. Now that his edited version had aired, I decided to allow the gathering to see portions of the rough cut I had been given. We rolled the video, and at the conclusion of the showing there was not a dry eye in the convention hall. In the years since, I have made firm friendships with many of those veterans, and of the scores of letters I sent to those who were not in attendance (both navy and army air force) I was astounded at the return rate. Stacks of packages arrived in the mail with detailed information and original photographs included. Invariably, also tucked inside I found my unused self-addressed, stamped envelope returned for future use.

Oscar Pilot Sei'ichi Yamada describing his attack on B-24 bomber flown by Captain Harrel Hoffman and crew.

I arrived at Tokyo's Narita International Airport on a cold, cloudy Thursday in February 2003 and caught a crowded train into the city. That evening I met with Dr. Hitoshi Kawano, who has a Ph.D. in sociology and has done extensive archival research for the U.S. Department of Defense. He now works as an instructor with the Japan Defense Agency. We met at the Navy Lodge on Yokosuka Naval Base, Yokohama, Japan. At the session, Dr. Kawano went over the series of interviews he had painstakingly set up after spending several months assisting me in tracking down Japanese veterans from the Kuriles. Only one of the men spoke English, so Dr. Kawano was to serve as interpreter.

The following day the former Ki-43 Oscar pilot Sei'ichi Yamada came down to greet us at the Tokyo train station near his home. A few months short of ninety years old, the five-foot, two-inch-tall veteran then led us slowly up the incline to his modest apartment. The epitome of politeness, he ushered us inside. His wife appeared for a brief moment to serve tea as we began discussing his experiences from long ago. Though frail, Mr. Yamada is still full of energy, using both hands in true fighter pilot fashion to describe the epic air battle during which he shot down the B-24 flown by Captain Harrell Hoffman and his crew. Mr. Yamada seemed to draw within himself as he described the last moments of the engagement. Transported back in time, he slowly related how he watched as the B-24 exploded, and the Americans descended in their parachutes toward the cold seawater below and their sad fate.

After the Japanese surrender in 1945, Warrant Officer Yamada obtained his commercial license and was hired by Nippon Airlines to fly helicopters until retirement. He accrued more than six thousand hours and continued to fly until age eighty-three.

The most startling revelation occurred during my next interview. Months before I arrived in Japan, I asked Dr. Kawano to try locating an antiaircraft gunner who served in the northern Kuriles during the war. My intent was to determine how the ground-based air defense system was orchestrated. He succeeded in finding a

Former Japanese soldier Toranosuke Ozaki survived bombings at Attu, Kiska, and the northern Kuriles, plus two years in Soviet gulags.

former machine gunner, Mr. Toranosuke Ozaki, whom we met for lunch at the Yokohama Bay Sheraton Hotel. Shortly after being seated in the lounge, Dr. Kawano explained my purpose in more detail. Upon his mentioning that I had visited Attu, Mr. Yamada spoke up rather excitedly. Dr. Kawano turned to me, "He said he has been there." I was mystified for a moment, but then recalled that in the late 1990s a group from Japan had visited the island to erect a memorial in memory of the deaths of Colonel Yasuyo Yamasaki and his men. Thinking that was the case, I asked Dr. Kawano to find out exactly when Mr. Ozaki had been there. "During the invasion in 1942," came the answer. Suddenly I found myself sitting across from a man who represented living history. Ozaki had seen Charles and Etta Jones. He had stormed ashore the very first day of the 1942 Japanese invasion. Since only twenty-nine soldiers had survived the American invasion in 1943, I was curious about whether Mr. Ozaki was one of them. He was not, but explained his extraordinary luck in being evacuated to Kiska in

September 1942, then being kept behind while the other troops returned to Attu two weeks later. His description of life on Kiska and of being evacuated during the miraculous rescue in August 1943 was detailed and riveting. During the course of the interview, I was able to obtain firsthand descriptions of Japanese life on Attu and Kiska in addition to later learning about the air defense setup on Shimushu and Paramushiro.

After the war, Mr. Ozaki was held on Shimushu, then sent to Magadan in December of 1945. From there he was moved to Nahotska, Irinka, Lake Baikal, and finally to an isolated gulag deep within the Soviet Union, where he was incarcerated for two years before Stalin approved the release of his group. He arrived back in Japan on December 4, 1947, the day after his father had passed away.

The most intriguing of the interviews had to be the two with Trueman Fukuno, who as a young man "wound up in the wrong navy." Here was a man who got caught up in one of history's monumental events, and like a leaf being blown about by a bitter wind, found himself cast in ever more dire circumstances. In spite of the hardships of being orphaned in his teens, then enduring the bombing on Shimushu, followed by four years of slave labor in Siberia's Kolyma region, Trueman Fukuno maintains a positive outlook on life. I suspect that was the key to his extraordinary survival. It certainly was not his size, at just over five feet tall and weight at 79 pounds the day of his release. "During my incarceration," Fukuno recalled, "I lost most of my teeth, which was worse than weight loss, because weight can, of course, be regained, while teeth cannot. I lost three to a sexy Russian female army dentist who visited our barracks at Camp 47. Her office consisted of a satchel in which she carried her pliers and vodka. She was plastered and pulled teeth like crazy while happily bragging about her sex life."

Upon Fukuno's return from Siberia, he was employed in the oil industry in Japan, where he climbed the corporate ladder and retired in 1989. He now lives in Tokyo with his wife, Ryoko.

According to Yasuo Wakatsuki's book *The Siberian POW Camp*,

Trueman "Turpy" Fukuno survived the bombings on Shimushu and four years in Soviet gulags.

Volumns I and II, there were an estimated 610,000 Japanese POWs (military personnel) taken inside the Soviet Union when the war ended. By April 21, 1950, the Soviets returned 527,940 to Japan. The last ship arrived from Nahotska on April 23, 1950. About 3,000 were still held in the gulags, and of those, 1,500 additional POWs were repatriated in six groups between 1953 and 1956, after the death of Stalin. About 80,000 perished during confinement.

Fleet Air Wing 4 commodore Leslie E. Gehres took a demotion back to the rank of captain in 1945 in order to command a ship. He was serving as skipper of the aircraft carrier USS *Franklin*, when it was hit with two bombs from a Japanese dive bomber on March 19, 1945. Gehres refused to leave the ship, even though the flight and hangar decks had become raging infernos. With the ship in danger of sinking or capsizing, Captain Gehres was not about to abandon more than three hundred sailors trapped belowdecks. The ship burned for fifteen hours during one of the worst U.S. naval disasters at sea but was saved by the actions of Gehres and his valiant crew. More than a thousand of the three thousand crewmen aboard were killed or injured. The men of the *Franklin* became the most decorated crew in U.S. naval history.

The "Silver Stallion of the Aleutians" General Simon Buckner, after leaving Alaska went on to command the Tenth Army during the South Pacific campaign. General Buckner hit the beach at Okinawa on Easter morning, April 1, 1945. *Time* magazine put the general's portrait on its cover on April 16. A superstition had arisen that being on a *Time* cover was a "jinx," reinforced two days later, on April 18, with the death of beloved war correspondent Ernie Pyle (*Time* cover, July 17, 1944), among others. Following the publication of his cover photo, Buckner led his men through two months of bitter fighting and on the eve of victory on June 18, 1945, went to a forward observation post, where the "jinx" caught up with him. Struck by shell fragments from a Japanese artillery round, Buckner died within seconds.

Lieutenant Douglas M. Birdsall, the pilot in the navy's first official *Empire Express* mission on January 19, 1944, survived the war, rose to captain in the navy and as an airline pilot, then retired in Palm Desert, California with his wife, Carla.

After the war, former POW corporal William Cavanaugh testified against Ofuna Prison Camp commander Aida, medical technician Kitamura Congochyo, and the guards Nakakichi, Nishi, and Mori. The War Crimes Tribunal found them all guilty. Aida and Congochyo received the death penalty and were hanged. Nishi and Mori received fifteen-year prison sentences. Nakakichi was sentenced to twelve years in prison.

Cavanaugh retired in Ocala, Florida, and POW lieutenant Milt Zack resides with his wife, Rayma, in Laguna Woods, California. Radioman ARM Petty Officer First Class Harold R. Toney, who survived a crash-landing on Kamchatka and internment in the Soviet Union, now lives in Byhalia, Mississippi.

Navy navigator Byron Morgan, who also survived internment, suffered a stroke in recent years and now lives in an assisted-living home in Long Beach, California.

Nona Fedorovna Solodovinova, the attractive Russian interpreter, contacted Byron Morgan in 1962, seventeen years after his release, to let him know she was living in Naro-Fominsk, southwest of Moscow.

The Attuans, who were never permitted to return to Attu, resettled on Atka after the war. They were awarded $79,500 for resettlement costs. The Aleut/Pribilof Islands Association in 1977 began an effort for war reparations and redress from the federal government. The Aleutian and Pribilof Islands Restitution Public Law, PL 100-383, was signed by President Reagan on August 10, 1988. Terms included a trust of $5 million to benefit Aleut evacuees and descendants. Reparations also included $1.4 million for destruction of church property, $12,000 awarded to each eligible Aleut for "damages for human suffering," and $15 million for damage to lands and properties on Attu Island that were placed into the National Wilderness Preservation System.

Regarding the wreckage of the PV-1 Ventura seen on Agattu, the U.S. Navy officer responsible for recovering aircraft made it known that the bomber was still considered government property. No attempt to recover the aircraft was, or is expected to be, in the works by the navy, and no civilian enterprise may recover and restore the plane without U.S. Navy agreement. As a result, the restoration of this aircraft presents a major challenge, such that the last of the rarest of war birds may disappear from history much like so many relics of the Aleutians campaign.

Missing since March 25, 1944, remains of the crew of Bomber 31 found in the Russian Far East were returned to next of kin in November 2003. This was made possible after an exhaustive search for maternal relatives needed to provide DNA samples to compare with that of the bones found at the crash site. Six of the seven families were located rather quickly, using navy personnel records, but Lieutenant Whitman's file mentioned only an aunt living in Miami Beach.

The navy sought help from the Miami Beach police but had no

luck hunting down any relatives of the pilot. Shirley Ann Casey, a private detective from Deerfield Park, Florida, was intrigued by the case. Casey locates missing persons for a financial firm in West Palm Beach. She began the search for Whitman's aunt but ran into one dead end after another. The aunt, Frances Williams McClain, married four times and lied about her age, leaving a confusing paper trail. In 1945, a year after the crash, she purchased a gravesite for him in Oak Hill, Ohio. The aunt died in 1977 at age 92, but Casey was able to trace a cousin mentioned in her will. More than fifty-two hundred men shared the cousin's name in one state alone, but knowing the cousin's age narrowed the search.

Finally Casey dialed the right number.

"I almost fell out of this chair," she recalled. "I couldn't believe it. I didn't expect to find him for two to three years."

The cousin was willing to provide the navy with a blood sample but demanded anonymity.

Had it not been for Casey's work tracking down a DNA sample from the maternal bloodline, the DNA investigation would have been inconclusive. The remains might have included Walt Whitman's, and no one would ever have known. But they did not. DNA from the recovered bones matched samples taken from maternal family members of Donald Lewallen, James Palko, and Clarence Fridley, according to the U.S. Navy Casualty Office. Some fragments were too small to refine for analysis and were placed together in one coffin for burial.

Clarence Fridley's family put his remains to rest on Veterans Day, November 11, 2003, in a cemetery in Eureka, California, near where they live. Walt Whitman's relatives have not scheduled a ceremony as yet; his grave site still awaits him in Oak Hill, Ohio. Donald Lewallen's family requested that his remains be interred at Arlington National Cemetery on November 19, 2003. The funeral service was held in the Old Chapel at Fort Myers. Afterward, the casket was taken to Arlington for burial. At the conclusion of the service by the grave site, the wind came up as the scene clouded over. It felt as if a williwaw had blown in from the Aleutians to signal acknowledgment at the honor bestowed on the navigator of Bomber 31.

The remaining bone fragments were buried together in a plot next to Lewallen's grave site the following day during ceremonies honoring the entire crew. James Palko's family requested that his remains be buried with those. The casket was drawn from the Old Chapel at Fort Myers by a four-horse caisson.

The many family members in attendance walked the short distance from the chapel to the grave site on a sunny autumn day. Relatives of the deceased and fellow servicemen were present to watch a missing-man formation of F-14 Tomcats fly overhead. Others hobbled along on the arm of a relation. The U.S. Navy band and a 21-gun salute also were part of the ceremony. Some of the elderly leaned on canes. But it was neither the valiant men and women who have come to be known as our greatest generation nor the heraldry that caught my attention. It was the daughters and sons who came with them, the granddaughters and grandsons, the great-grandchildren, the grandnieces and grandnephews. The men of Bomber 31 and all the 480,000 servicemen and servicewomen like them who did not survive World War II had been denied so much. They gave full measure, all their days and nights, so that we could wake up each morning in freedom, able to go about our lives having children, getting promoted, loving others, and growing into old age these many decades.

As I watched the proceedings honoring the crew, a profound feeling of gratefulness descended upon me for having had the opportunity to contribute to the realization of their story. It confirmed my opinion that when one of America's sons or daughters gives full measure—no matter how long ago—those fateful moments should not remain in obscurity forever. America's dedication to recovering our missing in action is well worth the effort. Approaching a crash site, I now sense the message from beyond: "At last someone has come to find out what happened to me."

Appendix I
Empire Express Squadron Deployments on Attu

August 10, 1943, to August 16, 1945

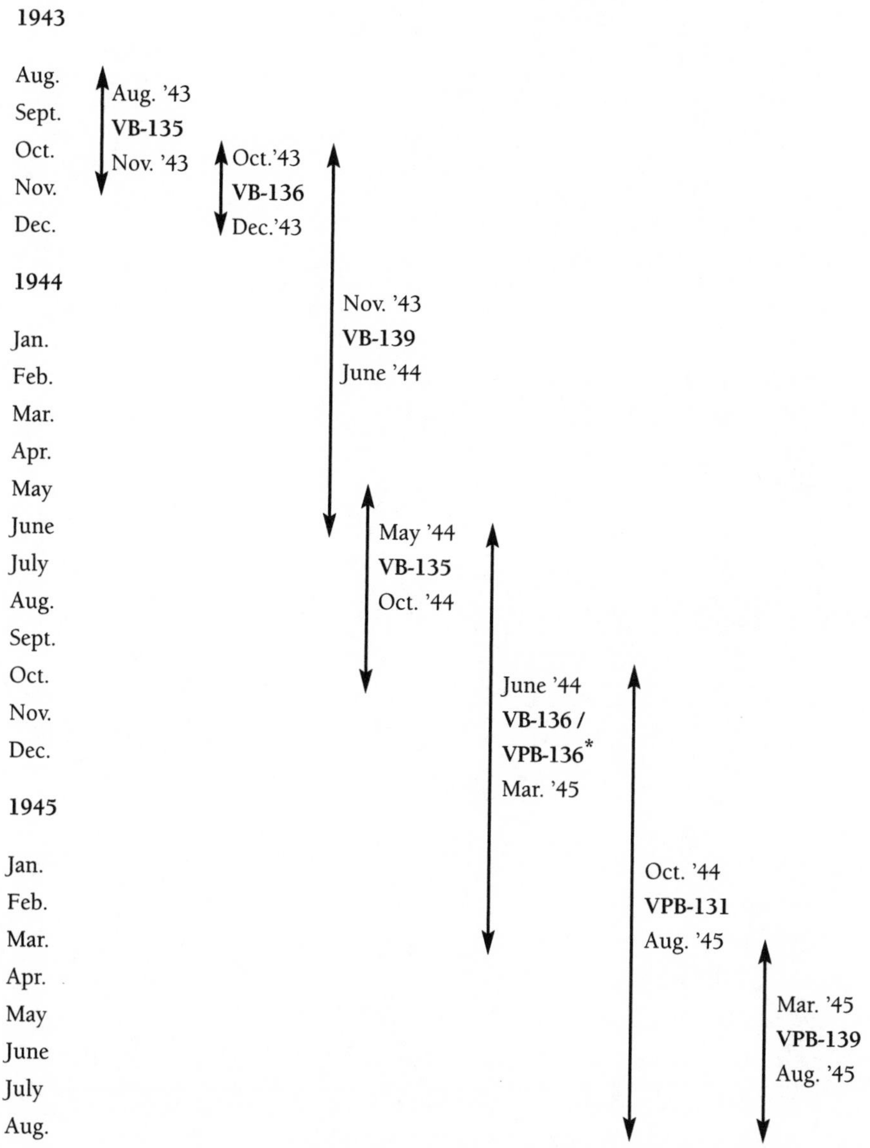

*On October 1, 1944, the designation of all PV squadrons was changed from Bombing (VB) to Patrol Bombing (VPB).

Appendix 2
Army Air Force Aircraft Losses

Date U.S.*	Tail No.	Type	Unit	Remarks
1. June 4, 1942	Unk.	B-17E	Unk.	Mansfield piloting and crew lost on bombing mission to Kiska.
2. June 11, 1942	41-1088	B-24D	21 B. S.	Jack F. Todd, pilot, and crew shot down over Kiska. Right wing broke off.
3. June 12, 1942	41-1090	B-24D	21 B. S.	George Rogers piloting. Crashed on takeoff.
4. June 18, 1942	40-2359	B-24D	21 B. S.	Ira Wintermute ran out of gas, ditched. Horace T. Freeman and Brooks C. Quattlebaum drowned.
5. July 22, 1942	41-1105	B-24D	21 B. S.	Pilot Edwin P. Heald and crew lost.
6. Aug. 10, 1942	41-11762	B-24D	21 B. S.	Attacked by enemy aircraft and AAA over Kiska. Pilot Ira Wintermute and crew bailed out eighty miles east. Clifford R. Brockman and Paul A. Perkins drowned. Eugene W. Latham's chute fouled on prop and he went down with aircraft. Second B-24 loss involving Wintermute.
7. Sept. 28, 1942	41-11802	B-24D	404 B. S.	Crash-landed on Adak due to battle damage from fighters and AAA over Kiska. Flown by Davidson. Sarenski wounded in face.

8. Sept. 30, 1942	41-1092	B-24D	21 B. S.	Waddlington crashed on landing.
9. Dec. 9, 1942	40-2365	B-24D	404 B. S.	Crash landed in Bechevin Bay near Atka with John Andrews, Louis Blau, W. E. Lynd, J. C. Beardsley, John A. Vertar, Thomas A. Nicholas, J. E Mecey, James W. Chamberlain, E. Balas, A. C. Meador, and J. V. Hart.
10. Dec. 25, 1942	41-23895	B-24D	21 B. S.	Damaged beyond repair after Thomas Archer in P-38 (41-2005) ran into B-24 aft section and was killed.
11. Dec. 31, 1942	41-23897	B-24D	21 B. S.	Damaged beyond repair after hit by P-40.
12. Jan. 18, 1943	41-23822	B-24D	21 B. S.	Shot down with Thomas F. Bloomfield and crew.
13. Jan. 18, 1943	41-23900	B-24D	21 B. S.	Lost near Great Sitkin Island; pilot Ernest C. Pruett.
14. Jan. 18, 1943	41-23908	B-24D	21 B. S.	Crashed on Great Sitkin Island with Linton D. Hamilton and crew.
15. Feb. 13, 1943	41-29748	B-25D	77 B. S.	Crashed on Adak after losing engine to AAA over Kiska. Steve Rouchak killed. Claimed one Jake.
16. Mar. 30, 1943	42-63752	B-24D	21 B. S.	Shot down over Kiska with Fred M. Smith and nine men aboard. The navigator lost his life on the flip of a coin.

17. Apr. 15, 1943	41-23970	B-24D	21 B. S.	Shot down over Kiska. Pilot Albert F. Danek and ten men lost.
18. May 15, 1943	41-23896	B-24D	21 B. S.	*Kiska Katie* shot down over Attu with Anthony Brannon and nine men. Could be May 14.
19. May 15, 1943	41-29741	B-25D	73 B. S.	Crashed at Amchitka with no fatalities.
20. June 18, 1943	42-40080	B-24D	36 B. S.	Crashed on Herbert Island Killed were James H. Jones and Willard F. Crippen.
21. July 10, 1943	43-36147	B-25D	77 B. S.	Ditched off Little Sitkin after fuel starvation following sub search.
22. July 15, 1943	41-11816	B-24D	36 B. S.	Crashed on Cape Adagdak, Adak.
23. July 22, 1943	41-29779	B-25D	73 B. S.	Ditched off Kiska from AAA. Crew rescued by PBY.
24. Aug. 6, 1943	42-53347	B-25C	77 B. S.	Crashed on Amchitka, no fatalities.
25. Aug. 12, 1943	42-40129	B-24D	404 B. S.	Shot down over Paramushiro; piloted by Harrell Hoffman plus crew of nine men.
26. Aug. 12, 1943	42-40309	B-24D	404 B. S.	Crash landed on Kamchatka by J. R. Pottenger. Thomas E. Ring died of injuries and Dimel injured.
27. Sept. 12, 1943	41-13260	B-25C	77 B. S.	Interned Kamchatka, R. E. Hurst and crew.

28. Sept. 12, 1943	41-29788	B-25D	77 B. S.	Crash-landed in Aleutians after battle damage over Paramushiro. All aboard killed except Ken J. Harris and Art Olsen.
29. Sept. 12, 1943	41-30171	B-25D	77 B. S.	Interned Kamchatka, W. A. Marrier and crew.
30. Sept. 12, 1943	41-30502	B-25D	77 B. S.	Crashed on Cape Lopatka after battle damage over Paramushiro. No fatalities. Interned, Salter and crew.
31. Sept. 12, 1943	41-23890	B-24D	36 B. S.	Shot down over Paramushiro. Pilot F. T. Gash and crew lost.
32. Sept. 12, 1943	41-23891	B-24D	404 B. S.	R. K. Putnam and crew interned, Kamchatka.
33. Sept. 12, 1943	40-2355	B-24D	404 B. S.	C. G. Wagner and crew interned Kamchatka.
34. Sept. 12, 1943	41-30473	B-25D	77 B. S.	Interned Kamchatka, N. R. Savignac and crew after battle damage over Paramushiro.
35. Sept. 12, 1943	42-53345	B-25C	77 B. S.	Shot down over Paramushiro with A. W. Berecez and crew.
36. Sept. 12, 1943	42-53349	B-25C	77 B. S.	Shot down over Paramushiro with J. D. Huddleson and crew.
37. Sept. 12, 1943	42-53352	B-25C	77 B. S.	Interned Kamchatka with J. T. Rodger and crew.
38. Sept. 12, 1943	42-53354	B-25C	77 B. S.	Shot down over Paramushiro with Q. T. Standiford and crew.

39. Nov. 18, 1943	41-1104	B-24D	21 B. S.	Richard E. Payne and crew of ten lost near Adak, including Tom Crump and Floyd Musa.
40. Nov. 18, 1943	42-53348	B-25C	77 B. S.	Crashed on Amchitka, killing eight men.
41. Feb. 22, 1944	41-23884	B-24D	36 B. S.	Crashed into two C-47s on Shemya; Ken H. Ristad was pilot. Five crewmen and Walsh, an electrician on the ground, were killed.
42. Mar. 25, 1944	41-11906	B-24D	36 B. S.	Lost with pilot James L. Harris and eleven men.
43. Apr. 26, 1944	41-23848	B-24D	36 B. S.	Crashed off Agattu with Wilfred W. Larson, William Gallagher and thirteen men.
44. Aug. 13, 1944	41-11850	B-24D	404 B. S.	Crash landed on Ilak Island After all bases fogged in. Piloted by Corbin U. Terry and Ted Buszek.
45. Sept. 3, 1944	41-23973	B-24D	36 B. S.	Blew up near Iliamna with Robert Geatches and eleven others. R. D. Moss and five others survived.
46. Sept. 9, 1944	Unk.	B-25D	77 B. S.	Lieutenant Albert D. Scott and crew of five crashed after striking ship's mast during attack. They were taken as POWs by the Japanese.
47. Sept. 10, 1944	Unk.	B-25D	77 B. S.	Interned on Kamchatka, with R. W. Head, Hammond, McIntosh, Lawton, Carr, Crowell.

48. Sept. 25, 1944	42-40977	B-24D	404 B. S.	Interned on Kamchatka with Jack Ott, Perlich, Arnold, Shimer, Martel, Clark, Petersen, Saigh, Austin, Shelton, Karkoszynski.
49. Oct. 25, 1944	43-3709	B-25D	77 B. S.	Crash-landed on Attu.
50. Nov. 1, 1944	43-3685	B-25D	77 B. S.	Interned Kamchatka with McQuillin and crew.
51. Nov. 6, 1944	Unk.	B-25	77 B. S.	Lieutenant Alfred Muldoon and crew lost near Torishima Retto with all hands.
52. Nov. 8, 1944	43-36151	B-25J	77 B. S.	Shot down over Paramushiro.
53. Nov. 16, 1944	43-36153	B-25J	77 B. S.	Shot down over Kurabu Zaki, Paramushiro, with Wagner and crew.
54. Nov. 18, 1944	42-40993	B-24D	404 B. S.	*Bugs Bunny, What's Up, Doc?* crash-landed on Cape Zhelty, Kamchatka, with Donald Taylor and crew.
55. Dec. 6, 1944	42-40976	B-24D	404 B. S.	Lost off Attu with Ellis Millard and crew while returning from Paramushiro.
56. Dec. 7, 1944	41-23782	B-24D	36 B. S.	Interned Kamchatka with Robert Weiss and crew.
57. Dec. 29, 1944	43-36128	B-25J	77 B. S.	Shot down over Suribachi Air Base, Paramushiro. Lieutenant Collier or Lieutenant Banker.
58. Dec. 29, 1944	43-36136	B-25J	77 B. S.	Shot down over Suribachi Air Base, Paramushiro. Lieutenant Collier or Lieutenant Banker.

59. Jan. 18, 1945	42-40996	B-24D	404 B. S.	Interned Kamchatka with Ken E. Elliot, Charles N. Talbot, Jr., and crew.
60. Jan. 23, 1945	42-41152	B-24D	404 B. S.	Went down over Shimushu with Charles Talbot and eleven men after left wing blew off.
61. May 11, 1945	41-11924	B-24D	36 B. S.	Interned Kamchatka with Richard Klienke and crew.
62. May 11, 1945	43-36149	B-25J	77 B. S.	Shot down by enemy aircraft over Paramushiro with Larsen and crew.
63. May 11, 1945	43-36158	B-25J	77 B. S.	Interned Kamchatka with Winter, Stifel, and crew.
64. May 16, 1945	42-40998	B-24D	404 B. S.	Interned Kamchatka with William D. Blakeway and crew.
65. May 20, 1945	43-36134	B-25J	77 B. S.	Interned Kamchatka with Beever and crew.
66. May 20, 1945	43-36140	B-25J	77 B. S.	Shot down over Shimushu Island.
67. May 20, 1945	43-36152	B-25J	77 B. S.	Shot down over Paramushiro with John Daughtrey and crew.
68. June 10, 1945	43-36160	B-25	77 B. S.	Interned Kamchatka during divert from Kuriles. Hit by Russian AAA over Kamchatka, too, with Wolbrink and crew.
69. June 10, 1945	44-29148	B-25J	77 B. S.	Shot down by Soviet AAA while diverting to Kamchatka.

70. June 17, 1945	44-50345	B-24M	404 B. S.	Shot down by bomb fragments from an exploding Japanese ship. Pilot Richard S. Brevik. Only tail gunner, William T. Cavanaugh survived.
71. July 13, 1945	44-36148	B-25J	77 B. S.	Shot down over Kamchatka by Soviet AAA during divert attempt from Kuriles, killing Raymond Livingston and crew.
72. July 17, 1945	43-36135	B-25J	7 7 B. S.	Interned Kamchatka after divert from Kuriles. Wampler and crew. Judd lost at sea when bomber ditched off Kamchatka.
73. July 17, 1945	43-36145	B-25J	77 B. S.	Crashed on Kamchatka after battle damage over Kuriles. No fatalities. Terris and crew.

* For aircraft shot down over the Kuriles or interned on Kamchatka, the actual date at the location of loss/internment is used, which is one day later than the aircraft departure date from the Aleutians.

Appendix 3
Navy Aircraft Losses Navy PV-1/PV-2

Date U.S.*	Tail No.	Unit	Remarks
1. Apr. 2, 1943	29735	VB-136	Circumstances Unknown.
2. May 4, 1943	29768	VB-135	Amchitka loss.
3. May 10, 1943	29847	VB-136	Spun in at Adak while making instrument approach; flown by Parmenter.
4. May 10, 1943	29794	VB-136	Flown by Lieutenant J. G. Malloy. Crashed into Kuluk Bay when returning from search.
5. May 23, 1943	29746	VB-135	Circumstances Unknown.
6. May 23, 1943	29787	VB-135	Flown by Ensign P. P. Patterson; crash on takeoff, Amchitka. Patterson, AMM 3C A. D. Shave killed. The rest were seriously injured.
7. June 26, 1943	29743	VB-135	Crashed on landing and destroyed.
8. June 28, 1943	29737	VB-135	Circumstances unknown.
9. Sept. 25, 1943	33133	VB-136	Flown by Throckmorton. "Throck" was cartoonist. Crashed during attempted takeoff on familiarization flight.
10. Nov. 9, 1943	33140	VB-136	Crashed on Shemya. Flown by Dinsmore.
11. Dec. 9, 1943	34774	VB-139	Flown by Edward Watson. Skidded on runway.
12. Dec. 30, 1943	33346	VB-139	Flown by V. C. Austin. Returning from sector search, ran out of fuel, landed gear-up on frozen lake on Agattu, where aircraft remains to this day. Minor injuries. Searched Sector George 8.

13. Mar. 25, 1944	33343	VB-139	Flown by J. H. Moore. Crashed on takeoff. Ensign Mitchel Lambert, Ensign Robert E. Janson, (VP-43) Gordon F. Heckendorn, Victor O. Mog killed; three live.
14. Mar. 25, 1944	34641	VB-139	Flown by Walt S. Whitman. Crash-lands on Kamchatka. Crew of seven missing.
15. Apr. 27, 1944	48937	VB-135	Flown by J. J. McNulty. Missing on training patrol out of Adak.
16. May 1, 1944	29749	VB-139	Circumstances Unknown.
17. May 6, 1944	48733	VB-135	Flown by Lieutenant (j.g.) A. A. Wheat. Missing on Paramushiro mission. Airdales newsletter says "blew up after TOT on night mission." Crew of seven.
18. May 13, 1944	48934	VB-135	Flown by Lieutenant Hardy V. Logan. Missing on Paramushiro mission. Crew of six.
19. May 18, 1944	34640	VB-139	Flown by Ralph J. Lowe. Crashed plane on takeoff.
20. May 18, 1944	33433	VB-139	Flown by Lieutenant Norem. Crash-landed from battle damage upon return from combat with shipping. Hydraulics, windshield shot out. Copilot Clifford Tambs shot in chest, killed.
21. May 23, 1944	48889	VB-135	Flown by C. E. Clark. Crash on takeoff. Loss of all hands.
22. June 8, 1944	33357	VB-131	Lieutenant Newby crashed due to undercarriage collapsing upon landing, Whidbey Island, Washington.
23. June 12, 1944	48923	VB-135	Flown by J. W. Clark. Ditched near Agattu. Crew recovered by VP-400 mail flying boat.

24. June 14, 1944	48930	VB-135	Flown by H. B. Schuette. Crew of seven diverted to Kamchatka due to battle damage.
25. June 14, 1944	48910	VB-135	Flown by Lieutenant Russell P. Bone. Crew of seven interned in USSR. Bone, Mantle, Stevens, Sommers, Gelber, Crow, Horvath.
26. June 19, 1944	48938	VB-135	Flown by George A. Mahrt. Fuel siphoned overboard during mission to Paramushiro, diverted to Kamchatka. Interned in USSR. Mahrt, Johnson, King, Dickson, Patzke, Strom, Everard.
27. July 10, 1944	48919	VB-135	Circumstances unknown
28. July 23, 1944	49505	VB-135	Crashed on Attu.
29. July 23, 1944	48928	VB-135	Interned at Petropavlovsk. Flown by J. W. Clark. Landed USSR due to fuel shortage and bad engine. Interned: Clark, Miller, Mathers, Simes, Brennan, Rowe.
30. July 24, 1944	48909	VB-135	Flown by Vivian. Landed Kamchatka due to battle damage. Crew of seven interned: Vivian, Wilson, Edwards, Anderson, Schasney, Virant, Nommensen.
31. Aug. 13, 1944	49525	VB-136	Flown by C. W. Lindell. Force-landed in USSR. Fuel low and bad engine. Crew of Six: Lindell, Head, Richardson, Williamson, Brown, Manthie.
32. Aug. 20, 1944	49507	VB-136	Flown by J. R. Cowles. Crash-landed on Kamchatka. Crew of five interned: Cowles, Panella, Parker, Toney, McDonald.
33. Aug. 28, 1944	49508	VB-136	Flown by J. A. Dingle. Landed USSR due to battle damage. Crew of six interned: Dingle, Petterborg, Dulan, Henry, Pollard, Leintz.

34. Sept. 11, 1944	33278	VB-136	Flown by Lieutenant (j.g.) D. F. McDonald. Landed Kamchatka due to damage from fighter attacks. Interned: McDonald, Miles, Broadwell, Ross, Rosa, Nicodemus.
35. Sept. 17, 1944	49472	VB-136	Flown by Lieutenant Commander C. Wayne. Landed USSR due to damage from fighter attacks. Interned: Wayne, Murphy, Ehret, Mulford, Baxter.
36. Nov. 4, 1944	49641	VB-131	Flown by Lieutenant Robert A. Ellingboe. Shot down by fighters over Parmushiro. Six killed: Ellingboe, Bird, Overturf, Marriot, Panetti, Rutter.
37. Dec. 16, 1944	34636	VB-139	Flown by A. G. Neal. Ran off runway at Attu.
38. Feb. 21, 1945	49654	VB-131	Flown by Lieutenant John W. Powers. Crew bailed out over Point Lopatka, USSR when weather prevents Petropavlovsk landing. Interned: Powers, Thomas, Pleasant, Timperman, Mann, Hosner.
39. Mar. 17, 1945	48891	VB-136	Lieutenant Moorehead ditches in darkness near Karcuk on west side of Kodiak, crew recovered by 28' dory, aircraft had radio failure en route Attu to Whidbey.
40. Mar. 26, 1945	37065	VB-139	PV-2 Harpoon flown by Lieutenant L. J. Dulin. Crashed and burned at Shemya after overshooting landing while on instrument approach during severe snowstorm. Two of crew seriously injured, the rest had multiple lacerations. All recovered.
41. Apr. 7, 1945	49648	VB-131	Flown by J. E. Patton. Crashed into Casco Bay, Attu. Stalled after go-around in gusty wind conditions one-quarter-mile from runway on second final approach. All killed.

42. Apr. 22, 1945	37075	VB-139	Flown by Lieutenant William D. See. Lost from radar contact 90 miles out from Attu. Crew of 6. PV-2 Harpoon

*For aircraft shot down over the Kuriles or interned on Kamchatka, the actual date at the location of loss/internment is used, which is one day later than the aircraft departure date from the Aleutians.

Appendix 4
Interned Crews, by Release Group*

Group No. 1. One crew (5 men); "escaped" May 11, 1943

Parent Unit	*Crew (pilot's name in italics)*	*Landed*	*Date Interned (USSR time)*
Doolittle	*York,*[a] Emmens, Herndon, Laban, Pohl	Vladivostok	Apr. 16, 1942

Group No. 2. Eight crews (61 men); "escaped" Feb. 18, 1944

1. Army 404th	*Pottenger,* Filler, Hanner, Wiles,[b] Homitz, Dixon, Ring,[c] Bernatovich, Day, Dimel,[b] Varney[b]	Kamchatka	Aug. 12, 1943
2. Army 404th	*Putnam,* A.T. Miller, Amundson, Dyxin, George, Albert, Bryson, Doyle, H. M. Hammond, Goode, Gross	Petropavlovsk	Sept. 12, 1943
3. Army 77th	*Savignac,* Keithley, Hodges, Fawcett, Vickers	Petropavlovsk	Sept. 12, 1943
4. Army 77th	*Rodger,* Fry, Eastmoore, Overby, Green	Petropavlovsk	Sept. 12, 1943
5. Army 77th	*Salter,*[d] E.H. Taylor, Koepp, Wiar, Graham, Lans	Petropavlovsk	Sept. 12, 1943
6. Army 404th	*Wagner,* Vandiver, Black, Corbett, Marx, Kerns, Waid, Saugestad, Carter, Everett, Vasquez, Daniels, Fuller	Petropavlovsk	Sept. 12, 1943
7. Army 77th	*Hurst,* J.M. Taylor, O'Dair, Wilcox, Huber, C.H. Field	Petropavlovsk	Sept. 12, 1943
8. Army 77th	*Marrier,* Sabich, Hahn, Billingsley, Dunwoody	Petropavlovsk	Sept. 12, 1943

* Reprinted from *Home from Siberia* by Otis Hays by permission of Texas A&M University Press.

Group No. 3. Seventeen crews (130 men); "escaped" Jan. 30, 1945

1. Navy VB-135	*Bone,* Mantle, Stevens, Sommers, Gelber, Crow, Horvath	Petropavlovsk	June 15, 1944
2. Navy VB-135	*Schuette,* Brassil, Morgan, Dunaway, Jage, Beggin, Morris	Petropavlovsk	June 15, 1944
3. Navy VB-135	*Mahrt,* Johnson, King, Dickson, Patzke, Strom, Everard	Kamchatka	June 20, 1944
4. Navy VB-135	*Clark,* Miller, Mathers, Simes, Brennan, Rowe	Petropavlovsk	July 23, 1944
5. Navy VB-135	*Vivian,* Wilson, Edwards, Anderson, Schasney, Virant, Nommensen	Petropavlovsk	July 24, 1944
6. Army 771st	*Jarrell,* Kirkland, Ogden, Golden, Losick, Earley, R. Price, Zuercher, Bailey, Hummel, Bost	Vladivostok	July 29, 1944
7. Navy VB-136	*Lindell,* Head, Richardson, Williamson, Brown, Manthie	Petropavlovsk	Aug. 13, 1944
8. Army 395th	*McGlinn,* Caudle, Turner, E.C. Murphy, Conrath, Webb, Stocks, Robson, Childs, Mannatt, Beckley	Khabarovsk Territory	Aug. 20, 1944
9. Navy VB-136	*Cowles,* Panella,[b] Parker, Toney, J.R. McDonald	Kamchatka	Aug. 20, 1944
10. Navy VB-136	*Dingle,* Petterbog, Dulan, Henry, Pollard, Leintz	Petropavlovsk	Aug. 28, 1944
11. Army 77th	*Head,* R.W. Hammond, McIntosh, Lawton, Carr, Crowell	Petropavlovsk	Sept. 10, 1944
12. Navy VB-135	*D.F. McDonald,* Miles, Broadwell, Ross, Rosa, Nicodemus	Petropavlovsk	Sept. 11, 1944
13. Navy VB-136	*Wayne*[d] Murphy, Ehret, Mulford, Baxter	Kamchatka	Sept. 17, 1944
14. Army 404th	*Ott,* Perlich, Arnold, Shimer, Martel, Clark, Petersen, Saigh, Austin, Shelton, Karkoszynski	Petropavlovsk	Sept. 25, 1944
15. Army 77th	*McQuillin,* D.A. Ward, Voland, Brishaber, Sylvester, Hermansen, Horin[e]	Petropavlovsk	Nov. 1, 1944
16. Army 794th	*W.H. Price,* Flanagan, Scherer, Morrison, Rutherford, Larkin, Pletter, Weed, Arentsen, Mann, Brownwell, Mertz, Sigrist, Hassinger	Vladivostok	Nov. 11, 1944

Group No. 4. Four crews (43 men); "escaped" May 27, 1945

1. Army 404th	*D.H. Taylor,*[e] Yelland, Wheeler,[e] Lodahl, J.R. Smith, Ruhman, Bendorovich, Burnett, Lakin, Divoky, Lutton, Newell	Kamchatka	Nov. 18, 1944
2. Army 404th	*Weiss,* R.C. Murphy, Michael, Bechtel, A.R. Miller, Williamson, Bingold, Reed, Kimsey, Leighton, Shuping, Centore, Herron	Petropavlovsk	Dec. 7, 1944
3. Army 404th	*Elliott,* Bacon, Bingham, Cohen, Schwierjohn, Hamann, Harrison, Wyberg, Fallows, Koller, Morris, Roth	Petropavlovsk	Jan. 18, 1945
4. Navy VPB-131	*Powers,*[a] Thomas, Pleasant, Timperman, Mann, Hosner	Kamchatka	Feb. 21, 1945

Group No. 5. Seven crews (52 men); released Aug. 24, 1945

1. Army 404th	*Kleinke,* Galleron,[f] J.S. Smith, Stella, Zakoian, Neet, Y.H., Smith, Raymond, Cutler, Jolly, Stakshus, Nutley	Petropavlovsk	May 11, 1945
2. Army 77th	*Winter,*[g] Tyler, David, Stifel,[e] Babb, Sargent, Wutchic[i]	Petropavlovsk	May 11, 1945
3. Army 404th	*Blakeway,* Kuehner, Hand, Potter, Cayon, Stevenson, Gleason, Burgess, Schwedtman, Lokey, Folkman, Leatherwood	Petropavlovsk	May 16, 1945
4. Army 77th	*Beever,* Osburn, Olah, Nichols, Jonasen, Parrish	Petropavlovsk	May 20, 1945
5. Army 77th	*Wolbrink,* Kroot,[h] B.F. Field, Caris, Glodek,[i] Dehaven	Petropavlovsk	June 10, 1945
6. Army 77th	*Wampler,* [g] Millar, Scherl, Prosuk, Judd,[j] Curley	Kamchatka	July 17, 1945
7. Army 77th	*Terris,* Earnheart, Drynan, Kurczak, Vaughn, Sorenson	Kamchatka	July 17, 1945

Notes

a Commanding officer of the group.

b Injured in crash.

c Died as a result of crash injuries.

d Commanding officer of the group and also commander of the parent squadron.

e Wounded.

f Injured in internment camp.

g Alternative commanding officer of Group No. 5. Later, Winter was released separately through Red Cross Action.

h Disabled.

I Dead on arrival at Petropavlovsk.

j Lost at sea when bomber ditched off Kamchatka.

Appendix 5
Mitochondria DNA Analysis of Human Bones

There are two kinds of DNA in most human cells. DNA found in the nucleus, called chromosomes, is a mixture of DNA from an individual's mother and father. The second kind of DNA is found in the energy center of a cell, called the mitochondria, and is identical to that of the individual's mother only.

As human remains age, cell DNA begins to degrade or fall apart. Since there are hundreds of mitochondria, each with many copies of the maternal DNA, but only two copies of chromosomal DNA in each cell, analysis of the mitochondria DNA is usually the only possible method for identification of aged remains.

The analysis process is difficult and time-consuming. First, recovered bone matter is cleaned to remove contaminants. Mitochondria DNA is extracted from bone material using enzymes and chemicals that break open cell membranes and release the DNA strings. From the extracted DNA, regions of mitochondria DNA that change frequently (and are thus good for identification) are isolated using a process known as polymerase chain reaction (PCR). PCR amplifies the DNA region of interest.

Then blood or saliva samples are taken from the subject's maternal side of the family. Specimens from brothers, sisters, grandmother, or mother all are usable. A sample from a child of an uncle would not be. The amplified sequence of the deceased's DNA is then compared to that of maternal relatives. If a match occurs, the percentage of similar sequences in the general population is calculated to determine the significance of the match. Thus, high probabilities can be obtained regarding the identification of missing individuals.

The analysis of mitochondria DNA is a relatively new idea, and only a handful of laboratories in the world examine them. Using this technique, they can determine family background in this manner regardless of how long a subject has been deceased— even hundreds of years. Generally, only about one inch of preserved bone matter is needed to conduct the evaluation.

Appendix 6
Aircraft Diagrams

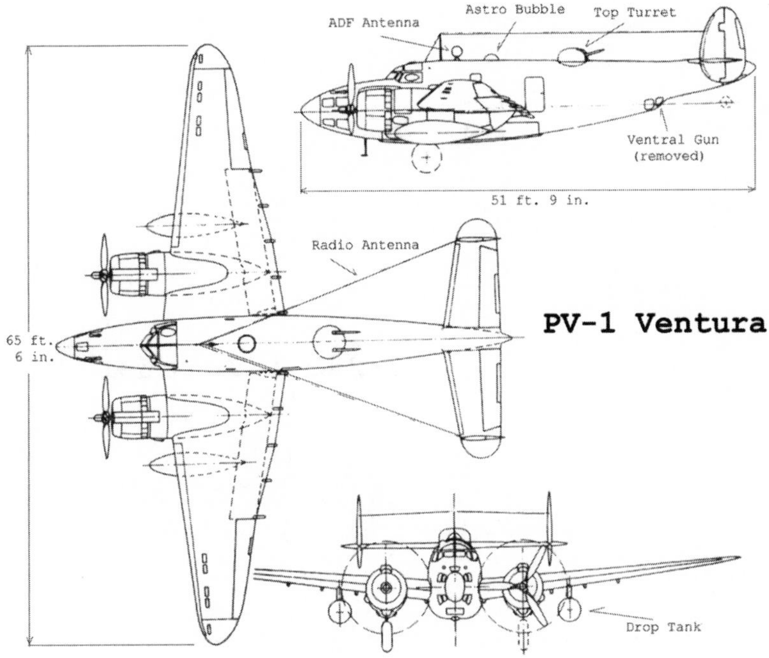

This diagram originated in *Japanese Aircraft of Public War* by Rene J. Francillon, Technical Illustrations by J. B. Roberts, Naval Institute Press. It has been modified by the author.

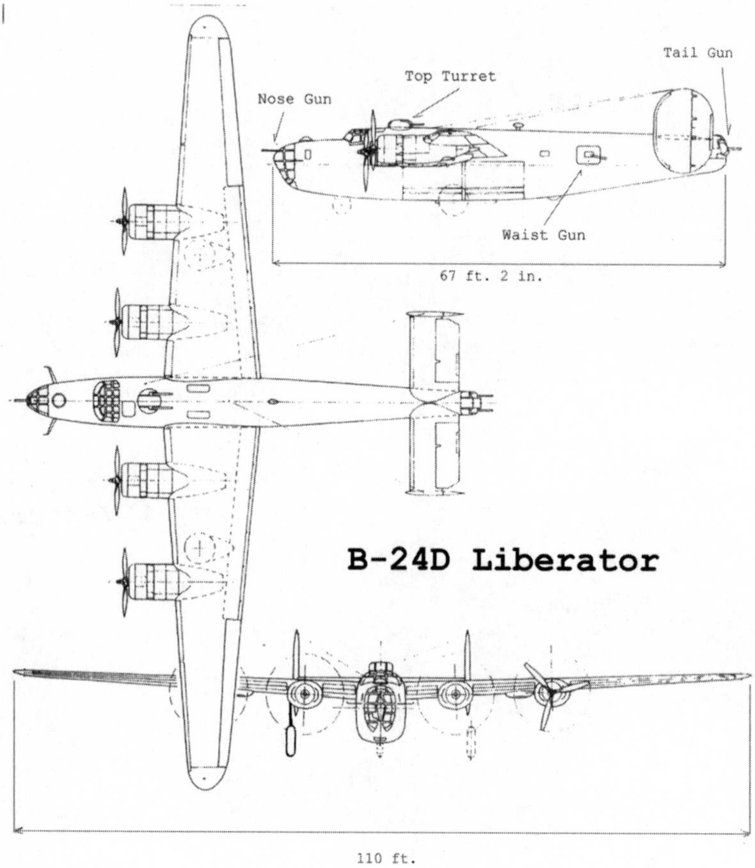

This diagram originated in *United States Military Aircraft Since 1909* by Gordon Swanborough and Peter M. Bowers, Smithsonian Institute Press. It has been modified by the author.

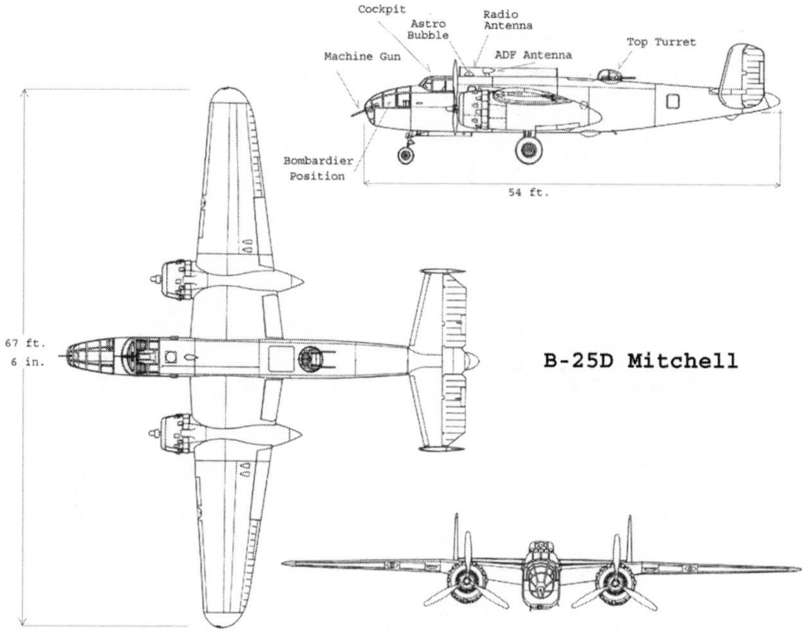

This diagram originated in *B-25 Pilot Training Manual*, Published by Headquarters, Army Air Force, Dayton, Ohio, 1944. It has been modified by the author.

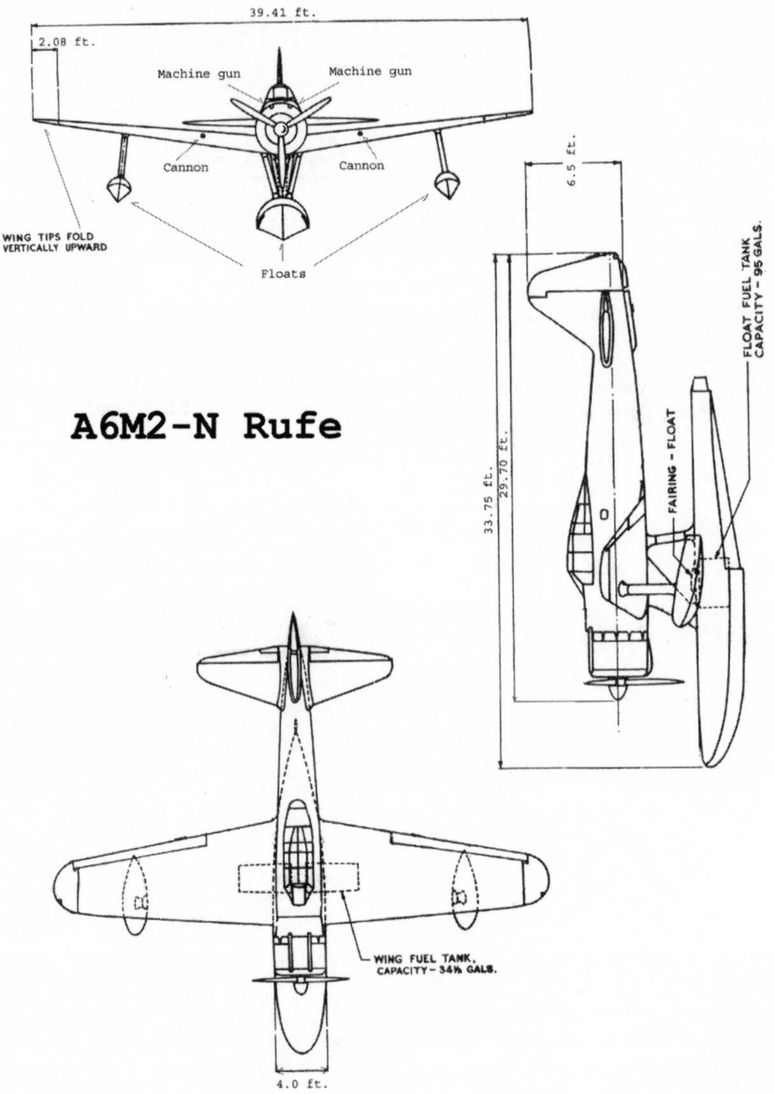

This diagram originated in *British Air Ministry's Secret Foreign Aircraft Bulletin No. 11*, December, 1943, Ministry of Aircraft Production, Whitehall, London. It has been modified by the author.

Ki-43 Oscar

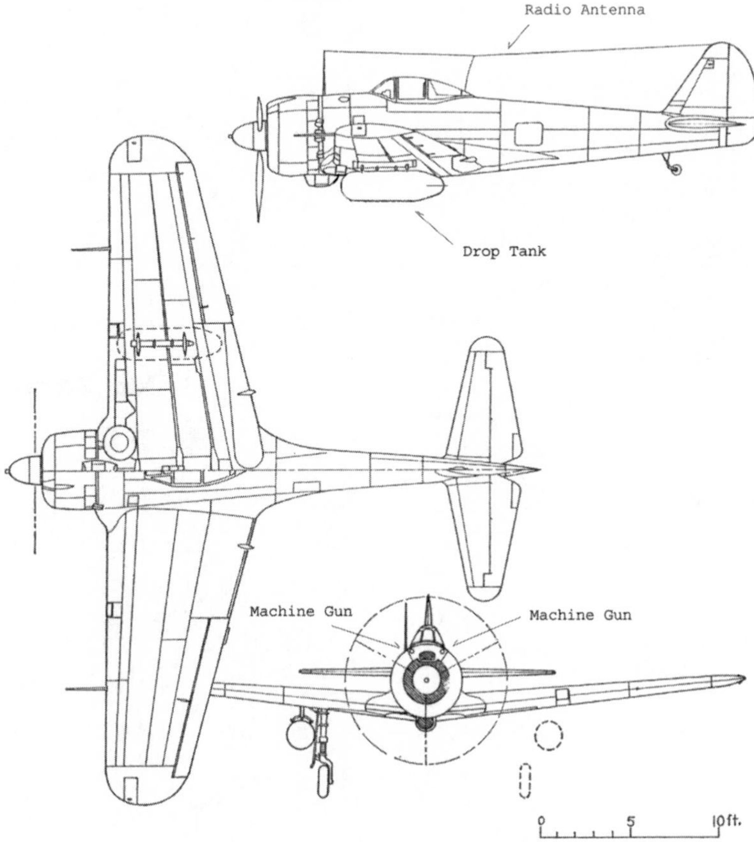

This diagram originated in *Japanese Aircraft of Public War* by Rene J. Francillon, Technical Illustrations by J. B. Roberts, Naval Institute Press. It has been modified by the author.

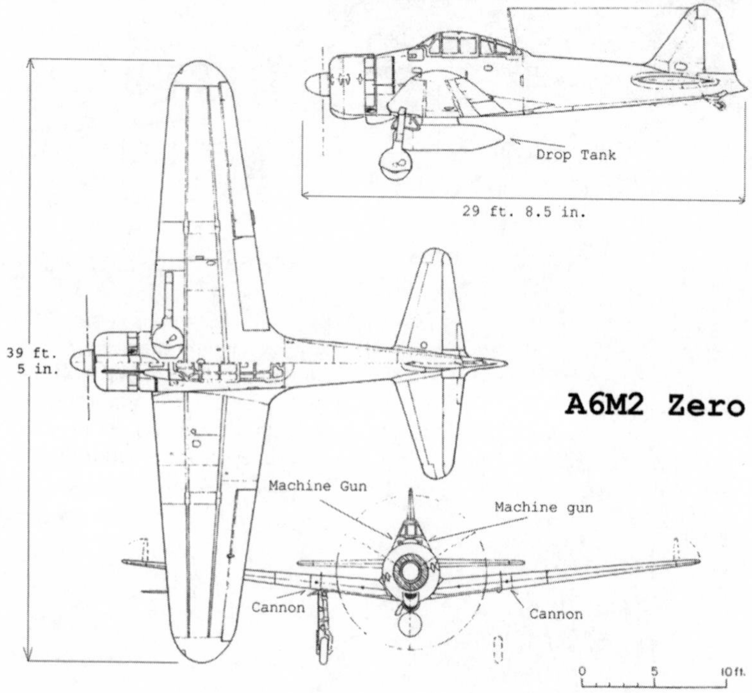

This diagram originated in *Japanese Aircraft of Public War* by Rene J. Francillon, Technical Illustrations by J. B. Roberts, Naval Institute Press. It has been modified by the author.

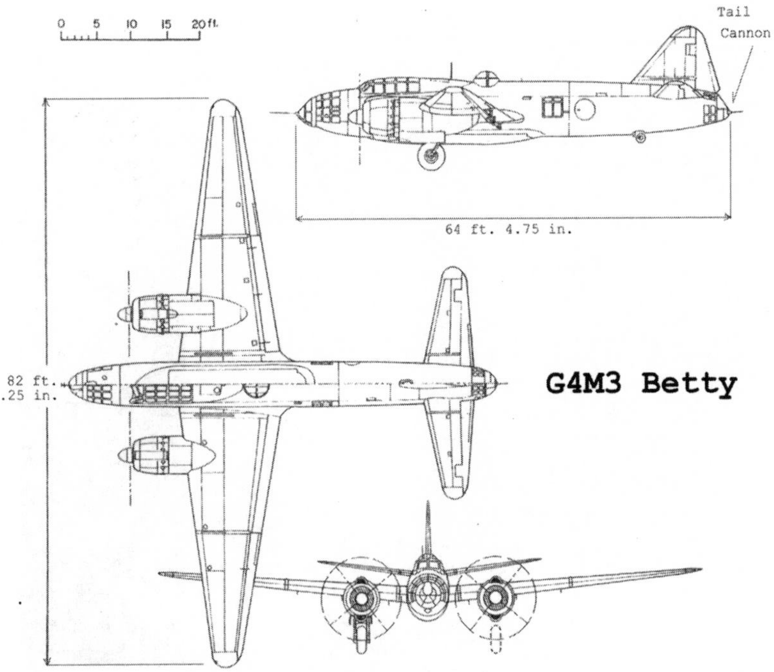

This diagram originated in *Japanese Aircraft of Public War* by Rene J. Francillon, Technical Illustrations by J. B. Roberts, Naval Institute Press. It has been modified by the author.

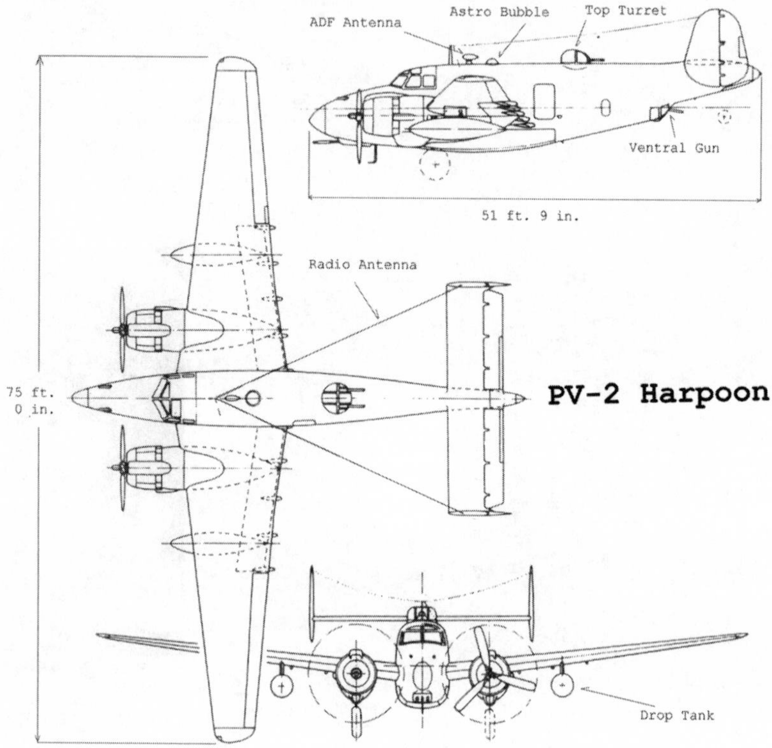

This diagram originated in *Lockheed Aircraft Since 1913* by Rene J. Francillon, Putnam and Company Ltd. It has been modified by the author.

Notes

Prologue

xxi-xxii. The Russians had . . . the first bodies.: Khotin, Mikhail Yurevich, interview, *Subject: JCSD-Moscow Interview with Mikhail Yuryevich Khotin,* January 26, 2000, Moscow, pp. 1–3, and interview in Moscow, August 2001, conducted by Michael Barnes.

Chapter 1

9. During World War . . . selected Soviet pilots.: Geust, Carl-Fredrik, *Lend-lease: Aircraft Deliveries to the Soviet Union.* Internet site: http://airforce.users.ru/lend-lease/english/articles/geust/aircraft_deliveries.htm, p. 1.

13. According to Colonel . . . back in 1962.: Khotin, Mikhail Yurevich, interview, *Subject: JCSD-Moscow Interview with Mikhail Yuryevich Khotin,* conducted by Joint Commission Support Directorate Moscow team members Matt Kristoff and Paul Riley, January 6, 2000, pp. 2–4.

Chapter 2

17. On the eve . . . he eventually did: The Japanese Association of International Politics, ed., *Road to Pacific War, Vol. 17*, "Opening of the War Between Japan and the U. S.," Asahi Shimbun, Tokyo, 1963, p.25.

17. That acquiescence was . . . referred to them.: Cloe, John Haile, *The Aleutian Warriors, A History of the 11th Air Force & Fleet Air Wing 4,* Anchorage Chapter–Air Force Association and Pictorial Histories Publishing, Missoula, MT, 1990, p. 62.

17-18. In Hirohito's Japan . . . during the depression.: Ibid.

18. Hirohito's naval aide . . . "a splendid mood.": Woollacott, Martin, *The Battle Over the Legacy of Pearl Harbor Rages On,* published Friday, May 25, 2001 in

the *Guardian of London,* and Internet site: http://www.commondreams.org/views01/0525-01.htm, p. 1.

18. After the successful . . . Rabaul (May 1942).: Hagen, Jerome T., *War in the Pacific,* Vol. 1, Hawaii Pacific University, Honolulu, 2001, pp. 33, 35, 41, 67, 80.

18-19. Following the Treaty . . . narrow and treacherous.: Stephan, John J., *The Kuril Islands: Russo-Japanese Frontier in the Pacific,* Clarendon Press, Oxford, 1974, pp. 2–4, found at Internet site: http://www.fortunecity.com/olympia/ince/698/rurik/kuril.html.

19. When the Japanese . . . the 50th parallel.: Ibid., p. 3.

20. The Japanese used . . . "in this area.": Japanese Monograph No. 88, p. 9, as cited in Cloe, 1990, p. 84.

21-22. Admiral Theobald departed . . . "of calculated risk.": Carrigan, Paul E., *The Flying, Fighting Weathermen of Patrol Wing Four,* Regal-Lith Printers, 2002, Vol. I, Ch. XIII, pp. 1–3.

22. 25 May 1942 coded message from Admiral Nimitz: Ibid., Vol. I, Ch. XIV, pp. 7–8.

22-23. Army major general . . . his scant forces.: Cloe, 1990, p. 101.

23. Theobald placed his . . . of the Aleutians.: Ibid.

23. Compounding Theobald's failure . . . or his staff.: Ibid. Commander Edwin T. Layton was Nimitz's intelligence chief. He was perplexed with Theobald's take on the warnings about the raid on Dutch Harbor and the taking of Kiska and Attu. "Without telling us, he decided to ignore our intelligence estimate."

23-24. The Japanese plan . . . thirty minutes later: U.S. Strategic Bombing Survey (Pacific) Interrogation No. 97, "Aleutian Campaign, Carrier Attack on Dutch Harbor," Capt. James S. Russell, USN with Cdr. Masatake Okumiya, IJN, Tokyo, Oct. 10, 1945; Letter Vadm. Hiroichi Samejima to Adm. James S. Russell, Mar. 5, 1969, with account of Dutch Harbor raid, compiled from records in War History Section, Japanese Defense Agency; Cloe, 1990, p. 110.

24. Spread out in . . . with the Kates.: U.S. Strategic Bombing Survey (Pacific), op. cit.; Samejima to Russell, op. cit.; Cloe, 1990, p. 110.

24-26. At 4:00 A.M. . . . "swarming among us.": Carrigan, 2002, Vol. I, Ch. XV, pp. 3–5.

26. Bombs began raining . . . were burning fiercely.: Ibid., Vol. I, Ch. XV, pp. 5–6.

26. The Japanese photographs . . . Cape was killed.: Cloe, 1990, pp. 120–121, 126–127.

26-27. A second wave . . . Lieutenant Jacob Dixon.: Ibid., p. 119.

27. The three others . . . gunner were rescued.: Carrigan, 2002, Vol. I, Ch. XV, pp. 9–10.

27-28. The U.S. Navy . . . (at 5:34 A.M.).: Love, Robert W., Jr., *History of the U.S. Navy, Vol. II, 1942–1991*, Stackpole, Harrisburg, PA, 1992, p. 34.

28. Yamamoto's carriers were . . . damaging the ships.: Ibid., pp. 32–34.

28-29. Nagumo recovered his . . . "about the same.": Ibid., p. 37.

29. The *Akagi* had . . . and 147 aircraft.: Hagen, Jerome T., *War in the Pacific*, Vol. I, Hawaii Pacific University, Honolulu, 2001, p. 88.

CHAPTER 3

31. The Northern Area Fleet . . . a submarine detachment.: Denfield, D. Colt, "The Air Raid on Dutch Harbor" in *After The Battle, Number 62*, Battle of Britain Prints International Ltd., London, 1988, p. 2.

31. At nine-twenty. . . . of the Aleutians.: Cloe, 1990, p. 145.

31. On the night . . . Commander Hikumi Mukai.: Denfield, 1988, p. 3.

31-32. Once this 550-man . . . up the radio.: Cloe, 1990, p. 144.

32. By noon on . . . a child's arms.: Ibid., pp. 145, 329. William House survived the war and retired from the Navy in 1959. His nine other companions also survived imprisonment.

33. The second element . . . a service unit.: Ibid., p. 146.

33. The first, a . . . toward Chichagof Harbor.: Ibid.

33-34. At that time . . . villagers become alarmed.: Ibid.

34. Major Hotzumi's main . . . of the village.: Ibid.

34. An Aleut woman . . . cease-fire was ordered.: Fukuzawa, Mikizu, Japanese journalist, "Attack on the Aleutians," newspaper report filed in Tokyo in 1943; Carrigan, 2002, Vol. III, Ch. XXII, p. 52.

34. The Japanese continued . . . had them beaten.: Carrigan, 2002, Vol. III, XXII, p. 45.

34-35. Toranosuke Ozaki commanded . . . not an eyewitness.: Ozaki, Toranosuke, interview, Yokohama, Japan, Feb. 2003. Ozaki took part in the invasion of Attu, then was transferred to Kiska before being evacuated in 1943.

35. Innkenti Golodoff stated . . . near Anchorage, Alaska.: Fort Richardson National Cemetery, Fort Richardson, Anchorage Borough, Alaska, Building #997, Davis Highway, P. O. Box 5-498, Fort Richardson, AK 99505 (907) 384-7075, "Jones, Charles F, d. 06/08/1942, CIVILIAN, Plot: A 2, bur. 08/19/1948."

35. No death certificate . . . in his skull.: Cloe, 1990, p. 329.

35. The bullet hole . . . been self-inflicted.: Carrigan, 2002, Vol. III, Ch. XXII, p. 46.

36. On June 10 . . . Wing 4 war diary.: *United States Navy Combat Narrative, The Aleutians Campaign,* June 1942–August 1943, "PatWing Four, War Diary for June 1942," Naval Historical Center Department of the Navy, Washington, 1993, Ch. 2, p. 18. Noted from Internet site: http://www.ibiblio.org/hyperwar/USN/USN-CN-Aleutians.html.

36-37. After returning to . . . bombs and fuel.: Ibid. *The Aleutians Campaign* was originally published without author attribution. Naval records indicate, however, that Naval Reserve intelligence officer Lieutenant Colin G. Jameson was the narrative's principal author, assisted by Chief Petty Officer L. C. Smith.

37. The missions served . . . Japan for repairs.: Cloe, 1990, p. 159.

37. When the *Gillis* . . . in the inferno.: Ibid.

37. On June 19 . . . exploded and sank.: Ibid., p. 163. William House, the navy aerographer, recalled seeing the bow of the *Nissan Maru* still above water when he surrendered after evading capture for 49 days. When he was taken off the island in September, only its mast protruded from the water.

37. Intelligence photos revealed . . . were rarely repositioned.: Ibid., p. 172.

37-38. On August 4 . . . in any theater.: Ibid., pp. 199–201.

38. Over vocal objections . . . suitable for airfields.: Ibid., pp. 190, 191.

38. Theobald held sway . . . on the fifteenth.: Ibid., p. 207.

38-39. On Attu, the . . . for these troops.: Ozaki, Yokohama interviews.

39. Then, after learning . . . of the war.: Cloe, 1990, p. 147. Of the forty-two original Attuans, only twenty-four along with Etta Jones would survive.

39. On September 23 . . . curtain of smoke.: Ibid., p. 223.

39. Two weeks later . . . back to Attu.: Cohen, Stan, *The Forgotten War* Pictorial Histories Publishing, Missoula, MT, 1981, Vol. I, p. 188.

39. One Japanese survivor . . . "with a broom.": Cloe, 1990, p. 254.

40. On November 9 . . . a formidable adversary.: Caidin, Martin, *Zero Fighter*, ibooks inc., New York, 1970, p. 68; Cloe, 1990, p. 169.

40. The four P-38s . . . the mission report.: Cloe, 1990, p. 242; Intel Summary No. 38, XI Fighter Command, Nov. 9, 1942.

40. Concurrently in November . . . abandoned the idea.: Cloe, 1990, pp. 258, 259.

40-41. A month later . . . back to Adak.: Ibid., p. 248.

41-42. Meanwhile, attacks were . . . surrounding Kiska Harbor.: Cohen, op. cit., Vol. I, pp. 208–209.

42. On the morning . . . luck ran out.: Cloe, 1990, p. 248.

42-43. The U.S. military . . . no reported casualties.: Ibid., p. 254.

43. In spite of . . . none to combat.: Ibid., p. 257.

43-44. On January 24 . . . a nearby foxhole.: Ibid., p. 258.

44. The first American . . . shot both down.: Ibid.

44. Between November 1 . . . the next morning.: *United States Navy Combat Narrative,* op. cit., pp. 34–35. Noted from Internet site: http://www.ibiblio.org/hyperwar/USN/Aleutians/USN-CN-Aleutians-8.html.

45. One convoy reached . . . the *Nachi* damaged.: Morgan, Michael, "Close Call in the Aleutians," *W.W.II* magazine, Feb. 2000, Parts 1 and 2.

45-46. General Hap Arnold . . . antishipping alert.: Cloe, 1990, p. 259.

46. Kodiak was a . . . weeks on end.: Garfield, Brian, *The Thousand Mile War: World War II in Alaska and the Aleutians,* University of Alaska Press, Fairbanks, 1995, p. 246.

46. At Atka Island . . . 5,000 to 40,000.: Ibid., pp. 246–247.

46-47. In considering a . . . the invasion plan.: Cloe, 1990.

47. Kinkaid moved his . . . one-star commodore.: Ibid..

47. During April 1943 . . . was a fatality.: Ibid., p. 275.

47. Due to frequent . . . military songs loudly.: Document, *What the Japs Think of Us,* extracted from Japanese diaries and documents captured on Attu, Larry Reineke collection, University of Oregon Library, Eugene.

48. Loss of personnel . . . their hitting efficiency.: Ibid.

48. Concurrently, the two . . . under the tail.: *American Combat Planes*, Third Enlarged Edition, Ray Wagner, Doubleday, 1982; *Post World War II Bombers*, Marcelle Size Knaack, Office of Air Force History, 1988; *United States Navy Aircraft Since 1911*, Gordon Swanborough and Peter M. Bowers, Naval Institute Press, 1990; "Victor or Vanquished?", Martin Bowman and Michael O'Leary, *Air Classics*, Vol. 32, No. 5, May 1996; *Lockheed Aircraft Since 1913*, Rene J. Francillon, Naval Institute Press, 1987; *British Military Aircraft Serials, 1912–1969*, Bruce Robertson, Ian Allen, 1969.

48-49. The two Ventura . . . "the prevailing wind.": Patteson, Pat, *A History of Bombing Squadron 135*, Ch. XXV, p. 2.

49-50. The assault was . . . at all cost.: Cloe, 1990, p. 279.

50. The Japanese positioned . . . any invading force.: Morison, Samuel Eliot, *Aleutians, Gilberts, and Marshalls*, Vol. 7 of *History of United States Naval Operations in World War II*, pp. 39–40; Final Report, Assistant Chief of Staff, G-2, Western Defense Command, "Reduction and Occupation of Attu from the Combat Intelligence Point of View," Aug. 9, 1942.

50. D-Day was set . . . Holtz Bay area.: *United States Navy Combat Narrative, The Aleutians Campaign*, op. cit., Ch. 11, p. 96.

50-51. At 3:09 A.M. . . . two thousand yards inland.: Ibid., Ch. 11, p. 100.

51. By the end . . . had been killed.: Ibid., Ch. 11, p. 103.

51. Progress inland had . . . and stopped it cold.: Cloe, 1990, p. 282.

51-52. In the northern . . . eleven men aboard.: Ibid., p. 283.

52. During the battle . . . roaring continuously.: Diary, Dr. Nobuo Tatsuguchi, discovered on Tatsuguchi's body on Attu. Text from Internet site: http://www.7thinfantry.com/pacific/diary02.html, p. 1.

52-53. Four F4F Wildcat . . . Commander L.V.K. Greenamyer.: Cloe, 1990, pp. 284–285.

53. Aboard the seaplane . . . "criss-crossing the backness.": Carrigan, 2002, Vol. 1, Ch. XXII, p. 23.

53-54. Carrigan and his . . . the killing ground.:Ibid.

54. The battle continued . . . days, was killed.: Cloe, 1190, pp. 286–287.

54. On the twenty-first . . . things became disorderly.: Tatsuguchi, op. cit., p. 2.

55. On the twenty-fourth . . . remaining Japanese troops.: Cloe, 1990, p. 287.

55-56. The next day . . . downing one bomber.: Ibid.

56. Dr. Tatsuguchi's entry . . . of Imperial Edict. : Tatsuguchi, op. cit., p. 3.

56-57. On the twenty-eighth . . . attack tomorrow.: Ibid.

57. As midnight approached . . . to commit suicide.: Carrigan, 2002, Vol. III, Ch.XXII, pp. 43–44.

57-58. During the next . . . for three months.: Cloe, 1990, pp. 291–292.

58. The last known . . . September 1, 1943.: 2002, Carrigan, Vol. III, Ch. XXII, pp. 36–37.

CHAPTER 4

59. On the night . . . the American lines.: Ozaki, Toranosuke, radio operator on Kiska, heard the report. From an interview, February 2003, Tokyo.

59. The nearly daily bombing . . . "delivery by Roosevelt.": Ibid.

60. Once resistance collapsed . . . August 15, 1943.: Cloe, 1990, p. 295.

60. U.S. Intelligence overestimated . . . a hundred warships.: Ibid., pp. 295–296.

60. U.S. construction in the . . . navy medium bombers.: Ibid., p. 297.

60. With Attu back . . . Japanese resupply efforts.: Ibid., p. 298.

60-61. On June 1 . . . inflict serious damage.: Ibid.

61. On the eleventh . . . than a year.: Intel Summary (Supplementary), Field HQ, 11AF, June 18, 1943; Cloe, 1990, p. 299.

61-62. Two squadrons of . . . the American unit.: Letter, Oliver Glenn to John Cloe, Nov. 8, 1978; Cloe, p. 301.

62. Not to be . . . about unauthorized flights.: Cloe, 1990, p. 301.

62. Several weeks later . . . of their graves.: In August 1991, Bering's grave and the graves of five other seamen were disinterred. The remains were transported to Moscow, where they were investigated by forensic physicians in an effort to re-create Bering's appearance, about which little is certain. In 1992, Vitus Bering and the other seamen were buried again on Bering Island.

62. While Soviet troops . . . about the affair.: Cloe, 1990, pp. 301–302.

63. Sensing a need . . . well-informed man.: Ibid., p. 303.

63. Missions against Kiska . . . the orbiting Kingfishers. : Morison, op. cit., p. 55, Cloe, 1990, p. 301.

63. The Japanese took . . . ground with shrapnel.: Ozaki, Tokyo interview.

63. Fearing a possible . . . ammunition/supply buildings.: Hutchison, Kevin Don, *World War II in the North Pacific, Chronology and Fact Book*, Greenwood Press, Westport, CT, 1994, p. 109.

64. Paramushiro Island, the . . . and fifty-five hardstands.: Ibid., p. 114.

64. The Kashiwabara area . . . light antiaircraft positions.: Ibid.

64. Kakumabetsu, on the . . . machine gun pits.: Ibid., p. 129.

64. On the southeast . . . machine gun pits.: Ibid., p. 128.

64. Even so, General . . . the North Pacific.: United States Air Force Office of History Internet site, Eleventh Air Force, http://www.geocities.com /tempelhof.geo/11AFHIST.html+aleutians%2Bhudelson&hl=en&ie=UTF-8.

64-65. The B-25 Mitchell . . . faster Japanese fighters.: U.S. Air Force Museum, North American B-25D, Internet site: http://www.wpafb.af.mil/museum/research/bombers/b3-6.htm.

65. The B-24 Liberator . . . maximum range.: *Jane's Encyclopedia of Aviation*, Michael J. H. Taylor, ed., Portland House, NY, 1989, pp. 258, 260–261, Internet site http://www.planestuff.com/b2libspec.html.

68-69. In the Aleutians . . . of the war.: Cloe, 1990, p. 304.

69. That same evening . . . in the air.: Mission Report, Fleet Air Wing Four, July 11, 1943; Amme, "Vp-45: The First Squadron Based at Attu"; Cloe, 1990, p. 305.

69. On July 18 . . . "in a year.": Cloe, 1990, p. 305.

69-70. The force turned . . . the Kurile Islands.: Ibid.

70. Bomb damage was . . . buildup was underway.: Intel Summary, Field HQ, 11AF, July 18, 1943; Wheeler Diary as noted in Cloe, 1990, p. 308.

70. With warning of . . . reduce response times.: Yamada, Sei'ichi, Warrant Officer pilot, Nakajima Ki-43 Hayabusa (Oscar) fighter, interview, February 2003; Ozaki, Tokyo interview.

70. To weather the . . . as "Roosevelt's Rations.": Garfield, 1995, pp. 360–361.

70-71. The Japanese High . . . on June 22: Dictionary of American Naval Fighting Ships, Office of the Chief of Naval Operations, Naval History Division, Washington, USS *Monaghan* II (DD-354), from Internet site: http://www.ibiblio.org/hyperwar/USN/ships/dafs/DD/dd354.html+monaghan%2Baylwin%2Bsubmarine+I+7&hl=en&ie=UTF-8.

71. Another submarine disappeared . . . Imperial Destroyer Squadron 1.: Garfield, op. cit., pp. 359, 361.

71. The Japanese were . . . in late June.: Cloe, 1990, p. 313.

71-72. On July 2 . . . Kiska wide open.: Ibid., p. 314.

72. Eighty nautical miles . . . the dense fog.: *U.S. World War II Battleships and Battle Cruisers,* from Internet site: http://www.geocities.com/Pentagon/Quarters/4289/Idaho.html.

72. Klaxons sounded, and . . . their radar targets.: Cloe, 1990, p. 314.

72-73. At dawn, the . . . a weather report.: Ibid.

73. After daybreak, Admiral . . . the northern side.: Garfield, 1995, pp. 370–371.

73. At midmorning . . . the assembly point.: Ozaki, Tokyo interview.

73-74. To the men . . . of abandoned dogs.: Cloe, 1990, p. 314.

74. While the fleet . . . and safely away.: Garfield, 1995, pp. 370–372.

75. On August 1 . . . "or shipping observed.": Cloe, 1990, p. 315.

75. Casco Field on . . . shortly after noon.: Cloe, John Haile with Michael F. Monaghan, *Top Cover for America: The Air Force in Alaska,* Pictorial Histories Publishing, Missoula, MT, 1984, pp. 124–125.

75. Just south at . . . "so we scrambled.": Yamada, op. cit.

76. At 11,500 feet . . . Japanese continued attacking.: Hays, Otis, Jr., *Home From Siberia,* Texas A&M University Press, College Station, 1990, p. 57.

76-78. Inside the stricken . . . the scattered formation.: Cloe, 1990, p. 309.

78. To the north . . . "sorry for them.": Yamada, op. cit.

78. Captain Wadlington's crew . . . back to Attu.: Cloe, 1990, p. 310.

78-79. Lt. Pottenger's B-24 . . . a shoulder blade.: Hays, 1990, pp. 57–58.

79. The crew was . . . of the crew.: Ibid., pp. 57–58, 214.

79. The Japanese suffered . . . thirty-three troops killed.: Hutchison, 1994, p. 114.

79. Overall results of . . . defenses even more.: Yamada, op. cit.

79-80. With two of . . . "Kiska Harbor area.": Craven, Wesley Frank, and Cate, James Lea, eds. *The Pacific: Guadalcanal to Saipan,* Vol. 4 of *The Army Air Force in World War II,* University of Chicago Press, 1948–1958, p. 390; Cloe, 1990, p. 316.

80. Though reports of . . . "eat 'em all.": Cloe, 1990, p. 316.

80. A few days . . . "and say so.": Price, Nancy, "11th Air Force Vets to Begin Reunion Today," *The Anchorage Times,* August 9, 1990; Cloe, 1990, pp. 316–317.

80-81. Captain Ruddell and . . . "for his motherland.": Intel Summary, Field HQ 11 AF, July 23, 1943; Winzeler, Historian, 18th Fighter Squadron, p. 19. Commander Mukai after the war stated that the body of a man who fell to his death from a bomber during the winter was also buried on North Head. Cloe, 1990, p. 311.

81. When Ruddell and . . . "ahead as planned.": Cloe, 1990, p. 317.

81. Even though Admiral . . . "for training purposes.": Ibid., p. 320.

81. For the next . . . others were injured.: Ibid.

Chapter 5

83. Before the fighting . . . "well trampled tundra.": Cohen, Stan, *The Forgotten War,* Pictorial Histories Publishing, Missoula, MT, 2002, Vol. II, p. 202. As reprinted from Frank Davis article, "Gracious Living on Attu Island."

83. Tent poles were . . . and cracked stoves.: Ibid., p. 202.

83-84. On July 6, 1943 . . . "30-knot breeze.": Ibid.

85-86. The ubiquitous Quonset . . . "of frontier days.": Ibid.

88. The Japanese defense . . . and antiaircraft batteries.: See photos on the Internet at: http://www.web-birds.com/11th/28th/28th.

88. As noted, on . . . "the Japanese population.": Ozaki, Tokyo interview, Feb. 27, 2003.

89-90. Assigned to Shimushu . . . ready for action.: Sakaida, Henry, *Imperial Japanese Navy Aces 1937–45*, Osprey, Oxford, UK, 1999, pp. 42–44.

90. The U.S. Army . . . in the chapel.: Hays, 1990, p. 64.

90. The plan discussed . . . "to Russian territory.": Ibid.

90-91. The briefer told . . . "will be lost.": Ibid.

91. Following the briefing . . . "through the barrage.": Ibid.

91-92. Major Frank T. Gash . . . "at us again.": Carrigan, 2002, Vol. III, p. 159.

93. Wright gained respect . . . behind the bomber.: Ibid., Vol. III, pp. 156–159.

93-94. Wright was flying . . . "it," Wright recalled.: Cloe, 1984, pp. 125–126; Carrigan, 2002, Vol. III, p. 161.

94-95. The other four . . . turned for home.: Carrigan, 2002, Vol. III, pp. 160–161.

95. As the five B-24s . . . his landing gear.: Hays, 1990, p. 65.

95-96. Major Salter's B-25 . . . to the field.: Ibid.

96. Back over Paramushiro . . . "in any way.": Ibid., p. 66.

96. Soviet soldiers stationed . . . the struggling airmen.: Ibid., p. 67.

96-97. Marrier and Sabich . . . wheels for landing.: Ibid., p. 66.

97. Lieutenant Marrier and . . . others had used.: Ibid.

97-98. Inside Captain Jones's . . . the completed portion.: Carrigan, 2002, Vol. III, Ch. XXV, pp. 8–14. Lieutenant Underwood recovered but lost the sight in one eye and 85% of the vision in the other. Captain Jones recovered from his shrapnel wounds. Lambe's injuries were relatively minor.

98. Damage to the . . . the Paramushiro Straits.: Hutchison, 1994, p. 118.

98. When Admiral Nimitz . . . "to those concerned.": Ibid.

99. Tokyo Rose, her . . . "in endless months.": Carrigan, 2002, Vol. III, Ch. XXV, pp. 27–28.

100. "Hundreds of innocent" . . . Tokyo Rose predicted.: Ibid., Vol. III, p. 176.

100. For the men . . . of the slaughter.: Ibid., Vol. III, p. 177.

100-101. In the early . . . "and massacre Bay.": Ibid., Vol. III, p. 180.

101. Then in November . . . the PV-1 significantly.: Larson, Robert R., *A Personal History of VPB-136,* Ch. XXIV, unpublished, p. 180.

Chapter 6

103. Three crews and . . . and a yeoman.: *Historical Survey of Patrol Bombing Squadron 139,* United States Pacific Fleet, 1 Jan. 1945, p. 4.

104. The Bat's skipper . . . to prove himself.: Annabel, Russell, "The Private War of Flairwing Four," *Liberty* magazine, 1944, p. 28.

104-106. Commodore Gehres sent . . . could be obtained.: Scrivner, Charles L., *The Empire Express,* Historical Navy Album, Temple City, CA, 1976, p. 7.

106. Meanwhile, on Attu . . . "like college kids!": Stevens, William R., letter to AMM2c Jack Miller, dated April 10, 1990, p. 1.

107. Gehres enjoyed his . . . utilize the excess.: Scrivner, 1976, p. 41, and PV squadron veterans too numerous to list.

107-108. That same January . . . ammunition/supply buildings.: Hutchison, 1994, p. 109.

108. The Japanese navy . . . in fog banks.: Ibid., p. 132.

108-110. Birdsall made a . . . and navigation skills.: Cary, Alan C., *PV Venturas/Harpoon Units of World War II,* Osprey, Botlen, Oxford, 2002, p. 26, and Birdsall, Douglas, interview, 2002

111-114. On January 19 . . . the starter problem.: Birdsall, Douglas, interview, 2002. By the time Birdsall landed, some eight hours later, the commodore had cooled off.

114-115. Out over the . . . were in weather.: Scrivner, 1976, p. 8.

115-117. Neraing Kamchatka, the . . . had been flown.: After Action Report, VB-139, 20 Jan 1944, Night Bombing and Photo Reconnaissance of Paramushiro and Shimushu, Report No. 1, pp. 1–7.

117-118. Starting in February . . . ship *Kokai Maru*.: From World War II History Internet site: http://warships.web4u.cz/history/histmain.php?language=&file=USN_1944_2E.

118-119. When asked the . . . by 200 bursts.: The official web site of the Kodiak Military History Museum, http://www.kodiak.org/faw4/meadows.html, Seattle *Post-Intelligencer*, Tuesday, February 15, 1944 edition.

119. The opinion of . . . "on the enemy.": Rearden, Jim, *Cracking the Zero Mystery,* Stackpole, Harrisburg, PA, 1999, p. 66; Cloe, 1990, p. 238.

119-121. On Shimushu, the . . . to his supervisor.: Fukuno, Trueman Shinyo, interview in Tokyo, Japan, February 28, 2003. In December 1944, Fukuno listened to the tragic ordeal later referred to as Halsey's Typhoon that claimed 778 men, the USS *Hull, Monaghan,* and *Spence,* plus more than 100 aircraft.

Chapter 7

123. She was built . . . in Burbank, California.: Sources for data on PV-1 production and specifications were taken from *American Combat Planes,* Third Enlarged Edition, Ray Wagner, Doubleday, 1982; *Post World War II Bombers,* Marcelle Size Knaack, Office of Air Force History, 1988; *United States Navy Aircraft Since 1911,* Gordon Swanborough and Peter M. Bowers, Naval Institute Press, 1990; "Victor or Vanquished?", Martin Bowman and Michael O'Leary, *Air Classics,* Vol. 32, No. 5, May 1996; *Lockheed Aircraft Since 1913,* Rene J. Francillon, Naval Institute Press, 1987.

123-124. The downside was . . . things got dicey.: Scrivner, 1976, p. 6.

124. Bureau No. 34641 . . . at Casco Field.: Ibid.

125-127 Weatherman Aerographer's Mate . . . Kurile combat assignment.: Carrigan, 2002, Vol. III, p. 277.

128. Moore restarted his . . . "cockpit was killed.": Moore, James, interview, 2001 for the NOVA documentary "The Last Flight of Bomber-31."

131. Raised in Manhattan . . . "in the dirt.": Townsend, O. Wendell. Internet site: http://www.arlingtoncemetery.net/ccfridley.htm, p. 1.

132-134. Well out in . . . results were negative.: *War Diary, United States Pacific Fleet, Bombing Squadron One Hundred Thirty Nine,* entry March 25, 1944, pp. 1–8.

134. Within days, Tokyo . . . nickname, "Moose" Hanlon.: VPB-139 Squadron Reunion, Wichita, KS, August 2002, comments by Swinney, Miller, and others.

Chapter 8

135. By April 1944 . . . support that effort.: *Homeland Operations Record,* Vol. IV, Fifth Army Area, Japanese Monograph No. 21, prepared by Military History Section, Headquarters, Army Forces Far East, Department of the Army, undated, p. 14. On August 27, 1943, Admiral Kinkaid wrote to Admiral Nimitz about General Buckner's desire to command a Kurile invasion, so the Japanese concern about invasions from both south and north was not without merit: from Hutchison, 1994, p. 117.

135-136. Japanese northern airfields . . . twenty medium bombers.: *Homeland Operations Record,* op. cit., Vol. IV, p. 15.

136. Two years earlier . . . in the Kuriles.: Hutchison, 1994, p. 112.

136-137. At Kitanodai Airfield . . . flight at Kitanodai.: Yamada, Sei'chi, interview in Tokyo, February 2003.

137. To prepare replacement . . . (to navigation) gear.: Morgan, Byron, *I'll Take My Vodka Straight,* memoir, unpublished, pp. 163–164.

137. A master station . . . longitude and latitude.: Zack, Milt, *Milt's Military*

Memoirs, Internet site: http://www.geocities.com/tempelhof.geo/miltch3.html, Part III, p. 2.

137-138. Ensign Byron Morgan . . . "this dead water.": Morgan, op. cit., p. 164.

138. Ensign Morgan arrived . . . the six-man Quonsets.: Ibid.

138-140 .Then on May . . . minutes of fuel remaining.: Ibid., pp. 165–166.

141. The Japanese did . . . return to base.: Hutchison, 1994, p. 141.

141-142. On May 18 . . . ammunition cooked off.: Birdsall, Douglass M., E-mail July 14, 2003.

142-144. Norem continued on . . . the way home.: Birdsall, Douglass M., interview August 2003.

146. On June 11 . . . armed with torpedoes.: Hutchison, 1994, p. 144.

146-147. The next day . . . regarding the deviation.: Morgan, op. cit., pp. 167–168.

147. At the radio . . . the communications building.: Fukuno, Tokyo interview, 2003.

147. Japanese Air Group . . . American strike force.: Hutchison, 1994, p. 145.

148-150. The *Ventura* formation . . . great beast beneath.: Morgan, op. cit., p. 170.

150-151. Schuette radioed his . . . a smooth landing.: Ibid., pp. 165–172.

Chapter 9

153-154. Lieutenant Schuette parked . . . getting shot over.: Morgan, op. cit., p. 173.

154. The crew was . . . "Suborta Lieutenant Dondekin.": Ibid.

155. Dondekin had suffered . . . "bomb monkeys . . . good.": Ibid., p. 175.

155. In addition to . . . of the internees.: Hays, 1990, p. 58.

155. The typical internment . . . units on Attu.: Ibid., p. 6.

156. After the Doolittle . . . of interned crews.: Ibid., p. 5.

156. The first of . . . May 11, 1943.: Ibid., p. 50.

157. Iran was selected . . . two occupation zones.: Ibid., p. 19.

157. The northern zone . . . "of vital importance.": Letter, Chief Military Intelligence Service to Commanding General, Army Air Forces, Subj: "Air Forces personnel Formerly Interned in Russia," May 22, 1943, Army Intelligence Documents.

157. The interrogations were . . . quiz sessions ended.: Hays, 1990, p. 58.

157-158. The crews learned . . . greatly appreciated luxury.: Ibid.

158. Medical treatment was . . . the Soviet Union.: Ibid., pp. 59–60.

Chapter 10

160. On May 13 . . . out of Attu.: Hutchison, 1994, p. 141.

160-161. Two of VB-135's . . . fuel than anyone else.: Scrivner, 1976, p. 8.

161. On June 17 . . . .50-caliber machine guns.: Ibid., p. 23.

162. On June 19th . . . was no fire.: Hays, 1990, p. 102.

162. To keep the . . . Zeros remained operational.: Hutchison, 1994, p. 147.

162-163. On the other . . . previous ten days.: Ibid.

163-164. For VB-135, the . . . there without difficulty.: Hays, 1990, p. 103.

164. The next day . . . Vivian swung west.: Ibid., pp. 103–104.

164. As Vivian's PV-1 . . . "correct on altitude.": Ibid., p. 104.

166. Meanwhile, in and . . . the destroyer *Usugumo*.: Hutchison, 1994, pp. 148–152.

Chapter 11

167-168. Roosevelt had backed . . . in the Aleutians.: Maylock, Tom, *FDR: Pacific Warlord,* http://users.erols.com/tomtud/wwwroot11.html, 2000, Ch. 11.

168. On August 12 . . . "was running rough.": Hays, 1990, p. 105.

168-169. On August 19 . . . "like easy pickings.": Toney, Harold R., Parallax Film Productions Inc. interview for the documentary "The Last Flight of Bomber-31," tape 204, 2001, p. 2.

169-173. Sixteen to eighteen . . . "long lost brother.": Toney, op. cit., tape 204, 2001, p. 5.

173. The crew was . . . Petropavlovsk and internment.: Cowles, Jack R., After Action Report, dated August 6, 1945, letter to Commander Leslie M. Gehres, former commander, Fleet Air Wing Four, pp. 1–6.

173. Eight days later . . . off the pavement.: Hays, 1990, p. 110.

Chapter 12

176-179. Both Eleventh Air . . . into the sea.: Scrivner, 1976, p. 25.

179. Two days later . . . to the crew.: Hays, 1990, p. 115.

179. With the loss . . . put on hold.: Larson, op. cit., Ch. XXIV, p. 183.

180. In fact, in . . . and antiaircraft fire.: Scrivner, 1976, pp. 26–27.

181. Starting on the . . . the recommended maximum.: Fleet Air Wing Order No. 5–44, Hutchison, 1994, p. 161.

181-183. On November 18 . . . touching the ground.: *Operational Summary for 21 November 1944,* 28th Bombardment Group (Composite), United States Army, dated 22 November 1944, p. 1; Intelligence Summary No. 427, 17 November 1944, 404th Bombardment Squadron, p. 4.

183. Fuel flames filled . . . after a while.: Hays, 1990, pp. 170–172.

184-185. At Sheyma . . . from the B-24.: *Operational Summary for 21 November 1944,* op. cit., pp. 1–2.

185. Before heading back . . . had turned back.: Hays, 1990, p. 172.

185. "The food, medical . . . in sleeping bags.": Ibid., p. 173.

185. The men sat . . . survive was over.: Ibid., p. 174.

185-186. On September 10 . . . ceilings and visibility.: Hutchison, 1994, pp. 158–161.

186. Warrant Officer Trueman . . . "dig ourselves out.": Fukuno, Trueman S., communication dated Oct. 12, 2003, subject: Shimushu, p. 1.

186-187. Antiaircraft gunners slept . . . positions were occupied.: Tanakura, Hiroichi, Imperial Navy 2nd Antiaircraft Battery, 51st Guard, interview, Tokyo, Feb. 2003.

187. Mail delivery was . . . "rank and file.": Fukuno, Oct. 12, 2003 communication, p. 2.

187-188. In addition, as . . . "battle" (Operation SHO-1).: Hutchison, 1994, p. 159.

Chapter 13

189-190. Sixty-one Americans who . . . responses in Russian.: Hays, 1990, p. 69.

190. When Lieutenant John . . . moved into each.: Ibid., p. 104.

190. The new internees . . . "a little rough.": Ibid., p. 137.

191. After numerous false . . . of the city.: Ibid., p. 116.

191. Stalin's approach was . . . "deserve to die.": At the time of the Moscow show trials, playwright Bertold Brecht told the philosopher Sidney Hook of Stalin's approach, "the more innocent they are, the more they deserve to die." Applebaum, Anne, *Gulag, A History,* Doubleday, New York, 2003, p. 89.

191-192. Many of the . . . Magadan, for example.: Ibid.

192. While walking the . . . "saw them yesterday.": Hays, 1990, pp. 145–146.

192-193. On the fifteenth . . . Tashkent, in Uzbekistan.: Ibid., p. 117.

193. Arriving at Tashkent . . . of two wires.: Ibid., pp. 63, 76.

193-194. The new arrivals . . . to the end.: Ibid., pp. 62–63.

194. Mealtime fare at . . . speculated was buckwheat.: Ibid., p. 136.

195. A week earlier . . . the Doolittle raid.: Pearson, Drew, "Washington Merry Go Round," syndicated newspaper column, United Feature Service, released Nov. 30, 1944. Pearson's account claimed the crew was rescued by a Russian tank crew from Japanese-controlled Manchuria, then brought to the Soviet Union and turned over to a man named Clyde Pangborne, who flew the crew to Alaska.

195. Someone in contact . . . the York crew.: Cassidy, Henry C., "'Escape' of Tokyo Raid Crew from Russia Revealed," *St. Louis Post-Dispatch*, Dec. 2, 1944, pp. 1, 5.

195. While the internees . . . alert Soviet guards.: Hays, 1990, p. 157.

195-196. The next day . . . "Soviet Union alive.": War Department "EX report No. 542, McGlinn, Richard M.," p. 10.

196. On the sixteenth . . . shipped to Tashkent.: Hays, 1990, pp. 158–159.

196. Christmas came and . . . of their release.: Ibid., p. 160.

196. Diplomatic efforts in . . . according to plan.: Lucas, Richard C., "Escape," *Aerospace Historian* (Air Force Historical Foundation), Spring 1969, p. 17.

196-197. Major Paul Hall . . . "of the war.": Letter, Maj. Gen. John R. Deane to Lt. Cdr. Charles Wayne, Jan. 11, 1945, "Internee" files; Hays, 1990, p. 163.

197. Weeks passed with . . . of his hair.: War Department "EX Report No. 542, Incidental Intelligence," p. 4; Hays, 1990, pp. 158, 164.

197-198. On January 25 . . . issued fresh uniforms.: Hays, 1990, p. 166.

Chapter 14

199-200. In November 1944 . . . to Allied use.: Hutchison, pp. 163–164.

200. The New Year . . . the Northern Kuriles.: Ibid., pp. 167–168.

200. On January 3 . . . the runway clear.: Kita, Wahei, war correspondent, interview, Feb. 2003, and journal entry dated Dec. 29, 1944, p. 2.

200. On the January 19 . . . with this eventuality.: Hutchison, 1994, p. 168.

200. Following it came . . . "the attacking barbarians": Ibid., p. 174.

200-201. And fight they . . . month was over.: Kita, op. cit., interview and journal entry, pp. 3–4.

204-208. Leading eight B-25s . . . glittering in the night.: Duncan, Ray, Sgt., staff correspondent, *Yank, The Army Weekly,* Aug. 31, 1945, "Stairway to the Kuriles," pp. 1–4; Zack, *Milt's Military Memoirs, Part III, Overseas,* pp. 6–10 and interview, Nov. 4, 2003.

208-213. Lewis brought the . . . "on Purple Hearts.": Hutchison, 1994, p. 179.

213. Bombing missions over . . . "a direct hit.": Fukuno, communication, Oct. 30, 2003, p. 1.

213. The Japanese government . . . "war, morale plummeted.": Fukuno, communication, Oct. 12, 2003, p. 2.

213-214. On June 16 . . . "to seven knots.": Ibid, pp. 1–2.

214. Kolva began his . . . around the ship.: Ibid, p. 2.

214-217. The nose of . . . and blew up.: Hutchison, 1994, p. 182. On 19 July 1945, the submarine *Cabezon* sank the 2,631-ton ship *Zaosan Maru* at 50-39 N., 154-38 E.

217-218. That night, a . . . in New York.: Cavanaugh, William, CPL, telephone interview, November 15, 2003.

218-219. Cavanaugh mentioned the . . . about to change.: *Case file, 2nd Lieutenant Richard L. Brevik,* 16 June 1945, Defense Prisoner of War/Missing Personnel Office (DPMO), undated, pp. 2–3; Hutchison, 1994, p. 181.

219-220. Confined in Ofuna . . . on at arrival.: Cavanaugh, William, CPL, telephone interview, November 15, 2003; *Warsailors.com* Internet sites: http://www.ussyorktown.com/yorktown/pow.htm, *Yorktown Aviator,* "My Experience as Prisoner of War by the Imperial Japanese," p. 2, and http://www.warsailors.com/POWs/imprisonment.html#ofuna, p. 1. William Cavanaugh testified against camp commander Aida, medical technician Kitamura Congochyo, and the guards Nakakichi, Nishi, and Mari. The War Crimes Tribunal found them all guilty. Aida and Congochyo received the death penalty and were hanged. Nishi and Mori received 15-year prison sentences. Nakakichi was sentenced to 12 years in jail.

220. Conditions such as beriberi . . . by Allied forces.: Cavanaugh, William, CPL, telephone interview, November 15, 2003. After the war, Cavanaugh learned that the prisoners were to be beheaded if Allied forces ever invaded the Japanese main islands.

Chapter 15

221. By war's end . . . the northern isles.: Garfield, 1995, p. 394.

222-224. Emperor Hirohito's statement, August: Kyoki Press, transcript, *Hirohito's Surrender Broadcast, 15 August, 1945,* p. 1, http://www.kyokipress.com/wings/surrender.html.

224. How could "god" . . . his surrender speech: Smith, James, and McConnell, Malcolm, *The Last Mission: The Secret History of World War II's Final Battle,* Broadway Books, New York, 2002, pp. 191–226.

225. In the northern . . . miles from Shimushu.: Hutchison, 1994, p. 188.

225. Tsutsumi set in . . . villages to Hokkaido.: Ibid., p. 188.

225-226 On Shimushu, Warrant . . . about to unleash.: Medlock, Dr. Robert W., memoir, *My Journal of Life,* unpublished, p. 18.

226-227. The Japanese on . . . Kamchatka Defense Group.: Nagashima, Mr. Atsushi and Mr. Ichikawa, veterans of the Soviet attack on Shimushu, from interview in Tokyo, Feb. 25, 2003; Hutchison, 1994, p. 189.

227. As things remained . . . in Tehran, Iran.: Hays, 1990, p. 209.

227. The Japanese POW . . . a free man.: Cavanaugh, William, telephone interview, Nov. 14, 2003; Balch, Jean, *Sea V 10,* Winter 1999 edition, *Yorktown Aviator,* "My Experience as Prisoner of War by the Imperial Japanese," pp. 2–5 and from http://www.ussyorktown.com/yorktown/pow.htm.

227. B-25 navigator/bombardier . . . a U.S. submarine.: Zack, Milton, interview at his home, Nov. 2003.

228. Etta Jones, whose . . . Otaru City, Hokkaido.: Hutchison, 1994, p. 198.

228-229. In the Kuriles . . . world by 1938.: Applebaum, 2003, p. 113.

229. Under NKVD chief . . . bridge construction projects.: Ibid., pp. 36, 89, 104, 109.

229-230. Following the surprise . . . "units of labor.": Ibid., p. 102.

230. By the time . . . war with Japan.: Ibid., p. 432. The Soviet Union captured 2,388,000 Germans between 1941 and 1945 and another 1,097,000 Axis soldiers, including Italians, Hungarians, Romanians, Ukrainians, and Austrians as well as a smattering of French, Dutch, and Belgians and 600,000 Japanese. The figures come from Overy, Richard, *Russia's War,* Penguin, New York, 1998, p. 297, and from a Soviet document dated 1956. Another Soviet document from 1949, reprinted in Zagorulko, pp. 331–333, contains similar numbers (2,079,000 Germans, 1,220,000 non-Germans, and 590,000 Japanese).

230. On arrival in . . . to be counted.: Applebaum, 2003, p. 186.

230-233. Fukono's group occupied . . . "with trembling fingers.": Ibid., p. 213.

233. Other prisoners killed . . . frogs near bogs.: Fukuno, taped interview, Feb. 2003, Tokyo.

233 . Spring comes late . . . poisonous, even deadly.: Kuznetsov, S. I., "The Situation of Japanese Prisoners of War in Soviet Camps (1945–1956)," *Journal of Slavic Military Studies*, Vol. 8, No. 3, pp. 613–618.

233 . Some sixty thousand Japanese . . . to Soviet records.: Applebaum, 2003, p. 432.

233. In summer, the . . . by the bugs.: Ibid., p. 223.

234. According to Fukuno . . . torture and abuse.: Ibid., pp. 221, 431–434.

234-237. When back in . . . never been clarified.: Fukuno, letter dated May 3, 1950, courtesy William Cavanaugh; interview, Feb. 2003, Tokyo.

Chapter 16

239-240. The report noted . . . of the plane.: Khotin, interview report, *Subject: JCSD-Moscow Interview with Mikhail Yuryevich Khotin*, conducted by Joint Commission Support Directorate Moscow team members Matt Kristoff and Paul Riley, Jan. 6, 2000, pp. 1–3.

256. Cowles's after-action report . . . prior to impact.: Cowles, 1945, pp. 1–6; Toney, tape 204, 2001, p. 2.

259. During this period . . . overheard by Norem.: *War Diary, United States Pacific Fleet, Bombing Squadron One Hundred Thirty Nine*, entry March 25, 1944, pp. 1–8.

260. One thing is . . . engine would freeze.: Ibid.

Epilogue

281. The "Silver Stallion" . . . died within seconds.: Garfield, 1995, p. 395.

281-282. Nona Fedorovna Solodovinova . . . southwest of Moscow.: Hays, 1990, p. 179.

282. The Attuans, who . . . Wilderness Preservation System.: Laughlin, William S., *Aleut Traditional Culture, Unangax People of the Aleutian Chain*, Internet site: http://www.uaf.edu/ans/faculty/aleut.html.

282-3. The navy sought . . . "to three years.": Bryan, Suzzannah, "Re: WW II Crash Site Found in Northern Kurils," South Florida *Sun-Sentinel*, Nov. 19, 2003.

Acknowledgments

Continued gratitude goes to ever-persistent agent Nancy Ellis-Bell, and to Herman Graf, Philip Turner, Keith Wallman, Claiborne Hancock at Carroll & Graf, and copy editor William D. Drennan. Instrumental in making this endeavor a success was the support of editors Warren Lacy and Heather Lyons at *Military Officer* magazine, plus George Larson and Linda Shiner at *Air & Space/Smithsonian. Parallax Film* producers Michael Barnes and Julie Crawford also played key roles, as did NBC correspondent Dana Lewis with his timely financial rescue of the stalled expedition team. Not to be overlooked is the assistance by Dr. James Connell from the U.S. Embassy and the many Russian participants in the Kamchatka recovery operation including Colonel Konstantin Golumbovsky and his professional colleagues Vadim Peretruhin, Ivan Samardich, Halid Mirzaev, Dima Eryshev, Dima Vlasyuk, Viktor Orlovsky, Anatolii Nikiforov, Slava Nikiforov, Volodya Vlasyuk, Denis Koshaev, Irina Filipova, Irina Galenchik, and Nina Tsyrul'nikova.

To the hundreds of hardworking members of the newly reorganized Joint POW/MIA Accounting Command (JPAC) in Hawaii, I render a hand salute for once again allowing me access to the hallowed sites where your dedicated work takes place. Likewise, plaudits go to the men and women of the Coast Guard who protect our shores and rescue those in trouble at sea.

This book could not have been completed without access to the books and research done by countless historians including John Cloe (*The Aleutian Warriors*), Otis Hays, Jr. (*Home From Siberia* and *Alaska's Hidden Wars*), Brian Garfield (*The Thousand-Mile War*), Stan Cohen (*The Forgotten War*), Charles Schrivner (*The Empire Express*), Byron Morgan (*Escape the Red Bear*), and Kevin Don Hutchison (*World War II in the North Pacific*), all well worth reading. Of the many who made significant personal contributions to my effort I wish to personally acknowledge Dr. Hitoshi Kawano, Trueman Fukuno, Will Swinney, Douglas Birdsall, William Cavanaugh, Milt Zack, John Bratten, Robert Johnston, Albert King, Jack Miller, Dr. Robert Medlock, Sei'ichi Yamada, Toranosuke Ozaki, Wahei Kita, Kenjiro Ichikawa, Hiroichi Tanokura and Atsushi Nagashima.

I also want thank the many other veterans on both sides of the conflict who gave so graciously of their time, recollections, and photographs. In addition to those whose names appear in the book, special mention must go to daughter Donna Lewallen and niece Marie Gosha (Donald Lewallen family); Ralph Carrigan, brother of Paul Carrigan; Charlotte Davis, sister of Jack Parlier; and Benjamin Badman (Walt Whitman family), and to investigator Shirley Ann Casey for the material and hours of assistance they provided.

Finally, I once again acknowledge the support of my family, especially my wife, Carol, who edits every draft and offered a wealth of cogent comments and suggestions.

Index

J

K

O

P

Z

About the Author

Colonel Ralph Wetterhahn (Ret.) is a trained aircraft crash investigator and the author of *The Last Battle: The Mayaguez Incident and the End of the Vietnam War*, about three marines captured and killed by the Khmer Rouge during the final combat action of the Vietnam War, and a novel about the search for lost airmen, *Shadowmakers*. His articles are widely read in *Air & Space/Smithsonian, Popular Science, VFW,* and *Military Officer Magazine*. In 2001, he received two Awards for Publication of Excellence for feature writing (an article revealing direct Soviet involvement in the Korean air war) as well as news reporting (the discovery of Bomber 31 in Kamchatka) from Communications Concepts, a professional writer/editors' organization. In 2003, he received the society's top recognition, their Grand Award, for writing an exposè about America's missing-in-action from the Korean War. During his military career he flew 180 combat missions for the U.S. Air Force and Navy. Wetterhahn, who was featured in the 2003 Nova documentary, "The Last Flight of Bomber 31," lives in Long Beach, California.